CONNECTED COMMUNITIES
Creating a new knowledge landscape

THE IMPACT OF CO-PRODUCTION
From community engagement to social justice

Edited by Aksel Ersoy

First published in Great Britain in 2017 by

Policy Press
University of Bristol
1-9 Old Park Hill
Bristol
BS2 8BB
UK
t: +44 (0)117 954 5940
pp-info@bristol.ac.uk
www.policypress.co.uk

North America office:
Policy Press
c/o The University of Chicago Press
1427 East 60th Street
Chicago, IL 60637, USA
t: +1 773 702 7700
f: +1 773-702-9756
sales@press.uchicago.edu
www.press.uchicago.edu

© Policy Press 2017

British Library Cataloguing in Publication Data
A catalogue record for this book is available from the British Library

Library of Congress Cataloging-in-Publication Data
A catalog record for this book has been requested

ISBN 978-1-4473-3029-5 paperback
ISBN 978-1-4473-3028-8 hardcover
ISBN 978-1-4473-3032-5 ePub
ISBN 978-1-4473-3031-8 Mobi
ISBN 978-1-4473-3030-1 ePdf

The right of Aksel Ersoy to be identified as editor of this work has been asserted by him in accordance with the Copyright, Designs and Patents Act 1988.

All rights reserved: no part of this publication may be reproduced, stored in a retrieval system, or transmitted in any form or by any means, electronic, mechanical, photocopying, recording, or otherwise without the prior permission of Policy Press.

The statements and opinions contained within this publication are solely those of the editor and contributors and not of the University of Bristol or Policy Press. The University of Bristol and Policy Press disclaim responsibility for any injury to persons or property resulting from any material published in this publication.

Policy Press works to counter discrimination on grounds of gender, race, disability, age and sexuality.

Cover design by Hayes Design
Front cover image: istock
Printed and bound in Great Britain by CMP, Poole
Policy Press uses environmentally responsible print partners

Contents

List of figures		iv
Notes on contributors		v
Acknowledgements		xi
Series editors' foreword		xii
Introduction Aksel Ersoy		1
one	Enabling conditions for communities and universities to work together: a journey of university public engagement Marina Chang and Gemma Moore	9
two	Understanding impact and its enabling conditions: learning from people engaged in collaborative research Alex Haynes	29
three	Emphasising mutual benefit: rethinking the impact agenda through the lens of Share Academy Judy Willcocks	47
four	From poverty to life chances: framing co-produced research in the Productive Margins programme Sue Cohen, Allan Herbert, Nathan Evans and Tove Samzelius	61
five	Methodologically sound? Participatory research at a community radio station Catherine Wilkinson	85
six	The regulatory aesthetics of co-production Penny Evans and Angela Piccini	99
seven	Participatory mapping and engagement with urban water communities Özlem Edizel and Graeme Evans	119
eight	Hacking into the Science Museum: young trans people disrupt the power balance of gender 'norms' in the museum's 'Who Am I?' gallery Kayte McSweeney and Jay Stewart	137
nine	Mapping in, on, towards Aboriginal space: trading routes and an ethics of artistic inquiry Glen Lowry and Mimi Gellman	155
ten	Adapting to the future: vulnerable bodies, resilient practices Deirdre Heddon and Sue Porter	179
Conclusion: Reflections on contemporary debates in coproduction studies Aksel Ersoy		201
References		213
Index		233

List of figures

1.1	Food Junctions Festival	16
1.2	Foodpaths Movement	16
7.1	The cultural ecosystem services framework	126
7.2	Cultural ecosystems mapping in the Hackney Wick focus	127
7.3	DEN-City, Hackney Wick Connected Communities Festival	130
7.4	Cultural mapping findings from Love the Lea Festival (volume of likes and dislikes)	131
7.5	Cultural mapping findings from Three Mills, National Mills Weekend (volume of meeting and heritage places)	133
9.1	'Cultured Nature' by David Garneau, 2012	157
9.2	'Mealy Mountains', by Amy Malbeuf, detail, 2013; caribou hair tufting and glass beads on map	161
9.3	Blueberry River Reserve: Hunting Map	165
9.4	Sketch II, Shawnadithit, The Taking of Mary March on the North side of the Lake, VIIIA-556	169
9.5	Dreamwalk #1, by Mimi Gellman, 2010	173
9.6	Maraya bus shelter poster	175

Notes on contributors

Marina Chang is a Research Fellow at the Centre for Agroecology, Water and Resilience (CAWR) at Coventry University, UK. Her research focuses on food and the city. Taking food as an entry point, her research focuses on the theory and practice of the commons as an alternative to the existing dominant neoliberal capitalism. She endeavours to integrate research, education, public policy, community development and enterprise into a coherent force for change.

Sue Cohen is Co-Investigator on Productive Margins, the large Connected Communities co-produced research programme based at the University of Bristol and the University of Cardiff. Sue has been involved in participatory grassroots programmes combatting poverty and discrimination at a local, national and European level. For more than 20 years Sue was CEO of the Single Parent Action Network set up under the Third European Poverty Programme, developing a network of self-help groups across the UK and involved in transnational participatory research exchanges in countries across the EU.

Özlem Edizel is a Senior Lecturer in Tourism and Events at the University of Westminster and Research Fellow at Hydrocitizenship project (AHRC) at the Middlesex University. Her research interests centre on sustainable development, cultural mapping and urban governance.

Aksel Ersoy is an urban planner who is interested in understanding the complex relationship between social and economic transformations taking place in developing economies, metropolitan cities and the built environment. At the moment, he is working as Assistant Professor in Urban Development Management at Delft University of Technology, Netherlands. His research experience has benefitted from a combination of theories and approaches in the discipline of planning and beyond. His PhD thesis explored two sets of theories on local economic growth, i.e. the endogenous growth theory of the economists and the institutional theories of economic geographers and sociology. Later on he became interested in STS literature. In particular, he looked at co-production of knowledge in cities and the role of communities. Recently, he has become interested in the concept of smart city, urban infrastructure and the circular economy. He grew up in Mersin, which is a port city in southern Turkey on the Mediterranean coast.

Graeme Evans is Professor of Urban Cultures & Design. He holds a PhD and MA from City University, Department of Culture & Creative Industries, and during the last 20 years has held senior academic posts as director of research centres in London and Maastricht. He is a founding editorial board member of the *Creative Industries Journal* and publishes in a wide range of international journals with work translated into Chinese, German and Turkish and contributions in over 100 books and journals. He has completed several major studies for the UK Cultural Ministry, Arts Councils and overseas cultural agencies, including the Organisation for Economic Co-operation and Development and the Council of Europe. Prior to academe he was co-director for an inner city arts centre and community technical aid centre, Inter-Action/InterChange Studios, and served as director of the London Association of Arts Centres. He is currently researching the evolution and role of the arts centre in architecture and design, artform innovation and social impact.

Nathan Evans is a Lead Officer working for the South Riverside Community Development Centre (SRCDC) on a Welsh Government anti-poverty programme in Cardiff South. Over the past 20 years he has been developing and supporting a range of UK/Wales national and area-based projects and activities covering the themes of community development, arts-based practice, engagement and participation, community auditing, youth development and race equality.

Penny Evans is a founding member and a director of Knowle West Media Centre (KWMC), an internationally respected media arts charity. KWMC develops bespoke citizen-focused programmes using traditional and digital media, including data. The projects that KWMC develops range from food production, health and wellbeing to data and digital literacy, skills and training, and business and enterprise development. Evans is a collaborator and developer on many of KWMC's academic research projects with universities and programmes with government agencies, European partners, the public sector and business, and is a Fellow of the Royal Society of Arts.

Mimi Gellman is an Anishinaabe/Ashkenazi (Ojibway-Jewish Métis) visual artist, designer and educator with a multi-streamed practice in architectural glass and conceptual installation. She is currently an Associate Professor in the Faculty of Culture and Community at Emily Carr University of Art and Design in Vancouver, Canada and is completing her research/praxis PhD in Cultural Studies at Queen's

University on the metaphysics of Indigenous mapping. Mimi's interdisciplinary work explores her interests in phenomenology and technologies of intuition through an embodied practice of walking and mapping and through works and installations that point to the existence of the animacy and agency of objects. The cross-cultural dialogue exemplified in her work suggests a pre-existing connection to the other-than-human worlds. It is her cosmological orientation, in other words, her Ojibway/Métis worldview and the language that expresses it that predisposes her to be open to the reality of the spirit and life of objects and their ability to communicate across diverse thresholds. She continues to exhibit internationally, with recent exhibitions in France, Germany and Tokyo and was included in the seminal exhibition at the Museum of Modern Art in New York in 2011. Her work can be found in the collections of Price-Waterhouse, Kraft/General Foods Corporation, the Toronto Transit Commission and Rogers Stadium, among many others.

Alex Haynes is the CEO of Whittlesea Community Connections, a place based community organisation. Prior to her CEO role she managed projects in the areas of learning and education, women's policy, cultural diversity, gender, eliminating violence against women, urban and community planning, climate change, food security and environment.

Deirdre Heddon is Professor of Contemporary Performance at the University of Glasgow (UK). She is the author of *Autobiography and Performance* and co-author of *Devising Performance: A Critical History* (both published by Palgrave Macmillan). Her edited collection, *Histories and Practices of Live Art*, co-edited with Jennie Klein, was published in 2012 by Palgrave Macmillan.

Allan Herbert currently manages a Welsh Government anti-poverty programme in South Cardiff as a staff member at South Riverside Community Development Centre, a grassroots organisation in Cardiff, Wales developing participatory anti-poverty initiatives, education, learning and childcare projects to local families and individuals. The centre is also a thriving hub for local community organisations and self-organising groups. Allan has been working for the organisation for 18 years and has a background in community organising and arts-based practice.

Glen Lowry is a researcher, writer, editor and publisher whose work investigates new forms of critical and creative practice, most often from the perspective of collaborative investigation. Trained as a cultural theorist (PhD English), Lowry works with artists and collectives on projects that look at questions of social justice and emergent publics. As a publishing advisor to the Aboriginal Healing Foundation (2011–14), Lowry travelled across Canada participating in discussions about Truth and Reconciliation among Aboriginal and non-Aboriginal communities. He is the Associate Dean, Outreach and Innovation, in the Faculty of Art at OCAD U in Toronto.

Kayte McSweeney is the *Object Journeys* Partnership Manager at the British Museum. This programme seeks to embed community-led exhibition development practice and research at the museum and explore new and meaningful ways to collaborate with the public. She has worked in the museum sector for over 10 years specialising in visitor research, audience engagement, participatory practice and community-led research initiatives. Having studied History at Trinity College Dublin, Kayte followed her ambition to work in museums through an MA in Cultural Heritage Studies at University College London (UCL).

Gemma Moore is an experienced evaluator and community engagement practitioner. Gemma works in the UCL Public Engagement Unit as the Evaluation Officer, a role she has been in since 2009. Her career has developed her skills in a number of areas: public engagement, community development, consultation, evaluation and social research methods.

Angela Piccini has followed an unconventional path through her academic career. Although she has focused always on the lively materialities on and of the moving image, she has pursued that through an undergraduate degree in art history, graduate degrees in archaeology, post-doctoral research posts in geography and in practice-as-research in performance and screen, and as a Reader in Screen Media at Bristol University. She has also worked in public sector heritage, commissioning photography, making postcards and designing guidebooks. She enjoys working in collaboration with different publics and is involved in a number of collaborative research projects that involve film and artists' cinema. Publications include *The Oxford Handbook of the Archaeology of the Contemporary World* (2013, co-edited with Paul Graves-Brown and Rodney Harrison), *Media Archaeologies of the Olympic City* (2016,

Public 53), and *Imagining Regulation Differently: Co-creating Regulation for Engagement* (in preparation, co-edited with Morag McDermont and Tim Cole, Policy Press). She grew up in Vancouver, swimming at urban beaches and feeding mussels to the sea anemones.

Sue Porter (1954–2017) was a Senior Research Fellow in the School for Policy Studies, University of Bristol. She was involved in a series of research projects during her career. Some of these included the D4D (Arts and Humanities Research Council; AHRC) project, Alternative Futures (AHRC), Tacking Disability Practices (Economic and Social Research Council), Walking Interconnections (AHRC) and Challenging Elites (AHRC). Sue was also involved in a wide range of disability networks including chairing the Vassall Centre Trust. She was a founder of the Disabled Staff Forum within the University, helping to ensure equality in the working environment for disabled staff.

Tove Samzelius is a Policy Advisor on child poverty for Save the Children Sweden and a PhD candidate at the School of Social Work at Malmö University. She was previously a Director at Single Parent Action Network (SPAN) in Bristol, where she was overseeing and developing front-line services for single parent families. Tove also worked with a number of collaborative research projects during her time at SPAN. Her current research focuses on poverty and homelessness among single mother families in Sweden.

Jay Stewart is co-founder and CEO of Gendered Intelligence, a Community Interest Company aiming to increase understandings of gender diversity and improving the quality of lives of trans people. He gained his doctorate in the Visual Cultures Department at Goldsmiths College, University of London with his thesis 'Trans on Telly: Popular Documentary and the Production of Transgender Knowledge'.

Catherine Wilkinson is a Lecturer in Children, Young People and Families in the Faculty of Health and Social Care at Edge Hill University, UK. Catherine has a BA (Hons) in Fashion Brand Management, an MSc in Marketing Management and a PhD in Environmental Sciences. Catherine completed her PhD in Environmental Sciences at University of Liverpool, UK, funded by an ESRC CASE award. Undertaking 18 months of ethnographic research, Catherine adopted a participatory mixed-methods approach to explore the ways in which young people use community radio as a platform to find and realise their voices, build stocks of social capital, and create their own communities and senses of belonging. Alongside completing her PhD, Catherine held a part-time role as Researcher in Residence, conducting ethnographic research at a performing arts café, funded by Artsmethods and the Faculty of Humanities, The University of Manchester, UK. Catherine is interested in ethnography and participatory action research and other creative qualitative approaches.

Judy Willcocks is Head of Museum and Study Collection and a Senior Research Fellow at Central Saint Martins, University of the Arts London. Before taking up post at the university Judy worked in national and independent museums. Her research interests include the possibilities offered by museum objects in supporting teaching and learning, and the landscape and ecology of university museum partnerships. She is co-founder of the Arts Council funded Share Academy programme, exploring the challenges and benefits of university museum partnerhips.

Acknowledgements

In early 2014, Bryony Enright, Nathan Eisenstadt and I sent out a call for papers for a session at the Royal Geographical Society (with the Institute of British Geographers) Annual Conference to raise concerns about the importance of interdisciplinarity and collaboration in community co-production and the potential for this to contribute deeper insights into debates around impact and engagement. The call struck a chord with current thinking that had not yet found a space for expression: such was the response that the single session was expanded to four over the course of a full day with a final panel session involving leading thinkers and practitioners in the area of collaborative and co-produced research. Discussion was lively and collegial, not only bringing academics, practitioners and community partners together in a new space, but also making connections between previously disparate fields of academic enquiry. The day received a high degree of positive feedback from participants and there was a keen desire to take the insights of the discussion forward. This book emerges from that desire and showcases a selection of high quality papers presented at the session and updated in light of the conversations and feedback on the day. The book provides a much-needed opportunity to get these insights to a wider audience and strengthens the growing network of people seeded by the conference session.

I would like to thank Wendy Larner, who not only chaired the 2014 RGS (with IBG) Annual Conference in that year but also contributed enormously to the development of my career in recent years. My gratitude also goes to my senior colleagues Morag McDermont and Keri Facer at the University of Bristol, who helped me engage with rich and compelling discussions of 'co-production'. Thanks, of course, to the contributors of this collection who have produced such timely, insightful and thought-provoking chapters and the two anonymous reviewers who helped to finetune the collection. Also I wish to acknowledge the late Sue Porter, who sadly and unexpectedly passed away in January 2017. Last but not least, I would like to acknowledge the support of the publishers, Policy Press, who have been a great help with the final production.

Series editors' foreword

Around the globe, communities of all shapes and sizes are increasingly seeking an active role in producing knowledge about how to understand, represent and shape their world for the better. At the same time, academic research is increasingly realising the critical importance of community knowledge in producing robust insights into contemporary change in all fields. New collaborations, networks, relationships and dialogues are being formed between academic and community partners, characterised by a radical intermingling of disciplinary traditions and by creative methodological experimentation.

There is a groundswell of research practice that aims to build new knowledge, address longstanding silences and exclusions, and pluralise the forms of knowledge used to inform common sense understandings of the world.

The aim of this book series is to act as a magnet and focus for the research that emerges from this work. Originating from the UK Arts and Humanities Research Council's Connected Communities programme (www.connected-communities.org), the series showcases critical discussion of the latest methods and theoretical resources for combining academic and public knowledge via high-quality, creative, engaged research. It connects the emergent practice happening around the world with the longstanding and highly diverse traditions of engaged and collaborative practice from which that practice draws.

This series seeks to engage a wide audience of academic and community researchers, policymakers and others with an interest in how to combine academic and public expertise. The wide range of publications in the series demonstrate that this field of work is helping to reshape the knowledge landscape as a site of democratic dialogue and collaborative practice, as well as contestation and imagination. The series editors welcome approaches from academic and community researchers working in this field who have a distinctive contribution to make to these debates and practices today.

Keri Facer, Professor of Educational and Social Futures,
University of Bristol

George McKay, Professor of Media Studies,
University of East Anglia

Introduction

Aksel Ersoy

The impact agenda and continuing debate around public engagement, impact and relevance (economic, political or otherwise) is having a significant influence on the global university sector. This debate has been fuelled by the banking failure in the late 2000s, which saw politicians, economists and (rather more unsettlingly) some academics seek justification for universities primarily through their contributions to economic growth (Rhoten and Calhoun, 2011). With their academic labour less evidently linked to economic outputs, academics working in the Arts, Humanities and Social Sciences have come under particular pressure. As a response to the dominance of the economic, other metrics of impact have been mobilised. These stress connection and engagement with, and responsiveness to, the needs of 'local communities' through increasingly participatory approaches to knowledge production. In the UK, the mechanisms for measuring and embedding 'community oriented impact' have begun to take hold through the Research Excellence Framework (REF) and bodies designed to support universities in their public engagement strategies such as the National Co-ordinating Centre for Public Engagement (NCCPE), The Wellcome Trust, Catalyst Public Engagement Beacons and embedded university public engagement departments. Meanwhile, new funding streams have opened up, including the Research Council UK (RCUK) Connected Communities programme, designed to promote collaborative endeavours and co-production between academics, artists, public service providers and a range of community groups.

Similarly, the focus on collaborative working and co-production has been subject to scholarly discussions. In August 2014, Wendy Larner's Royal Geographical Society (with Institute for British Geographers) keynote address heard by a number of scholars pointed to the multiple sites where co-production was adopted within the discipline of geography. The range of submissions emerged from a number of disciplines to speak about the topic of co-production. Almost 1800 participants contributed to more than 380 individual sessions. They reflected on the challenges, opportunities and interdisciplinary understandings that arise when different perspectives have been brought in the field of geography. Some examples came from cultural geographers who had been working with museums or other cultural institutions to create new forms of knowledge between academic researchers, cultural institutions and publics – co-production is the term used for the opening up of cultural institutions. Others emerged from policy co-production where different constituencies are being brought together in processes to produce new policy formation in much more engaged and diverse processes. Co-production of sites, such as water geography, brought together scientists, social scientists, policymakers and the public to reshape science in scientific knowledge. Last but not least there were examples of co-production of institutions in 'engaged universities' initiatives or new forms of activism to speak with alternative methodologies within the discipline of geography.

Outside geography, the term co-production speaks to social sciences in a number of different ways. It is very comfortable with social sciences and humanities as it emphasises dimensions of meaning, discourse and textuality. It addresses a number of disciplinary enquiries:

> To political scientists, particularly those working in post-structuralist frameworks, co-production offers new ways of thinking about power, highlighting the often invisible role of knowledges, expertise, technical practices and material objects in shaping, sustaining, subverting or transforming relations of authority. To sociologists and social theorists, the co-production framework presents more varied and dynamic ways of conceptualising social structures and categories, stressing the interconnections between macro and the micro, between emergence and stabilisation, and between knowledge and practice. To anthropologists, it offers further tools for analysing problems of essentialism and stereotypic reproduction, showing how the cultural capacity to produce and validate knowledges and artefacts can account for long-term stability, as well as creativity and change. Finally, co-productionist accounts take on the normative concerns of political theory and more philosophy by revealing unsuspected dimensions of ethics, values, lawfulness and power within the epistemic, material and social formations that constitute science and technology (Jasanoff, 2006: 4)

At a more strategic level, it has been argued that co-production can offer alternative ways for academics to work with policymakers on the basis of creating alternative urban visions (Perry and Atherton, 2017;

Polk, 2015). This would stimulate longer-term transformations while contributing to sustainable urban development. While environmental governance is one of the ways in which the concept of co-productive capacities can be implemented, it can also bring science and governance together in a way to demonstrate the potential of diverse capacities (Van Kerkhoff and Lebel, 2015). Although universities are one part of these discussions, they have recently been asked to become more proactive in terms of collaborating with citizens, public institutions and community organisations (Facer and Pahl, 2017). A city–university partnership has referred to talk about the co-production of knowledge by practitioners and academics as an alternative to implementing best practice solutions across cities (Patel et al, 2015). In fact, the Bristol Method,[1] which came out of the European Capital Award in 2015, built on the idea that the Bristol Green Capital Partnership module would drive change towards Bristol becoming a more sustainable city over the next decades.

From a managerial perspective, the concept of co-production has a longer standing. Elinor Ostrom is credited with having originally coined the term 'co-production' in the 1970s when she noted that most public services were not delivered by a single public organisation but rather by several actors across the public and private sectors. Co-production has been defined as 'the process through which inputs used to produce a good or service is contributed by individuals who are not 'in' the same organisation' (Ostrom, 1996: 1073). The term was imported into the public management literature after the 2000s and it is now being used widely in discussions of the role of the third sector, democratic participation, and the institutional structuring of the concept. Such accounts being accompanied by case studies cover a wide range of service sectors, such as housing, education, healthcare, sanitation and water supply. The co-production discourse has replaced a long tradition of partnership and contractualism, and it is interested in exploring how public services are delivered in new ways in new times. Individuals and groups have turned to co-production owing to the fact that it is presented as offering an efficient solution to a range of political tensions associated within the complex social, political and economic orders of advanced liberal societies and it is functioning as a particular form of regulation (Innes et al, 2016. There is now a growing debate against traditional ways of designing policy that are seen as inadequate to cope with complex challenges (Durose and Richardson, 2015). There is a need to move towards exploring more democratic involvement which not only generates change in policy processes but also empowers community oriented practices.

Even though the increased institutional focus on community oriented research has now been recognised, the implementation of such practices has been complex. This kind of research emerges as response to the privileging of the economic as the dominant measure of impact and hence the rationality underpinning it can be understood as equally technocratic: research is about problem solving, not about questioning who defines 'the problem'. This shift to 'community oriented' and 'participatory' research comes shortly after a profound critique of the very terms of these discourses. In the last decade, scholars articulated rigorous criticism of the concepts and practices of 'community' (Joseph, 2002), 'empowerment' (Li, 2005) and 'participation' (Cooke and Kothari, 2001). The 'empowerment' of communities, as a process through which unpaid 'active citizen-subjects' take responsibility for social provision, has been analysed as an important technology of neoliberal governmentality that fails to address the material inequalities that foreground disempowerment (Hall and Reed, 1998; Herbert-Cheshire, 2000; Marinetto, 2003; Larner and Butler, 2005). Similarly, discourses of community engagement have been criticised as offering participation without substantive decision making or, worse, for cultivating consent for decisions that were not, nor ever could have been, to the benefit of the communities they claimed to help (Cooke and Kothari, 2001).

In spite of and alongside these problematic dynamics, increased funding and recognition for community oriented research appears to be opening the way for opportunities and initiatives that cannot be reduced to 'participation as governmental/technocratic response'. Building on traditions of feminist, post-colonial, critical race and participatory action research praxis, researchers are seizing the opportunity to push community oriented research beyond the technocratic rationality that currently places it in the limelight. Deploying tools from performance (Pratt and Johnston, 2013) and forum theatre (Brookes et al, 2012) to community mapping (Amsden and Van Wynsberghe, 2005; Perkins, 2007) researchers, practitioners and 'community partners' are co-producing (to varying degrees) an array of non-traditional 'outputs', from crowd-sourced digital archives, exhibitions, festivals and training opportunities to a plethora of community toolkits (Askins and Pain, 2011). The emergence of this work is exciting, but not unproblematic. While researchers are reflexive about the limitations and drawbacks of community oriented research, reflexivity does not insulate them from these very limitations and drawbacks. Feminist, critical race, post-colonial and Participatory Action Research (PAR) emerge from philosophical and practical trajectories and with radical social justice aspirations that do not sit easily with institutionalised community engagement. Such engagement seeks solutions to problems framed within the present order, whereas PAR, in particular, not only produces knowledge towards a radically egalitarian reshaping of society, but also move towards an undoing of the concepts through which particular practices are rendered 'problematic'.

This book explores the possibilities and tensions for co-produced research practices that emerge from the collision of long-established community oriented research practices, an increased institutional emphasis on community co-production in Academia, and the ongoing critique of the key terms of these practices. These three trajectories are subject to lively and topical debate in Academia but have not, thus far, crossed paths. Among long-established approaches to community oriented research scholarship, PAR is squarely oriented to a particular vision of social justice and community-defined methods and research questions. However, it tends not to engage with questions around the extent to which discourses and practices of community and empowerment work to produce particular kinds of governable subjects. While governmentality scholarship is acutely attentive to these dynamics, it is deeply reticent to offer a more empowering, or more socially equitable proposal. Such reticence is duly grounded in a critique of technocratic science and the moral universalism implicit in prescriptions for the lives of others. The problem is that this leaves the space for proposals for other modes of being and researching to less critical traditions: on the one hand to PAR, where what constitutes 'social justice' is often left assumed or unclear and, on the other, to institutionalised engagement practices that respond to pre-defined problems with technocratic solutions and rarely question the deeper relations of inequality that foreground disengagement. This book provides a range of case studies about what co-production looks like and some of the challenges that arise. It opens up the field and begins to illustrate in practice what the tensions and challenges of co-production are.

The chapters in this book represent subjects and specialisms that have shaped community oriented research practices, the institutional emphasis on co-production, and some of the critiques that are pertinent to the future direction of the field. In the first half of the book, they discuss the increasing importance of collaboration and engagement as a part of the impact agenda. In Chapter One, Marina Chang and Gemma Moore provide a context for the evolution of the concept of public engagement within the UK higher education sector focusing on a specific initiative: the Beacons for Public Engagement programme at University College London. They highlight the dynamic nature of public engagement in the process of community and university collaborations. In Chapter Two, Alex Haynes illustrates two examples of collaborative research with women's groups, from an Australian research study, exploring how people make their lives in new places. With her examples, Alex draws attention to some of the challenges and opportunities of collaborative social research. In Chapter Three, Judy Willcocks examines the relationship between universities and museums in the UK. By focusing on two case studies, namely Peckham Cultural Institute and the 'Local roots/global routes: the legacies of British slave-ownership' project, she illustrates some of the challenges and opportunities Share Academy has experienced. In Chapter Four, Sue Cohen, Allan Herbert, Nathan Evans and Tove Samzelius talk about how they engage with co-produced research and participatory practices from a community perspective. As 'representatives' from three different community groups in Bristol and Cardiff, they discuss how co-produced interdisciplinary research experiences and knowledge exchanges facilitate interaction with members of the community, with academics and with artists as a part of the Productive Margins project. In Chapter Five, Catherine Wilkinson discusses the nature of participatory research by giving a case study of KCC Live, a volunteer youth-led community radio station in Knowsley, UK. She talks about the co-production of audio artefacts in her project and illustrates how the young participants change the way she approached the term 'participatory'.

In the second half of the book, the chapters emphasise the role of arts practices and how such practices can advance co-produced research for interdisciplinary studies as well as stimulate inclusion and transformation. In Chapter Six, Penny Evans and Angela Piccini discuss three case study projects that came out of University of Bristol and Knowle West Media Centre (KWMC) collaboration. Within those projects, they look at the positioning of arts practices as knowledge producing, rather than instrumental or facilitative. They address some of the issues around collaboration and regulation and explore how arts-based projects are shaped through institutional structures. In Chapter Seven, Özlem Edizel and Graeme Evans focus on the application of cultural ecosystems mapping as a participatory, co-produced visualisation and engagement method. Using a case study of the Lee Valley in London, they investigate how local communities relate to and engage with urban water environments using arts and humanities methodologies. In Chapter Eight, Kayte McSweeney and Jay Stewart reflect on the partnership between Gendered Intelligence and the

Science Museum. They discuss how co-produced research impacts on both organisations and conversations around the ways in which museums posit particular values and 'norms' around gender identity. They highlight the importance of gender diversity in collaborative projects. In Chapter Nine, Glen Lowry and Mimi Gellman discuss the project of Trading Routes, an art/research project seeking to engage with the contested geographies in Northern British Colombia, Alberta and relations of Indigenous and non-Indigenous ways of knowing. They highlight the need for the ontological differences between Indigenous and non-Indigenous/Western maps. They call attention to new coalitions, among artists, academics, community leaders, that are respectful of land-based knowledge systems. In Chapter Ten, Deirdre Heddon and Sue Porter discuss the 'Walking Interconnections: Performing conversations of sustainability' project. They talk about the interventions that the project and its outcomes have staged not only in environmental discourse and debate about inclusive public space, but also in representations of walking practices. They focus on the potential contributions of disabled people to sustainability planning. The conclusion chapter discusses the contribution of this book in relation to process oriented research and institutional dimension of co-production debates.

By bringing practitioners, academics, artists and 'community activists' together at the intersection of these otherwise divergent trajectories, *The Impact of Co-production* stimulates novel thinking around the compatibility of current institutional support and models of funding in relation to research focused on social justice. In so doing it contributes to and pushes forward topical debates on contested approaches to 'impact' and community – co-production that has, as yet, lacked empirical study and tended to be articulated solely by and for academic researchers. Threading a line between celebratory accounts of institutionalised community engagement, self-professed 'radical' scholarship for social change and critical accounts of the governmentalisation of community, the book makes an original contribution to all three fields of scholarship. The individual chapters make different contributions to the agenda as they represent a mix of academic and practitioner contributions and offer interesting insights into the actual processes and methods used, the issues arising and the value that the authors place on their work. There are differences between the chapters in terms of how they use references and link to the literature – with some chapters written with minimal referencing and others following a more traditional academic style. This has not been an issue for the book as the contributors have viewed impact not as an outcome of research but as a praxis during which they have collaborated in order to reflect on their practices.

Note

[1] http://bristolgreencapital.org/the-bristol-method-how-to-use-partnerships-to-drive-change/

ONE

Enabling conditions for communities and universities to work together: a journey of university public engagement

Marina Chang and Gemma Moore

Introduction

Within the current climate, UK higher education institutions are facing a challenging time operating against a backdrop of financial, cultural and political change. One thing we know for certain is that universities will need to work more closely than ever with policy, business, non-governmental organisations and the multiple communities that make up the society we live in. Now more than ever it is considered pivotal to rethink the relationship and interactions between higher education and society. Simply, there is a pressing need for universities to communicate and engage effectively with the world. The result is a movement in agendas within the UK higher education sector where ideas of 'participation', 'engagement' and 'involvement' are becoming prevalent.

In this chapter, we provide a context to the evolution of the concept of public engagement within the UK higher education sector and focus on a specific initiative: the Beacons for Public Engagement (BPE) programme at University College London (UCL), which aimed to embed public engagement within such institutions. We draw on a journey of public engagement as the case study (three collaborative projects: Food Junctions, Foodpaths and *The Food Junctions Cookbook*). Two particular reasons make this journey an interesting case study. First, it is exemplary of the wider approach to public engagement at the UCL-led Beacon. Second, it illustrates a nuanced evaluation processes that provides enabling conditions for communities and universities to work together.

We highlight that public engagement is changing and dynamic – it is a journey; however, whatever the scope or scale of the journey there are some challenges to be addressed if public engagement is to be effective. Moreover, we expose the enabling conditions for communities and universities to work together; the authors recommend the five conditions to generate effective engagement, particularly through nuanced evaluation and support. In this case, evaluation and support can be seen as a pathway – bridging the gaps between theory and reality of engagement, between strategy and practice, and between the communities and academia – to ensure communities and universities to work together to impact on the university, research practice, communities and ultimately society. The key themes that have arisen from our learning provide a base for critical awareness, for those with a role or responsibility in the process of community and university collaborations.

We, the authors, also recognise that our own experience and positions cannot be ignored: it has influenced the practice and the knowledge produced. We have been working at UCL in the field of university public engagement from very different, but not opposing, perspectives. One of us has been working within with the UCL Public Engagement Unit (PEU) as an Evaluation Officer since 2009, responsible for assessing the effectiveness of the UCL-led Beacon. In practice this has involved devising an effective way to evaluate UCL's BPE; evaluating past, present and ongoing UCL public engagement activities (at programme and project level); and learning from and sharing knowledge on evaluation practices and experiences with practitioners, academics and researchers. The other author started her PhD on community-based sustainable food systems in London in 2009. Based on her research and activism she was the initiator, leader and co-organiser of three collaborative projects – a journey of university public engagement – at UCL, from 2009 to 2011, all funded by the UCL PEU under the BPE. Through the UCL-led Beacon the authors have developed a critical collaboration; here we bring together valuable and collective knowledge and experience from our own work.

Public engagement in higher education in the UK

Universities and communities interacting and working together is not a new concept. Authors including Grand et al (2015), Bauer et al (2007) and Stilgoe et al (2014) have traced the history of 'public engagement', in one form or other, through the lens of higher education, from the 1980s to the present day. What they indicate is that the trajectory of university public engagement is not simple or consistent. There are significant differences in perspective on what constituted engagement within higher education. Thus, it is important to define what we mean when we talk about 'public engagement'. It can be used to obscure the differences between and within activities that are radically different, potentially fundamentally diverse in concepts and theories i.e, science communication, community participation, consultation, volunteering, social enterprise, education. A useful definition is from the National Co-ordinating Centre for Public Engagement (NCCPE, 2010), which describes engagement as '… the myriad of ways in which the activity and benefits of higher education and research can be shared with the public. Engagement is by definition a two-way process, involving interaction and listening, with the goal of generating mutual benefit'.

There have been critiques of the models of public understanding of science or research, particularly on models that rest with the assumption of a deficit of knowledge within the public, which needs to be filled by scientists or researchers. Instead, there is a feeling that now:

> We need to engage the public in a more open and honest bidirectional dialogue about science and technology and their products, including not only their benefits but also their limits, perils, and pitfalls. We need to respect the public's perspective and concerns even when we do not fully share them, and we need to develop a partnership that can respond to them. (Leshner, 2003: 977)

Furthermore, it has been argued that engaging the public and researchers in a way that allows the researchers and the public to learn strengthens both parties and allows for mutual benefits (Lehr et al, 2007). As a result of this movement, new conceptualisations of academia and society are emerging. Post Normal Science, Community-Led Research, See-through Science and Sustainability Science all question nature of the production of academic or scientific knowledge (Nowotny et al, 2001; Stilgoe, 2003; Wynne et al, 2005). In summary, they argue for the co-production of knowledge by researchers and other stakeholders (in the broadest sense). These ideas are receiving attention in a variety of fields, including the understanding of the value and role of higher education. Many studies have made the case for public engagement in higher education activities. The theorised benefits include: improved quality and legitimacy of decisions (achieved through including a range of knowledges); an understanding of a broader set of views; engendering trust between the different groups involved (expert and lay); and building capacity of those involved (skills, knowledge) (Funtowitz and Ravetz, 1993; Rowe and Frewer, 2000; Stilgoe 2003). We contribute to this debate; exploring the involvement of a diverse range of stakeholders to question and understand how universities and communities can work together effectively.

Public engagement can take many different forms, so rather than consider a 'one size fits all approach' it might be helpful to contemplate a spectrum of engagement. Authors such as Trench (2008) and Rowe and Frewer (2005) have developed analytical frameworks for engagement. Trench (2008) focuses on public engagement with science, specifically, but the framework could be applied much wider. Within the analytical framework Trench picks out three underlying concepts:

1. Dissemination: which is the idea of types of engagement where the researchers tell the public, or public groups, about science/research.
2. Dialogue: two-way communication, listening to what people have to say and tell them what is happening in the university (a more consultative or involving practice).
3. Conversation or participation: the building of knowledge 'with' public groups (a more collaborative practice).

It is important to raise the differences between the various types of public engagement, as the purpose behind any public engagement activity informs what actually happens in practice. Thinking carefully about the purpose of engagement helps to distinguish between the different options and goals of engagement activities. We argue that public engagement is most effective when it is taken beyond informing or consulting and towards collaborative, participatory activities. These engagement driven processes are considered pivotal to demonstrating the deeper impact of higher education institutions reaching out to their communities. It is on the basis of this historical context that the BPE programme was created, and thus the UCL-led Beacon and the case study outlined in this chapter initiated.

Championing a culture of public engagement: UCL's Beacon for Public Engagement

Against this background of public engagement in higher education in the UK, the BPE was a programme launched in 2007 within the UK to support public engagement by higher education institutions. The initiative was funded by the Higher Education Funding Council for England (HEFCE), Research Councils UK (RCUK) and the Wellcome

Trust. At the core of the programme was the concept of culture change; the programme aimed to encourage a culture change within UK universities to recognise, reward and support public engagement. HEFCE offered a definition of public engagement, for the purpose of the BPE programme, which was:

> bringing together Higher Education specialists and non-specialists to develop new channels of communication and mutual understanding. The 'public' includes individuals and groups who do not currently have a formal relationship with a higher education institution through teaching, research or knowledge transfer (HEFCE, 2007, cited by Hussain and Moore, 2012).

Six BPEs were set up across the UK to pilot a programme of public engagement activities. Each BPE was made up of one or more higher education institution, £9.2 million was invested into the BPE programme by the RCUK, the UK funding councils and the Wellcome Trust (over 4 years). UCL was awarded £1.2 million. The NCCPE was also established to disseminate and share the learning from the programme. UCL was one of the six Beacons. In 2008 a Public Engagement Unit (PEU) was set up within UCL. The remit of the PEU is to support activities that encourage a culture of two-way conversations between university staff, students, and groups outside the university. The UCL-led BPE programme aimed to encourage a culture change at UCL with regard to public engagement and to facilitate and coordinate public engagement opportunities, through identifying and building on best practice. The UCL-led Beacon took the strategic aims of the BPE programme to build the foundations and a clear vision for delivery of its operations.

At the beginning of the BPE initiative in 2008, UCL was already involved in a range of public engagement activities and many staff and students were passionate about this area of work. However, a key challenge that been at the forefront of public engagement activity is the conflicting demands placed on researchers and students within the university. There is an underlying need for public engagement to be embedded within teaching, research and learning at any higher education institution. When public engagement is no longer seen as an 'add-on' to existing work, but instead an integral part of the role of staff and students in higher education, then the longer term impact of public engagement work will be recognised. The research consultants FreshMinds were appointed by UCL to undertake an investigation of public engagement at UCL. This research provided a background to staff attitudes towards public engagement and a snapshot of public engagement activity at UCL. The study revealed that there was an opportunity to coordinate public engagement activities at UCL, and build on the existing strengths in public engagement being undertaken by the institution (FreshMinds, 2008). The findings from this study were used to inform the BPE programme implementation at UCL.

The Beacons initiative at UCL has provided an array of opportunities for staff and students to carry out public engagement activities: funding and facilitating public engagement projects, running public events, training and mentoring staff and students to give them the skills and confidence for public engagement, providing support and advice, awards for best practice in public engagement, developing networks and influencing university policies. The achievements of the UCL-led Beacon, from the period of its inception to completion in December 2011, are outlined within the final evaluation report (Hussain and Moore, 2012). To give some context, these include: 91 public engagement projects funded through various grants; one completed Fellowship completed and five public engagement mentors appointed; a total of 237 partner groups/organisations linked to the programme; creation of the Annual UCL Provost's Awards for Public Engagement; over 37,560 people attending programme and project activities; over 1600 UCL staff and students and 530 people outside UCL participating in training and mentoring on public engagement. Now, public engagement is included as a requirement in the UCL academic staff promotions criteria.

The UCL-led BPE programme represents a complex interplay of strategies and practical actions to formalise and embed public engagement within UCL. Overall, the PEU was committed to increasing the activity in, capacity for and understanding of public engagement across the university. The BPE programme strived towards providing support, reward and recognition to staff and students involved in public engagement activities.

The role of evaluation and learning in the UCL Beacon

Monitoring and evaluation are considered a fundamental part of good practice in university public engagement. Many of the arguments for monitoring and evaluation public engagement focus on its role in collecting 'evidence of impact'. However, here we focus on evaluation role in questioning, understanding and learning. There are various approaches to programme and project evaluation, ranging in focus (assessing processes, outputs, outcomes and impacts), timing, audience (funders, stakeholders, beneficiaries) and methods used (quantitative and/or qualitative). Ultimately, decisions over what to investigate, for whom and for what purpose determine how evaluation is approached. Within the UCL-led Beacon evaluation and learning was integrated within and considered essential to its practice: an Evaluation Officer (one of the authors) was based within the PEU working within the BPE programme. The Evaluation Officer had a dual role: to evaluate the contribution to culture change and to support and advise on the evaluation of public engagement activities by UCL staff and students. Evaluation of the UCL-led Beacon was not an activity that happened at the end of the programme but was an embedded and ongoing learning and iterative process. Within the UCL-led Beacon the Evaluation Officer played a role at the start of the programme and throughout in the shaping and questioning of aims and intentions.

The evaluation model was built around a theory of change for the UCL-led Beacon, and from this it aimed to collect data that would contribute to an understanding of the changes resulting from public engagement: what has changed, why it has changed, how changes relate to activities and how these changes fit within the aims of the programme. A responsive, qualitative evaluation approach was adopted, which is grounded in the interpretative philosophy of science, one that recognises and focuses on understanding multiple experiences and values, a diversity of stakeholders and perspectives, both inside and outside UCL. Qualitative evaluation offers an alternative to approaches that only seek to describe and measure quantifiable outputs of a programme.

The Evaluation Officer worked with key stakeholders to develop a critical framework, which determined the focus of the evaluation of UCL's public engagement programme. The framework aimed to: provide a structure and a skeleton for the appraisal of the programme and projects undertaken; clarify the programmes' strategic aims; break down what they mean; and describe how they might be achieved. The framework, therefore, was designed to capture outcomes and impacts as well as quantifiable outputs. It was believed that articulating and capturing the outcomes and impacts of projects would provide a richer understanding of the achievements of the engagement activities taking place under the BPE. This framework was also used by the Evaluation Officer when providing nuanced support and guidance to staff and students undertaking engagement activities.

University public engagement in practice

A journey of university public engagement is our case study, focusing on a series of public engagement projects undertaken under the umbrella of the UCL-led Beacon. This is a particular kind of a journey, yet one made amid the ebbs and flows of people, disciplines, communities and ideas in a globalised world. The focus of the journey is not solely public

Figure 1.1: Food Junctions Festival

Figure 1.2: Foodpaths Movement

engagement; it tells us how we (i.e, including the funder, the PEU, and the staff and students involved in the case study) came together to share a passion for food and all that it means, and how that passion was translated into action. These were experiences of embodied engagement in a concrete reality. We began this collective journey with the Food Junctions Festival (Figure 1.1), continued with the Foodpaths Movement (Figure 1.2) and ended with *The Food Junctions Cookbook*.

Food Junctions Festival: igniting a moment

Food Junctions Festival began with a response to a funding call for proposal from the UCL PEU to contribute to the Reveal Festival[1] from 22 April to 2 May 2010, in which UCL was one of the key local partners. From the outset, we – a team of students at all levels at UCL – wanted to keep Food Junctions as a genuine collaborative project and the discussion – the dialogue and the interchange of ideas. A number of strategic decisions were made in the initial planning stage. First, we took advantage of food as a broad and inclusive topic that would allow a wide range of involvement across the entire university at all levels (from students to senior member of academic and supporting staff). Second, as a reflection of university–community engagement (another kind of 'junction'), we tried to ensure a balanced involvement from both the university and communities around King's Cross and beyond. Third, following the theme of 'revealing' we thought it would be more appropriate that we organised Food Junctions outside the campus – with our key community partner, Camley Street Nature Park, located close to King's Cross Station. We came to call ourselves 'Food Junctions: a festival where nature meets culture' indicating it was a nested enterprise within the Park and the Reveal Festival but also that many connections (junctions) would be explored, invented, animated and imagined far beyond.

Indeed, we were confident Food Junctions was no ordinary festival. Over the course of four and a half days in the ten-day period of the Reveal Festival, we coordinated 60 activities, involving over 200 contributors (mostly UCL staff and students and over 30 local community food initiatives) and around 1500 participants came to the Festival. These activities included providing a free healthy breakfast to start the day, hands-on gardening and cooking sessions, presentations and debates on topics ranging from urban agriculture, food tasting (wine, home-made jam, chocolate, wild honey), art workshops, architectural installations, poetry reading, walks and tours, film screenings and all ending with a dance performance as a kind of harvest celebration.

The works presented opportunities for contemplation and discussion, a space for socialising, and having spontaneous conversations about how to cross-disciplinary boundaries and develop future collaborative projects for both research and practice.

It is important to mention that all our work in progress described here was shared and discussed with all members of staff at the UCL PEU, who was funding and supporting our project. In so doing, we were able to discover many additional resources and expertise, which helped to ensure a smooth delivery of the project. It also helped us to conduct an evaluation of the project throughout the process and, above all, to embrace UCL PEU staff as part of our collaborative team, much beyond the normal division of funders and grant recipients. However, such an evaluation needed to reconcile the multiple layers of stakeholders involved the Reveal Festival, the Food Junctions team, collaborating individuals and organisations, festival participants and of course our personal reflections. The feedback was mostly positive and all felt that much has been learnt by working together. In this regard, the Santander 1-UCL Award might be a good example of a synergistic outcome generated from the Food Junctions. The Award called Food Junctions 'a ground-breaking festival'. It recognised our contributions to open up UCL's activity to our neighbours, offering a human face to a university that sometimes presents only buildings. Moreover, ownership of Food Junctions was shared with community groups, providing opportunities for local people to advocate for and represent their communities in a wider public context. However, with a more critical assessment from the evaluative process, a direction for ways forward was developed which included:

1. taking advantage of the momentum to extend and prolong ephemerality into continuous university–community engagement;
2. and focusing on further mobilising and bridging food knowledge, especially some of the more radical issues.

Foodpaths Movement: transforming a moment into a movement

Based on the critical assessment of the Food Junctions Festival, there was a crucial need for introducing and mobilising a variety of food knowledge for developing more sustainable food systems in London. This time, we decided to collaborate with another key local community partner – The Calthorpe Project – a community garden and a community at the heart of King's Cross. With the success of the Food Junctions, we were encouraged to participate in another bid for the funding, also offered from the UCL PEU. We decided to call it 'Foodpaths: the King's Cross Movement' to politicise the whole process. Inspired by new social movement theories and particularly the notion of 'everyday activism', we wanted to make the King's Cross Movement a particular kind of urban food movement – more inclusive and accessible at an everyday level through our lived experiences.

Foodpaths aimed to create paths to do two things: first, to support our desire to change current unsustainable food systems especially around the area of King's Cross; and second, to encourage university and community to help each other to develop a vision and action plan for long-term and sustainable collaboration rather than only having one-off projects or events. Once again, we were blessed with the luck to be chosen as one of the six winners of this grant, which enabled us to plant and grow our new seeds of enquiries regardless of all kinds of uncertainties and challenges ahead.

Unlike the Food Junctions Festival, we deliberately prolonged our project to a six-month period, which allowed us to communicate better the elaborated notion of 'path' and 'movement'. Five major themes for each month were decided: (1) growing food in the city; (2) food and cooperatives; (3) food and women; (4) food and health; (5) food and spirituality. Of course these five themes were not definitive, yet as a catalyst project, we thought this selection could already indicate the complexity of food system and our relationships with it.

At Foodpaths, we elaborated the notion of an 'urban food movement' as 'everyday activism' through ordinary practices such as gardening, cooking and sharing a meal around a table. And yet, Foodpaths was not a fully signposted journey to a utopia, but paths that we all had to seek and find, like any other adventurous journeys full of mud and swamps as well as uncertainties and insecurity, but at the same time excitement and fun. Above all, it was not merely about any individuals but us together, creating new paths towards a more sustainable food system in London. Through sustaining, widening and deepening the engagement between university and community, we managed to deliver our second university public engagement project.

From the beginning of Foodpaths, we set up a systematic evaluation mechanisms that helped to capture what was happening at the event and could be accessed via our blog. After each event, we managed to incorporate some of the feedback into the next event. In order for our learning to be effective, we needed to be critical and realistic about our evaluation. A list of things that did not work out can be long. We were not achieving our original goal in terms of engaging a more marginalised population and realised that a deeper structural barrier (basic material security) made inclusive community participation much more difficult. Similarly, we lacked representation from mainstream food corporations. And it was hardly surprising that sustaining and widening engagement still depended on the committed work of the core team members rather than making it more institutionalised.

However, we tried to facilitate learning, share knowledge and information, and encourage collaboration and dialogue around goals, means and expected outcomes. We also experimented in innovative ways to build capacity at different levels from individuals, to core team members and also organisations. Foodpaths was succeeding in joining more projects together and was helping participants link various themes (co-ops, growing, food waste, the role of women). However, all these networks were still quite personal, and time and place-bound. New thinking emerged. How could we create a legacy at UCL with recognition and legitimacy that would inspire more students and staff to continue our journey or even challenge us with much better ideas and effective organisations? How could we have our stories heard by a much wider audience?

The Food Junctions Cookbook: celebrating moments and movements

Throughout the Festival and the Foodpaths Movement, we had generated a huge amount of material. Ever since we started to organise the Food Junctions Festival, an idea of producing a cookbook had always been with us as an alternative to a conventional project report, which has been well received and supported by the funder – UCL PEU. This cookbook would represent the continuity and variations of our collective journey – a process of engagement to create something dynamic, innovative and sustainable over time. After an initial period of preparation, we sent out a call for contributions across a diverse range of networks. Half of our contributors were from the university, mainly from UCL but with a small numbers from other universities. The other half of the contributors were from the community, both groups and individuals. We welcomed people from all walks of life.

In *The Food Junctions Cookbook* (Chang and Meusburger, 2011), some 70 contributors share their 'living recipes' for things to cook, things to think about and above all things to do. The book mixes practice, politics and pleasure, and ties people together through a common interest in food. With elaborated notion of 'recipe' both literally and metaphorically, the book combines insights and inspirational stories from all round the world: how to taste wine, open up a catering coop, deal with food waste, prevent childhood obesity, make delicious dishes from wild plants and grow food in the city. We were pleased that all these stories and recipes and memories of producing them are now stored in this *Cookbook*.

The book is licensed under the Creative Commons and a PDF version can be downloaded for free. While printed copies can be bought on Amazon, we decided to donate our cookbooks to local libraries, community centres and community groups for wider engagement. Since the publication of the *Cookbook*, hundreds of people have told us that they were encouraged and strengthened by knowing that other people were doing similar things and that change was not only possible but under way.

To begin with, our *Cookbook* was seen as a social text revealing the new democratisation and cosmopolitanism of cookery, which broke through all the old monopolies – of professional gatekeepers who decide what should be cooked, and how, and how it should be presented. Also, *The Food Junctions Cookbook* was particularly important in two notable ways. First, it has the potential to impact local and national government for a more progressive framework for food policy and regulation with a vision positively to affect the lives, health and wellbeing of the working class, marginalised and most vulnerable. Second, it provides a new paradigm for community-oriented social innovation – beyond food security and food sovereignty, addressing sustainable resource management (water, air quality, housing, health, work and education) – where the autonomies, the rights and the responsibilities of urban dwellers could also benefit from similarly imaginative activity. This will help UCL to make a distinctive contribution not only to the global debate on the challenge of feeding an increasingly populous world in the cities but more widely on the challenge of developing sustainable cities as a whole.

Since *The Food Junctions Cookbook* was published at UCL, much has happened. What we have learnt is the fact that under the surface of differences, we all have common hopes and dreams and what it means to work hard on a common goal. Once again, it was believed that we are in a stronger position to fulfil what was stated in our original bid for the funding of the Food Junctions Festival, in which we said that 'we want to tell our stories, as students within particular departments and across the UCL community; as local residents around King's Cross and as global citizens'.

Learning from the journey

As described in the previous section, although the three university public engagement projects took place one after another, changes never appeared in a linear manner. The perspectives have incorporated views from key stakeholders involved in the journey, which gained from an inductive, interpretative and qualitative approach within the UCL-led Beacon Evaluation Framework. In effect, this can be seen as one of the many examples that produced close relationships and mutual learning between funding organisation and grants recipients.

Through the university–community collaboration, we endeavoured to challenge the predominant approach to knowledge, which has been based on a hierarchical, bureaucratic, individualistic and/or corporate-driven governance system. Rather, we promoted a more horizontal and interactive knowledge governance system where a multiplicity and interdisciplinarity of knowledge as well as a variety of channels for learning were created and sustained. In particular, developing embedded, flexible and inclusive evaluation mechanisms, with a higher priority given to the evolving process of university public engagement and its transformative impacts, should be integral to an innovative knowledge governance system. Our learning resonates with literature within the field on the subject of engagement, acknowledging the role of transparency, reflection and clarity to ensure effectiveness of the process (Rowe and Frewer, 2000).

We recommend the need to consider who should be involved (the evaluation team, if any) and how to work through this co-enquiry in order to evaluate the success and failures of, and learn from, any activity or project undertaken throughout the 'embedded' process: planning, coordination, implementation, documentation and dissemination. While the criteria of evaluation should follow a bottom-up approach among the evaluation team, the overall assessment should go beyond the judgement on the basis of the narrow criteria of positivist social and natural sciences alone and emphasise more transformative outcomes through the process of engagement.

While it is important for all stakeholders to agree on a set of clear parameters for university public engagement, in practice we sometimes had to alter the process of university public engagement to accept different outputs and outcomes from the original aims and objectives. For instance, in the public engagement projects outlined in this chapter, originally we had a normative aim to create a sustainable food system in London through our community–university engagement. However, it became an unrealistic gaol to achieve as simply not everyone shared the same vision of a sustainable food system. Instead, our collaborative projects created spaces for all stakeholders to express and reflect on how they might reimagine a sustainable food system from their own perspectives. Acknowledging that conflicting differences between stakeholders were not negatives to be eliminated but diverse values to be recognised was helpful in developing a balanced view in terms of evaluation. For example, the PEU, recognised that there were opportunities to break new ground in the field of public engagement, so they were more flexible with the terms and conditions of their funding.

One of the key factors that allowed the journey to continue was a more inclusive and long-term perspective from those involved. What really mattered was that there were multiple monitoring and evaluation mechanisms (including evaluation from UCL PEU, from partnering community organisation and core team internal evaluation). Unlike many people who see this inclusive approach as problematic and chaotic, our case study has demonstrated such evaluation can generate positive engagement with and interactions among different stakeholders if a coherent engagement framework exists. Indeed, such evaluation acts to create a learning culture and a learning organisation that can provide enabling conditions to experiment and innovate without concerns about making mistakes. To this end, there has been a variety of learning reports and reflective accounts produced by the case study, together with conferences, seminars and workshops. We were also continuously building and nurturing networks of communication, bridging organisations on the edge, creating mutual trust and mutual support and above all, through everyday practices such as growing, cooking and sharing, we provided the conditions for learning and exchanging knowledge about university public engagement.

Enabling conditions for effective public engagement within higher education

The previous sections scrutinised engagement in practice within one public engagement journey, a case study of three collaborative projects. Here, we draw on the case study to demonstrate that, while engagement is valuable in principle, it can, in practice, be problematic. We translate the learning from the journey into enabling conditions for universities and communities to work together. A number of conditions ensure the effective delivery of public engagement activities. The UCL-led Beacon final evaluation report synthesised the knowledge from the programmes' evaluation, and this was a first step in developing a practical guide that sets out how to bring about culture change within a higher education institution (Hussain and Moore 2012). Within this section we build on the themes raised through our evaluation and learning, and the authors' critical collaboration, with a focus on our case study in question, to outline enabling conditions for effective public engagement.

Flexibility of definitions and interpretations

Within the UCL-led Beacon there was a commonly agreed strategic approach to public engagement – what it was and what it was not – however, despite some 'definition boundaries', what was demonstrated in the actual projects was flexibility in definitions and interpretations of engagement and public groups, or communities, who were engaged. It is this flexibility that has been key to the delivery of effective engagement activities. The case study recognised and acknowledged the differing agendas, or goals, within their projects. This helped to ensure that partners and key stakeholders knew each other's interests and understood varying perspectives.

Within a university, departments, research groups, staff and students involved in public engagement generally know their audiences or partners already, and as such they are able to tailor activities. If the term community is interpreted broadly to include the variety of stakeholders, residents, local authority officers, project managers, then the case study is an excellent example of the 'creation of communities', social relationships, associations, networks through the fostering of social ties, interaction, local attachments, physical and social involvement around the particular project activities, be that a festival or workshops or the creation of a cookbook.

Diversity of opportunities

Underlying the flexible nature of public engagement, there are a variety of methods in which to carry out public engagement projects and our learning indicates that these should be drawn on. With the PEU at UCL, it was made clear that public engagement can range from informing the public about one's work, to taking part in two-way dialogue about the direction of research and teaching – there is a spectrum of purposes for engagement. The underlying ethos within the UCL-led Beacon was that one-way engagement (informing) should lead to deeper understanding and two-way dialogue. As illustrated within the journey presented within this chapter, the range of activities within the case study (festival, workshops, writing) gave opportunities for a diversity of people to get involved and allowed a wider scope of public engagement to take place. The case study illustrates that engagement methods can be tailored to certain factors and audiences; the production of a 'cookbook' is a wonderful example of tailoring the output, so to speak, of a project to fit with the key connecting theme. The team running Food Junction and Foodpaths took time to carefully select the stakeholders, to identify and approach the right people, consider what interests them and why should they be involved.

Coordination and support

Through the establishment of a PEU, the Beacons initiative enabled UCL to create something in the field of public engagement that is greater than the sum of the numerous public engagement activities undertaken. The public engagement activities had, and still have, an umbrella through which they were coordinated. This hub of activity is a necessary body that is needed in order to develop and maintain effective university public engagement (Hussain and Moore, 2012). Our learning indicates that it is key to champion an approach that encourages the formation of relationships between a funder or supporter and those undertaking the public engagement projects. The development of effective working relationships between the PEU and staff and students was fundamental to achieving the broader, strategic goals of the operations of the UCL-led Beacon in terms of building capacity for, and sharing experience and learning from, public engagement within UCL. However, without strong leadership within a project or department, the engagement activities are unlikely to achieve impacts among the wider organisation. We found that it is important to get support from senior leaders, such as heads of departments; if they are 'on board', they can recognise the importance of such work and the benefits it can bring to departments, the research and the communities.

Sustainability

The case study within this chapter illustrates a public engagement journey over a period of years. Not all engagement activities have this kind of lifecycle. Maintaining public engagement activity within researchers, or departments is a continuous challenge. Due to conflicting demands on time, public engagement activity is an area that needs to be an ingrained part of academic life. The evaluation of the UCL-led Beacon showed that, in reality, once a public engagement project has ended, it was difficult to keep staff and students involved in further public engagement activity (Hussain and Moore, 2012).

Unlike the case study outlined in this chapter, many of the public engagement projects funded under the UCL-led Beacon did not, in general, have a degree of forward planning, particularly around what happens when the grant finishes. Hence there was evidence of deterioration in engagement between some of the community and university collaborations. There is need to encourage and sustain 'engagement' to prevent the breakdown of such relationships. The UCL-led Beacon evaluation report noted that there is potential for staff and students to gain skills and confidence while undertaking public engagement projects, and this should in theory make it easier for them to do it again; therefore, consistent support and encouragement is an essential element to ensure sustainable public engagement.

Evaluation

In brief, evaluation plays an important role to bridge the gaps between the programme and the practices to ensure and enhance enabling conditions for communities and universities to work together as a pathway to transformative impacts on university, research, practices and communities. Within the case study it was the evaluation that fostered discourse across the potential divides (between funder and funded, between the academic and the communities, between strategy and practice). The evaluation facilitated constructive conversation, and ultimately the integration of knowledges created from a multitude of disciplinary perspectives. We cannot emphasise enough the importance of evaluation to the achievement of effective university public engagement. Any attempt to categorise any of the public engagement activities as 'successful' will depend on what criteria are being applied – and by whom. Our case study illustrated that the projects had open and even multiple aims for the engagement; however, they thought through what they wanted to achieve. The failure to specify success criteria (in terms of desired outcomes) in advance not only impairs the transparency of the projects but also hampers attempts to evaluate their 'success'. Hopes and aspirations for such projects need to be translated into tangible goals by which success can be measured.

Rather than a feeling among stakeholders that such projects have a positive impact on the people involved or research agenda, with each inferring on what the projects achieved, there is a need to collect evidence. This involves building in time for reflection, throughout the life of the activity, both for the person managing the process of engagement and those engaged. Within the case study, evaluation was embedded from the very start. Rather than be a target or output obsessed funder, the PEU, under the UCL-led Beacon, gave recognition to the multiple results that public engagement activities produce, even if these are not those originally expected. This mindset encouraged learning, and the sharing of learning, at all levels within Food Junctions and Foodpaths, culminating with the production of the *Cookbook*. All those involved in the case study were encouraged to build evaluation into their plans at the beginning of the project in order that they could learn valuable lessons for any future public engagement activity. Furthermore, as illustrated through the case study, there were plenty of opportunities for sharing of experiences (both internally within UCL and externally with those outside of UCL); this ensured that the knowledge gained did not just stay with individuals, predominately the core team, but was shared.

Conclusion

The engagement driven movement will continue to contribute significantly to the structure and strategies of the UK higher education sector. We feel that there will be increasing pressure to demonstrate the effectiveness and impact of such processes and strategies. Within this chapter we have discussed a university public engagement journey, a journey made up of different routes: the transition from theory to practice, the jump between strategy and practice, the movement from idea to action, the collaboration of academia and communities, a series of activities, a rethink of what it means engage effectively. By reflecting on the opportunities and challenges of the UCL-led Beacon we propose the enabling conditions for communities and universities to work together, noting five key contributors: flexibility of definitions and interpretations; sustainability; diversity of opportunities; coordination and support; and evaluation. These enabling factors are differently combined and interrelated. We have utilised structured evaluations and personal reflections to identify strategies for universities and the higher education sector to consider when supporting communities and university collaborations in the form of public engagement projects.

A key principle underpinning this journey was questioning: questioning what we are doing and why, thinking about how theory is translated into practice and how practice informs theory. Here, within this chapter, we have undertaken further critical reflection closely examining a case study from different perspectives. The key themes that have arisen from our learning provide a base for critical awareness, for those with a role or responsibility in the process of community and university collaborations. The chapter demonstrated the jump between the policy intentions and the practical delivery of the 'public engagement agenda'. We highlight that public engagement is changing and dynamic – not to mention that it is challenging. We provide a more differentiated conception of engagement within universities, one that acknowledges that certain conditions are required to generate effective ways of working between universities and communities, with a more sophisticated notion of the effectiveness and appropriateness of it in this field. It feels odd writing the heading 'conclusion' as our work is not concluded here; the journey for both authors and their practice continues. The UCL PEU has been centrally funded by the university after the BPE programmed finished, and continues to encourage and support staff and students to undertake engagement at UCL; while the practice of engagement, through universities and communities working together, positively moves forward.

Acknowledgement
The work presented in this chapter builds on work undertaken within collaborative projects. The authors would like to acknowledge the contributions of the teams involved in these projects. We have drawn on some of the key outputs produced, notably the UCL-led Beacon final evaluation report (Hussain and Moore, 2012) and the PhD thesis entitled 'Growing a Commons Food Regime: Theory and Practice' (Chang, 2013). We build on our learning and use this chapter to combine our experiences.

Note

[1] Reveal Festival was produced by Creative King's Cross, which is working with a huge range of local partners to take participants to a creative journey through the changing landscape of King's Cross.

TWO

Understanding impact and its enabling conditions: learning from people engaged in collaborative research

Alex Haynes

Introduction

This chapter speaks to several of the key questions outlined in this book, such as what are the lessons and challenges of collaborative research? What do we mean by impact? What does it look like on the ground? Can what we learn from people's experience of being involved in collaborative social research, the ways they describe impact, and what they value about their involvement and the outcomes help us to articulate the positive impacts of collaborative social research? The increasing emphasis on research impact, the way it is being variously defined by research councils across the globe,[1] and the influence of this agenda on institutional structures and research funding underlines the importance of examining in more detail the theory, practice and impacts of collaborative social research. This examination can draw from the extensive body of theoretical work on social, participatory and activist research, community engagement and development practice, and the ongoing critique of these endeavours. Equally this examination can be informed by the direct experiences of people engaging in collaborative social research and the impact and value they identify. As with much community development practice, collaborative social research seeks to make a positive difference in people's lives, generate change or support social action so the drive for impact is embedded in the research intent. In this context research impact may be described as understanding, influence and action for positive social change.

Banks (2001: 119) suggests that 'all first hand research of any kind, must be collaborative to some extent ... the researcher's very presence amongst a group of people is the result of a series of social negotiations'. While these negotiations vary between projects, in some cases the process of negotiation becomes fundamental to the research methodology. This negotiation also offers opportunities for the researcher to understand existing group protocols, rules and social norms or local cultures (Holcome, 2008; Davis and Holcombe, 2010). Engagement, negotiation and compromise are particular features of collaborative research that may make it well placed to deliver individual and collective impact.

Collaborative research in practice

This chapter draws from an Australian research study exploring how people make their lives in new places. The study is focused in an area of northern Melbourne (Australia) that is a mixture of suburbs established in the 1950s and 1960s and new housing estates. The area is culturally and ethnically diverse, and has a significant place in Aboriginal people's lives, the history of Melbourne and in the story of both humanitarian and skilled migration to Australia.

In this study I define collaborative social research as inquiry that is cooperative, ethical, shared, multi-directional and mutual. It is a form of research in which engaging with people, and perhaps the wider public, is foundational rather than added on like a one-off public event, workshop or results sharing activity. As with all engagement I have been mindful that involving people in research processes is not necessarily an empowering approach, similar to the critique of the assumed emancipatory character of participatory research. I also reflected on the assumption that cooperation or collaboration produces new critical insights or new knowledge.

The exploratory research question 'how do people make their lives in new places?' lent itself to research methods that enable discovery of people's experience of place, their meaning making in relation to place and the continual transition and revision of these meanings and experiences. A participant directed combination of methods was used, including participant-led walking tours, photo and video elicitation, participatory video, interviews, group dialogues, blog writing and observation. The flexibility of methods enabled the participants to choose the ways we progressed the research together, and to create content and outputs the individuals and groups own and can use.

One of the key findings of the study is the importance of groups, particularly for people seeking asylum, refugees and new migrants, to explore different interpretations, to see the world in new ways and to reflect on how the values and beliefs they bring intersect with their new realities. In this way perhaps they can begin to see themselves as protagonists in their own families, communities and their new country. Two women's groups involving more than 80 women who are, or have been at some stage, seeking asylum, refugees or migrants to Australia were part of the overall study. These groups are used here to help to draw attention to some challenges and opportunities of collaborative social research and illustrate how participants describe impact, which leads into a discussion of how impact was enabled through this particular study. This enabling has a methodological rather than a theoretical focus. I include some particular moments or encounters from my field notes that reveal the processes by which our positionalities were constituted and knowledge produced. The encounters hint at the range and depth of the women's dilemmas and tensions concerning faith, freedom and family, and reveal my own dilemmas about the purpose of research and the opportunities and responsibilities we have when we undertake it.

Persian women's group

The Persian women's group included women who were Persian, others Kurdish, some Muslim, others Bahai, some refugees who had spent time in refugee camps in Turkey, some asylum seekers who had spent time in offshore detention and community detention, many with no work rights[2] and most with limited English language. They were a relatively new group, having only formed six months before I met them.

I was invited by the facilitator to join their weekly gatherings, and through an interpreter I introduced myself with photos and explained my research question, my motivation and intent. They asked me to explain what I thought research was, what it was for and how it could be used and we talked about ethics and consent. For the first few weeks I observed the group, engaged with the women in breaks through those who spoke some English, I worked with those with very limited or no English by using a Persian Farsi dictionary and a translation app on our mobile phones.

While I was building some rapport I wanted to understand more about what was going on with the group and for them individually. I met with a Persian colleague to help me understand more of the nuances of Persian culture and conversation. I invited her to the group to see if that enabled different conversations. The Persian women were very pleased to have someone who could not only speak Farsi fluently but had grown up in Iran and still had family there but had lived in Australia for more than a decade.

From my observations and debriefing with my colleague it was clear the women were eager to learn more about social, cultural and political issues and they enjoyed the opportunity to have a more inclusive dialogue instead of the instructional dynamic that was part of the existing group format. In our reflection we discussed the idea of having more purposeful conversations – moving beyond capturing their experience to exploring social issues together. I wanted to start a conversation, encourage questions and interaction, share experiences and opinions. My colleague suggested that while Persians do not completely say what they think they will give some indication of it in discussion and that we can build on that.

To begin the purposeful conversations I chose a public issue that I thought might have personal interest and be provocative. In October 2014 the Australian Government Department of Parliamentary Services issued a statement that anyone wearing a burqa and trying to enter Parliament House will be now asked to temporarily remove their facial covering. This developed into a controversial plan[3] to make Muslim women wearing a burqa or niqab sit in glassed enclosures at Parliament House. While the plan was quickly dumped, it did ignite a media frenzy and divisive public opinion and commentary emerged.

Within the group meeting we talked about the issue as it was being presented in the media and gave the women a copy of a video, a mainstream weekly television programme that had shown a story 'Choosing the burqa, Beyond the Veil',[4] which profiled several women born in Australia who wore the burqa. At our next meeting we watched the video together and my Persian colleague explained the content and interpreted the dialogue. We had many of the same reactions to the video, and the same or similar questions.

Research diary extract

Initially the women discussed the general experience of women in Iran.

> 'Many of us come from Southern Iran where there are more Arabs. The situation for women is – if they refused to marry their first cousin chosen for them or wear the burqa they would be killed and a small fee paid by family to clear their guilt.'

The conversation turned to what happens in Australia. Most of the group wanted to know why the women in the video would do that here in Australia? And I was asking the same thing. We moved on to talking about how our laws and culture interact, intersect and their impression of life in Australia. We discussed the value we place on individual freedom and choice. One of the women said,

> 'Here it seems so easy to separate [marriage] for the flimsiest reason, or no reason. The slightest tremor is enough. In Iran there are practicalities and consequences of separating, family gatherings are important and impossible if people are not together.'

The Australian-born coordinator of the group replied,

> 'We have an individualistic society where we put our own needs and wants above those of others, family and community. You see it as flimsy but we see it as exercising choice. We put our own parents in nursing homes!'

Today was the first time I felt we engaged in dialogue as a group ... our interaction was no longer centred on the women being recipients of information or English language support. We created a shared platform that enabled broad ranging discussions and a place where everyone's views are welcomed.

When we met again they talked about feeling isolated, not knowing their neighbours, not seeing friends and not understanding social norms, particularly those around hospitality. In Iran they would see their friends and neighbours every day. I intuitively responded and invited them to my house for lunch which significantly changed the dynamic.

Research diary extract

Many of the group wore hijab, even one woman who was not wearing it when we first met. Over lunch one woman talked about the possibility of being sent back to Iran [if her claim for asylum was rejected], and how her family member had told her how much harder that would be for everyone if all her Facebook photos from her time in Australia had no hijab. Another shared

> 'I don't want to wear it (hijab) and my husband doesn't want me to wear it either but my family does. My brothers say they will kill me if I don't [the brothers live in Australia]. I haven't seen them for nine months – that's not right but they don't want to come, fuss over whether the meat is halal or haram. My husband says 'they don't need to come if they don't like our meat'.'

They often seemed to me to have a very binary notion of good and evil, right and wrong...

> 'It's confusion, the structure in Iran makes everything black and white, right and wrong. Here there is just a lot of grey. How do we make decisions? What do we base those decisions on? We are getting mixed messages?'

They explained that they have been part of a very closed society where religiosity is tied to goodness so it is confusing when they come here as there are many more and different choices, the path is not so direct or clear and their family members deal with these choices differently. Some are afraid so they hold back and they close their minds, others haven't come here to see new things they want to operate exactly as they were in Iran or Iraq, others are saying,

> 'we are in a place that we can pose questions to aspects of the religion that we don't understand, that we were too afraid to even think about before, but now because of the relative stability of our mind and heart, now we can think about these things'.

The conversation we had over lunch, sharing stories and experiences, indicated they are open to reflecting on new experiences, they are ready to ask, 'What is our purpose? Where have we come from and where are we going to?' The video discussion about life in Iran and Australia generally gave them enough confidence to bring the lunch discussion back to their own life, to the individual, specific and here and now. Some felt that they were really starting to push through the confusion and limbo and reach out for new understanding while others were unsure, being constrained by themselves, family members or the threat of going back.

Arabic-speaking women's group

The Arabic-speaking women's group has been established for 15 years, is multi-ethnic with women from a range of countries of origin and time in Australia. Some have been coming to the group since it started, some are straight out of immigration detention, and some are now permanent residents and Australian citizens. They come for friendship, to build connections, to access information and to learn English, even those who have spent 20 years in Australia. Most weeks there are 25–30 women but some weeks I came in to the former school classroom where they meet and was greeted by 50 women.

The coordinator of the group, herself a refugee from Iraq several decades ago, shared her story of arriving and making a new life in Australia with me in an 'interview', a series of three unstructured conversations. She suggested I come to the group, join in and talk with them and hear their stories. Over the next six weeks I worked with the group on a number of research activities (timelines, place diagrams and group discussions for example) and quickly identified some universal themes that framed the women's experiences of making their lives in a new place.

Research diary extract

There was animated chatter (in Arabic) across the four groups in the room and the nominated scribe was busy taking down comments and themes, the things the women thought were important for making their life in Australia. One woman said:

> 'for the first four years we did not socialise with anyone outside our culture. We were afraid to mix as maybe people won't accept us, or we won't accept them, and we couldn't really understand or speak enough English. But it's not just learning the language; you need to learn about culture, what is expected when you visit someone, in their home, at a workplace. You know safety, that feeling of being safe, comes from familiarity, knowing, understanding and communicating.'

The themes included some well documented practical things like the importance of, and difficulties with, learning English, difficulty in finding work, securing recognition of skills and qualification, the lack of cultural awareness and the need to interact and mix with others. There were also a range of relational themes related to the significant change in family and gender dynamics (between husband/wife, with children and extended family, family separation and reunion), and the different pace of transition and change in roles that happens.

> 'Here wives becomes equal so it is bad for men and good for women, 'bad luck for him'. I lived my whole life in Iraq and the government didn't give me anything. When we were offered public housing after two years in Australia my husband saw it from the outside and said the bedrooms are too small. I said 'This is my house, I am living here and if you don't like it you can live outside'. And now, well this is my time ... in Iraq once you reach 40 you are not allowed to wear makeup, paint your nails, etc. your time is up, you stay inside and wait to die. Not here, this is my time.'

Today I sensed the group dynamics were strongly influenced by the mix of women who had been in Australia for a decade or two and those who were much more recent arrivals. There were some strong attitudinal themes summarised succinctly by one woman when she said to her small group, as if giving advice,

> 'You need to make a choice to be happy ... you need some sympathy and understanding, some mercy when you first arrive but then you need to make a go of it yourself! Everything is here you just need to get out there, use the skills you have. Friends, and go betweens are critical for this, you know ... people to take you out, to connect with.'

The women arriving 20–30 years ago when there were no services, help, support and they had to work think the new ones are lucky. The new ones don't feel lucky, particularly the women on bridging visas. One describes her life as living in limbo, and

> 'after 3 years we still cannot work, we don't know what's going to happen to us. It has affected our mental health, our children ... but we don't want to go back, and luckily I found this group.'

A significant amount of the group discussion revolved around the expectations the women had and the reality within which they found themselves. Again as if sharing her story and then giving advice another woman said,

> 'you know before I came I had a beautiful image of Australia – I was shocked. My qualifications (teacher in home country) were not recognised, language was difficult and cultural differences made it hard to understand, or adapt. It was also difficult as I was middle class in my country so my social position changed dramatically. Despite my disappointment and difficulty I worked as a cleaner, I sacrificed everything for my children, so they could get a good education and qualifications. I am grateful I stayed here – we have everything we need now. Don't regret – one day you will reach your goals but you have to be patient. Live your life day by day and don't worry about what comes.'

I returned to the group with a summary of the themes we had developed so far for discussion. This seeded the idea of 'Alsadeqa Alqariba Afdel Min Alaqut Albaieda – The friend that is close to you is better than a sister far away'; a video of group members sharing their advice for newly arrived Arabic-speaking women.

I got a strong sense from the beginning that the women wanted the message of the video to be positive and 'a mix of practical advice and emotional advice (how to manage feelings for example)'. Over the next five months we workshopped the video content, learnt how to use the video equipment, interviewed and filmed each other and other significant things that happened in the group. The video dialogue was in Arabic as it was designed for Arabic-speaking women arriving in Australia and it enabled the women contributing to the video to speak freely and with the scope and nuances of their own language. The content was truly theirs and I could not influence or intervene because I did not know what they were discussing at the time of recording.

Research diary extract

I was standing at the side of the room observing the group watch a preliminary cut of the video that showed seven women sharing their experience and advice. Several times a woman looked towards me and made a positive comment about how helpful the video would be for women when they first arrive in Australia. As the last woman on the video started to speak a silence came over the group, they stared at the screen and tears rolled down some of their faces. It was in Arabic so I couldn't understand what the woman on the screen was saying, so I didn't know what the women in the room were having such a powerful reaction to but I felt it acutely, a tension, a sadness, disbelief. When the video clip had finished the women all turned to the one who had just been on the screen and she responded, moved around to face the women and addressed them in what I thought was quite an assertive, powerful tone. I watched as the women had a long discussion, some were visibly upset, a few sounded angry or confused and there was a lot of empathetic gesturing.

As they left that day they gave me a hug or a knowing nod and thanked me and I still didn't know what had been the subject of their discussion. The group facilitator and I had a long debrief about what had happened and the conversation that had followed the video viewing. The young woman on the video had shared her journey to Australia, which included how her children had drowned along with 90% of the other people on the boat. She also shared the impact that had on her life here in Australia and the importance of having the group to come to. Her husband still doesn't leave the house and blames himself. I expressed my concern for the young woman and the facilitator assured me she was 'ready to share', she needed to share, to be able to grieve, heal and move forward. The group would support her and there were referrals to specialist services available.

> I asked what the animated discussion had been about. After watching the video another woman shared the horrible suicide of a close family member in an offshore detention facility and had asked the group why the Australian government was doing this to them. This generated a discussion about why they were in the position they were, was it really the Australian government or was it because they were Arabs. 'Look at us, we are Arabs, all over the world we are doing it to each other, to ourselves.'

The video project gave the women an opportunity and context to share their stories, experiences and insights. The young woman sharing her journey took a huge step in her grieving and recovery and provided the group with an opportunity to support her and grow as a group through discussing how their personal circumstances and experiences fit within broader social and political issues. I wondered if I had known what the young woman was talking about would I have included it in the first cut video, would my actions and decisions have been any different. Through experiencing the intensity of the emotion in the room, the care and concern, the generosity of the women towards each other I felt the individual and collective power of sharing personal stories and the power of a women's group ... a group that enables women to feel valued as group members, to offer support and guidance to each other, to hear others stories which give their own story more context and meaning, and to make positive change in their own lives and in others' lives by producing a video to help women like them.

In terms of impact it is hard to know whether I was observing good community development and groupwork create positive impact or if, and to what extent, the research intervention had contributed to the impact. The facilitator generously suggested the focus and relevance of the research question and the self-direction of the research activity had led to the outcomes for the individual women and the group.

Identifying and articulating impact

This research was evolutionary and iterative, building on existing conditions, relationships and responding to the dynamic context within which the research is happening. This is particularly important when discussing impact, as it may be problematic for researchers to claim impact (or credit) when building from existing social platforms and the foundational work of others. There are many influences and factors that generate, complement or accelerate impact – these are not necessarily planned, and while they may happen throughout the research process they may not be a direct result of it. Impact conceived as unidirectional cause and effect has real limitations.

Impacts identified by the women

The impacts valued by the women in the two groups described in this chapter and attributed by them, at least in part, to the research process and outcomes included an increase in individual confidence, individual and collective learning and capacity building, group strengthening, increase in group profile and broader awareness raising in their local community about issues surrounding women seeking asylum and the importance of groups in providing social connection and information. The increase in the women's confidence generally related to the opportunity to discuss their lives and challenges and hear others and progress their thinking. As the impact agenda is further embedded and measured we risk losing sight of the value of the profound impact social research and researchers can have on one person's wellbeing (McDermott, 2002).

When asked directly about the experience of being involved in the research, one woman said

> '... these discussions gave me more confidence to ask questions, to understand how it works here and to reconsider my own priorities, beliefs and behaviour, ... I am more ready now to make changes.'

Another woman shared

> '... I have been here [Australia] for 6 years and you are the first person I have met who was born here. No one else has spent the time to get to know me, ask about me, share about themselves, ... just talk to me like I belong here ... it's made such a difference to the way I feel.'

Several of the women involved in the research spoke of an exchange; an exchange of knowledge, of experiences and opinions. Through that exchange they gained a deeper understanding of their position; their place or role in the group, in their family, in the broader community and Australia and they felt a stronger connection; connecting their story with others, to the place they had come to and with larger social, cultural and political forces. They spoke of finding a voice and speaking again – not just another language, but finding a new voice in a different context, a different place.

Another impact that was identified by the women was a better understanding of research and its potential to enable, to empower and "to create knowledge and things like the video to share across the community, to learn to use technology for good, to inform and support others we may never meet" (Participant, Arabic-speaking group).

Impacts identified by me

Being with the women through this research journey helped me to understand the context and content of their lives. It also had a profound impact on my confidence as a researcher to see that with empathy, genuine interest, suspended assumptions, and a clear orientation to justice and social action collaborative research and researchers can influence and encourage positive change in people's lives. I saw the research processes, ideas and outputs flow out from the groups to influence the community agency that supported the groups and how the outputs can be used in advocacy and to secure funding for groups. There is potential for the research findings to contribute to the policy discourse about settlement services in Australia once they are published.

By taking the research outputs into the public arena (showing the women's video at a Refugee Week event for example) and by engaging others from outside the groups we were able to directly address the need for social connection the women identified in the initial stage of research. I observed how the women were growing in capacity through interacting, reflecting and doing things together, how they were able to move from the theoretical to the tangible … the real experience of it. They were making sense of their journeys, to begin to address the misalignment of their physical and psychological journeys and to see intersections between their journeys and those of others, like the researcher. This was confirmed when they requested we do more together, perhaps start a new conversation group. Some of them now saw Australia and its culture as a platform to access information, see the world, raise their consciousness, understand what they are part of and explore how their values correspond to this newly discovered reality. I would also suggest that the knowledge, insights and expertise that emerge through collaborative research should also influence the debate around impact, value and relevance. To contribute to our understanding of how the insight and expertise was enabled, the following section describes the enabling conditions.

The conditions and context that enabled impact

To address the question of challenges and opportunities of collaborative research I think it is important in our discussion of impact to articulate the enabling conditions for impact, to keep the process, outcomes and impact connected. In the two groups that form the basis of this chapter these enabling conditions included

1. creating a shared space for social learning and action
2. developing a shared agenda and
3. using project specific and contingent methods.

1. Creating a shared space

> 'Where are the places for women to come, we need spaces so we can do things, we can laugh, we can ... I don't know. There is a scarcity of spaces, not only to reflect but to do things together, decide things together, to be and to experience, to stay connected.' (Group member)

The space already created within, and around, the two existing women's groups provided a clear entry point for the research. I felt the research might disrupt the existing group so it was necessary to create an intermediate space within that group space so the research did not risk subsuming the groups. I not only had to make the space but also hold it open. This involved give and take, compromise, extra effort, trust and confidence to push the boundaries. Space obviously has an element of physicality – the physical spaces where the group meets and the stability and amenity of that physical space is important but context is also critical. Meeting with the Arabic-speaking women's group reinforced the importance of being mindful of where people are, what else the group is doing, has just done or plans to do. In their case some of the group had just done six weeks of art therapy so the thought of more activities was not appealing nor was breaking into smaller groups. They were all interested in the research idea but hesitant unless they could do it in their normal group setting, as a group, all together.

The context also involves underlying group dynamics, power relations and the particular issues or sensitivities that impact on what is discussed and what happens during group activities. The Arabic-speaking women's group is well established and has rules that everyone knows about. They are used to discussing things in certain ways.

After the first week with the group I saw several of the women at a community event. They thanked me for joining in with the group and went on to explain the need to allow time in each meeting to recap on the research, the starting point, as there were new women joining the group all the time and it was important to 'keep the level of democracy in the group'. They explained that the 'group rules' are really important and only become visible over time and through actions and behaviour.

The Persian women's group had not established explicit rules to the same extent and was much more homogenous in terms of age, time in Australia and country of origin. They are more reliant on the coordinator from the community agency for leadership and setting the agenda. The existing context influenced the research process – the Arabic-speaking women were more confident, able to direct and suggest while the Persian women waited to be led.

2. Developing a shared agenda

I came to these two groups with a research question, albeit an open-ended exploratory question. There was already an overlap between my interest in how they were making their lives and the role the groups played in making their lives but there was a lot of work to do to establish a shared research agenda around what we were doing and why it was worth spending time on. The research question gave my initial conversations with the groups some framing and the research had a generous quality, it opened itself up, encouraged progressive interpretations and enabled me to find something to pursue together with the women.

With the Arabic-speaking women's group the agenda came through an iterative and reflective process that led to the idea of making the video to help other women. With the Persian women the agenda was almost tangible from the beginning, it just needed to be teased out with the showing of the burqa video and subsequent discussion. Through this our shared interest became visible to me as the women struggled to resolve the tensions around faith and family and connecting the personal with the political.

Developing a shared agenda does take some work but it may not always be the researcher who does the work and it may not be overt or explicit. One group member shared a poetic description of the skills required when she said

> '... having the skill to facilitate that from behind, for it not to be seen – it's like the breeze, so the leaves are shaking but nobody is actually seeing the breeze ...'

While talking about the difficulty in bridging the gap between their native culture and adopted culture one woman said 'you need to be like a person who can live inside and outside the water, able to survive in two worlds'. This analogy could equally apply to how I felt living inside and outside the group, between researcher and practitioner, between participant and observer. At first the Arabic-speaking women wanted me to ask questions so they could answer but during the video making I was in the background, observing, offering some technical support. I started 'helping out' with the Persian women learning English, getting to know them, and with the help of the colleague I introduced to the group, it became more like a peer group learning about and from each other through engaging in discussion around issues, having purposeful conversations.

3. Intuitive methodology and using project specific and contingent methods

> Intuitive methodology is a combination of ordered and wholly responsive approaches to soliciting information. The task is to sense the occasion; to be fully empathetic to the mood and the qualities of knowledge and emotion in respondents; and to allow opportunities to be created and seized. Intuitive research applies as a sensitive and exploratory process to the discovery and interpretation of artifacts as much ... as human contact. (O'Riordan, 2001: xxi)

The exploratory nature of the research question, how people make their lives in new places, encouraged the women to consider different ways we could work together to create ideas, knowledge, content and produce outputs people 'owned'. It gave me the ability to take processes and methods and determine how best to apply them in any given context, at any given time. Time is important – not just having enough of it but having a sense of timing, an ability to sense the mood, know when to do what, which requires some reliance on intuition, but was also made easier through the involvement of others from outside the groups in the research.

The flexibility of methods allows different people to participate in a way that is not threatening and may even be enjoyable. I am also more comfortable inviting people to participate, as I know I can align the methods more closely with how they would like to be involved. Collaboration and flexibility with methods enables spectators to be participants, then co-producers, then audiences. If I had tried to initiate a facilitated process with the Arabic-speaking women's group using video activities to structure and mediate social processes and build voice through group interaction there is a high risk they would not have engaged at all or would have lost interest. Overall, I adopted a research orientation towards creating opportunities and providing resources for women to have new experiences and conversations (Feldman, 1998; Gadamer, 1992).

While I have focused on the three enabling conditions that were identified in this particular study I also acknowledge that the production of outputs is conducive to impact. The ability to share, distribute, advocate with tangible outputs or products and tailor them for specific audiences enhances the potential for broader impact. It enables the social embedding of research findings, insights or results through circulation in other forums before landing in an academic context or format.

Conclusion

Collaborative research in the study described is not a discrete project, with a clear beginning or end. It is evolutionary in the sense that it builds on existing conditions, is dynamic and makes a ripple within and beyond the groups that is difficult to keep sight of or recreate. Collaborative or shared research allows things to come together, creates an intensity, an ongoing event that is relationally meaningful. The negotiations, compromises and collaborations involved are part of a process by which understandings are reached, knowledge is produced and impact generated.

According to Nyden (2006) the real value of collaborative research is the emphasis on 'what could be' rather than the traditional research emphasis on 'what is'. Limiting settlement support for refugees and those seeking asylum to introducing government systems (health, financial, legal systems for example), services and learning English does not allow for the exploration of new experiences, and social, cultural and religious differences that are critical for making a new life. As a secular society the spiritual is not foundational to policy or community life in Australia but left to personal, individual choice. Collectively we are loathe to look at, analyse and discuss religion and spirituality as it relates to broader society so when it does happen it is often awkward. The question I was asking was: can we create more spaces for people to explore different interpretations, to see the world in new ways and to reflect on how the values and beliefs they bring intersect with others and their new realities … and can we create the conditions so they can see themselves as protagonists in their own families, communities and their new country, rather than observers and economic beneficiaries? Enabled by their participation in the group and prompted by the research conversations they have been able to recalibrate the personal and societal … to join the personal with the public.

With thanks to the participants I share this example of collaborative research to add some detail to the overall impact conversation. By describing the challenges and the messiness, capturing the impacts women valued from their engagement and by considering what enables impact we might further develop the way we think about and demonstrate impact.

Acknowledgement

The intention was to co-author this chapter with one of the women from the Arabic-speaking women's group. Our initial discussions revealed her preference to work with me on telling her story and the story of her ethnic group from northern Iraq rather than spending time writing an academic book chapter. Through the research experience and our relationship she has recognised the importance of documenting her own biography in the context of 'her people', their life in Iraq and Australia and the larger social, political and historical forces that have influenced their collective story.

Notes

[1] Most government agency definitions of research impact encourage researchers to consider who or what could benefit from their research, how they can help to realise these benefits throughout their study, and how they can document or demonstrate these benefits. For example the Australian Research Council (2015) defines research impact as 'the demonstrable contribution that research makes to the economy, society, culture, national security, public policy or services, health, the environment, or quality of life, beyond contributions to academia'.

[2] While recent changes in Australian asylum seeker policy have extended temporary work rights to over 20,000 asylum seekers in Australia, not all asylum seekers are permitted to work and pathways to permanent settlement for asylum seekers have become increasingly more difficult to obtain.

[3] Read more: 'Controversial Parliament House burqa ban dumped', *Sydney Morning Herald*, 20 October 2014, www.smh.com.au/federal-politics/political-

news/controversial-parliament-house-burqa-ban-dumped-20141019-118j5h.html#ixzz43xdurQI6

4   Watch: 'Choosing the burqa', Yahoo News Australia

THREE

Emphasising mutual benefit: rethinking the impact agenda through the lens of Share Academy

Judy Willcocks

Introduction

The early 21st century brought considerable changes to the way museums and universities were constituted and understood. Initiatives like the UK government-funded Renaissance in the Regions programme encouraged museums to broaden their audiences and think of themselves as lifelong educators, situating learning at the centre of museum practice. However, ongoing funding problems within the museum sector continued to contribute to an erosion of curatorial skills as specialist roles were replaced with more general posts. At the same time, the university sector saw an increasing emphasis on the importance of the Higher Education Funding Council for England, which wanted academics in the UK to share their work beyond the academy. In addition, the introduction and steady increase of student fees and the rapid expansion of the student body (Arnold-Foster and Speight, 2010) led universities to place a greater emphasis on student employability and 'real world' engagement.

Decreasing public subsidy has been an issue for both sectors, with teaching grants rescinded for all but science, technology, engineering and maths subjects and some of the social sciences in 2011, placing particular strains on arts, design and humanities departments. Museums have suffered similar problems, seeing a reduction in Renaissance funding, cuts to the Department for Culture, Media and Sport, pressure on local government spending and increased competition for grants from the Heritage Lottery Fund and Arts Council England. These circumstances have encouraged museums and universities to think creatively about ways of delivering their core obligations of research, knowledge exchange and public engagement through collaborations with new partners. This chapter aims to explore how museum-university partnerships can be activated to form mutually beneficial, sustainable relationships through two case studies from the Share Academy initiative.

Share Academy

Share Academy, a partnership between University College London, University of the Arts London and the London Museums Group, was set up in 2012 in response to the emerging cultural and economic landscape. Share Academy was born of a belief that, in a world where everyone was being asked to do more with reduced resources, universities and museums had a lot to offer one another. Universities tend to have greater experience of managed risk taking, critical thinking and academic research while museums bring their incredible collections, subject specific knowledge and a superior understanding of how to take complex subject matter and render it in ways the general public can understand. The aim of Share Academy is to encourage collaborative partnerships between universities and small to medium-sized museums; those who might not otherwise have the confidence or the resources to engage with higher education. Lannin et al (2014) identify the fact that 'academics can be unaware of the potential held within small museums' yet they have much to offer in terms of subject specialist knowledge, unique collections, community engagement and fleetness of foot. Since 2012 Share Academy has been funded by Arts Council England to explore the challenges and benefits of partnerships between museums and universities, broker new partnerships and evaluate ensuing activity.

Between October 2012 and April 2013, the first pilot project was funded through Arts Council England's Strategic Fund for promoting excellence and raising standards within regional museums. The pilot delivered three exploratory case studies and a scoping study outlining the landscape and ecology of museum–university partnerships in the London region. Semi-structured interviews in the museum and higher education sectors identified the level of collaboration already taking place and the potential for further activity. The scoping study revealed that much good work was already happening, but that relationships tended to be ad hoc and personal rather than strategic or institutionally embedded (Hannan and McNulty, 2013). Relationships also tended to be predictable (museum studies students doing work placements) rather than creative or interdisciplinary. The pilot project concluded that there was potential for further partnership working and room for improvement in the way partnerships were brokered and managed.

This was followed by Share Academy II (April 2013–March 2015), funded by a grant from Arts Council England's Resilience Fund, which supports the provision of developmental opportunities across the museum sector. During the two-year period of the grant Share Academy was able to broker and fund 15 partnership projects with grants of up to £10,000 with a view to exploring what works well in museum–university partnerships, what challenges arise and what constitutes best practice in partnership working. Meyer (2010) argues that in a knowledge economy we need to know how knowledge is made, translated or transacted across boundaries. The Share Academy team was able to offer support from experts in partnership working from both the museum and university sectors. While the brokerage element of Share Academy was cost intensive, it did lead to a number of new (in certain circumstances unlikely) partnerships. It also ensured that the partnerships supported common goals.

As part of the application process Share Academy ran a number of 'sand pit' events to give academics and potential museum partners an opportunity to meet face to face and discuss ways of working together. This was modelled on activities developed by The Cultural Capital Exchange, an organisation set up to promote the exchange of knowledge and expertise between higher education, business and the cultural and creative sectors in London. The sand pits proved highly successful with many of the funded projects meeting at the events. Unsurprisingly, given that Share Academy was encouraging collaborative practice between universities (large scale, business-minded, self-confident, articulate) and small to medium-sized museums (can-do, generous-spirited organisations less used to fighting their corner), it was not unusual for the university partner to emerge from initial negotiations with the upper hand. Comunian and Gilmore (2015), who have explored how universities work with the creative economy, identify a need to acknowledge and address 'power relationships in these collaborations'. Share Academy's grant application and monitoring processes were designed to enhance the museums' negotiating position and ensure that projects carried mutual benefit for both partners.

Funding was awarded through an open application process and the resulting projects were diverse in their range and scope from student-led projects to testing ideas or engendering debate. From the outset Share Academy anticipated that most of the projects brokered and funded would be around researchers looking for ways to prove public impact and public engagement outside the academy but it was left entirely to applicants to decide how projects would be constituted. Ultimately research impact proved to be a relatively small part of the portfolio of projects, many of which were a blend of teaching, learning and research outputs.

Case studies

Between 2012 and 2015 Share Academy funded 18 projects in total. The projects included testing of new digital technologies in gallery environments, research into how health and wellbeing can be improved by interaction with museum collections, the creation of new publications and exhibitions for museums, using oral histories to explore inspiration and using drawing as a way of understanding medical specimens. A series of universities collaborated with a wide range of museums including independent, local government funded and university museums. There is a long history of archaeology and museum studies courses working with museums so Share Academy deliberately encouraged more creative partnerships. Some of them included BA Jewellery Design, and MA Fashion and the Environment (creating new material for exhibitions), MA Art and Science (exploring drawing as a way of understanding), MA Design (building new audiences), MA Publishing (designing and printing a book) and BA/MA English (contributing to a literary festival). In this section, two case studies are illustrated to give a more in depth view of what was achieved. They are the *Peckham Cultural Institute* and *Local Roots/Global Routes: the Legacies of British Slave-ownership*.

Peckham Cultural Institute

The Peckham Cultural Institute was a partnership between the South London Gallery, an international gallery whose mission is to 'bring art to the people of south London', and MA Culture, Criticism and Curation at Central Saint Martins, which offers students a unique framework for critically engaging with culture. The objective of the Peckham Cultural Institute was to create a counter offer to Google's Cultural Institute, effectively challenging the notion that Google (or those who use the Google search engine) have the right to define what might be considered culturally valuable. Google's mission is to 'organise the world's information and make it universally accessible' and in recent years Google has come to wield enormous power, both as the world's most used search engine and the instigator of highly successful projects such as Google Maps, Google Scholar and Street View.

The Google Cultural Institute is based on a model developed by Google when it launched the Google Book Search project (later renamed Google Books) in 2004. The Google Book Search project initially aimed to digitise some 15 million books from the collections of Stanford University, the University of Michigan, the Weidener Library at Harvard and the New York Public Library. In 2007 Jean-Noël Jeanneney, then president of the Bibliothèque National de France, published a critique of the project. Jeanneney acknowledged the value of attempting to open up a centuries old treasure trove of knowledge, but was concerned that Google – an institute in which 'the cultural impulse and the commercial impulse' were at odds – should be the driving force behind the project. In his view, Google's dominant motivation is to ensure revenue for shareholders rather than genuine cultural or public benefit. Jeanneney refused to accept that culture should be treated as 'just another piece of merchandise' where Google's algorithms rank, index and order content in a 'system in which success breeds success, at the expense of newcomers, minorities, the marginal' (Jeanneney, 2007).

While offering participation and access, the Google Cultural Institute could also be accused of representing culture in its narrowest and highest form. The Peckham Cultural Institute wanted to offer a critique of the Google Cultural Institute and represent a different and more democratic view of culture based on locality and community participation. From the start the project was built on democratic principles, being led by students from the MA Culture, Criticism and Curation course (who come from a wide range of cultural backgrounds) and members of South London Gallery's REcreative Editorial Board. REcreative was launched by the South London Gallery in 2011 and has developed into an online community exploring contemporary art and design. REcreative is led by young people aged 16–25 and aims to connect young creatives to free cultural opportunities in London and further afield. The Editorial Board meets every month to discuss content for the REcreative website and contributes to the South London Gallery's educational programme.

With the help of MA Culture, Criticism and Curation, the project partners were able to develop a good understanding of research methodologies and research processes. The partners agreed that they wanted their project to challenge Google's perceived hegemony and articulate a counter argument to the 'mechanistic point of view' computers impose on their users (Lovink, 2011). The project started with an introductory meeting followed by four study sessions, each with a guest speaker including gallerists, a designer and cultural historian and representatives from Culture 24, Arts Council England and Google Cultural Institute. Each session went part way to challenging whether

Googlers – or Google's algorithms – should be left to decide what constitutes culture. The study sessions served to give the group time to gel, to think about the subject and discuss key issues within it. They also offered an opportunity for those leading the project to see how the group was thinking and to be reassured about the quality of the work.

Participants in the workshops debated key issues such as what happens to a work of art when it is posted online, how a digital curation project can involve local residents in a meaningful way, how to generate content that is genuinely reflective of counter-culture and how to reflect a 'crowd-sourced' version of culture back to Google. Ultimately the project culminated in a digital think tank titled WYSIWYG? (What you see is what you get?) hosted in the South London Gallery's Clore Studio in July 2014. Artists, curators and digital experts from the Victoria & Albert Museum, Barbican and Lighthouse were invited to discuss the impact of the digital world on art and culture in the 21st century. It was interesting (perhaps even ironic) that a project about digital curation and archiving which at first anticipated a digital output ultimately culminated in an event where real people debated the issues associated with digital curation in real time. This was, in part, a reflection of the difficulty in creating online resources that represent culture in its widest sense in any meaningful way. It is also a result of the fact that the project was allowed to develop in line with the thinking of the project participants rather than the host institution. While the project did produce a modest website, the real value of the project was in the face-to-face engagement with the local communities, which attended the event in considerable numbers.

In her work *The Participatory Museum*, Nina Simon (2010) describes the importance of co-creative or collaborative practice for cultural institutions in terms of giving local communities a voice. In seeking to present an alternative and more egalitarian or counter view of culture through the REcreative project, the South London Gallery brought its embeddedness with the local community and long standing relationships with a group of young people who could provide an alternative viewpoint. This is a good example of a university benefiting by linking into a gallery's existing (and in this instance highly developed) public engagement processes. Simon (2010) also stresses the importance of creating a level playing field within collaborative or co-creative projects so the institution and project participants meet as equals. While the Peckham Cultural Institute had clear goals and structure, the project's outcomes were not prescribed by either Central Saint Martins or the South London Gallery. The brief for the project was offered 'in the spirit of study, debate, critique and participation' and asked participants to spend six months creating an alternative model for representing culture through digital curating in response to Google's offer to 'host the world's treasures online'. Beyond that there was no expectation of what the outcome might look like.

It would be unrealistic to suggest that the Peckham Cultural Institute can launch a serious challenge to the international corporate hegemony of Google. However, on a local scale the project has given young creatives in south London a voice and a framework for challenging seemingly unassailable cultural narratives. Members of the ReCreative Editorial Board have expressed an interest in rolling the model of the Peckham Cultural Institute out to other areas of their work and are using the Facebook group from the panel debates to continue the discussion. The project has also had an impact on the MA in Culture, Criticism and Curation course at Central Saint Martins, as research and practice models have been integrated into the course alongside a newfound belief in the value of participatory enactments and community engagement. In a world where new cultural norms are emerging in response to digital technologies, it is important that young people are provided with the tools to remain independent of thought and develop frameworks for countering overarching narratives. By bringing together groups of young people and engaging them (and their local communities), the Peckham Cultural Institute engendered new ways of thinking and encouraged ongoing and meaningful participation in cultural debate.

Local Roots/Global Routes: the Legacies of Slavery in Hackney

The second case study is a partnership motivated by the desire to share research beyond the boundaries of the academy through the building of meaningful community relationships at a local level. The project's focus was the impact of transatlantic slavery; something which has recently been brought to public consciousness through the marking of key anniversaries including (in 2007) the 200th anniversary of the abolition of slave trading in the British Empire. Exhibitions in the port cities of London, Liverpool and Bristol and the representation of slavery in films such as *Twelve Years a Slave* have gone some way to making enslavement a topic for mainstream discussion. However, Donington et al (2016) note that slavery is all too often considered a distant phenomenon and argue that because 'British slavery happened, in large part, on the plantations of the Caribbean, geographic distance has enabled a distancing of the mind'. In reality the slavery business was much more far-reaching than people assume. One of the key issues associated with narratives of slavery in the UK is the nation's reluctance to engage in discussions about just how many British citizens (and British institutions) profited from slave-ownership or business activities associated with slavery.

The Legacies of British Slave-ownership project run by UCL is seeking to change that by focusing on the 3000 or so slave owners who lived in Britain when slavery was finally abolished in 1833. In 2013 the project launched the Encyclopedia of Slave-ownership, pulled from thousands of records detailing the compensation paid to slave owners when their slaves were emancipated. This searchable database shows that the exploitation of enslaved people had links uncomfortably close to home. Proactive users can visit the project's website and search for the slave owners by name or geographical location. However, academics at UCL were keen to explore ways of sharing their research with those who might not know of the database or be motivated to make a search. With this in mind academics from UCL reached out to Hackney Museum and Archives to explore the possibility of working together on a programme of activities that would bring the Encyclopedia of Slave-ownership to life. Hackney was chosen as it is a diverse borough with a relatively large proportion of Black African, Black Caribbean and Black British residents compared to other London boroughs. The local museum has a strong track record in designing innovative projects to engage with local audiences. They have expertise in the delivery of educational activities for young people, working with creative practitioners on difficult historical subjects and (most importantly) the trust of their local community. Representatives from UCL and Hackney Museum and Archives attended one of the Share Academy sand pit events in the hope of working up some ideas about how they might work together.

At the outset of the project the partners were planning to work with a community consultant, a creative art practitioner and three secondary schools to produce an interactive educational resource for Key Stage 3. It was anticipated that the resource would have a performative element and would complement the Black History Season already offered by Hackney Museum and Archives for Key Stages 1 and 2. The proposed resource would address a number of issues including UCL's ambition to engage with local communities around issues of enslavement, Hackney Museum and Archive's continuing efforts to build meaningful and sustainable relationship with the public and a request from local school teachers for more resources addressing issues of race and identity. The project appointed a research intern who used information from the Legacies of British Slave-ownership database to trace Hackney's links with transatlantic slavery. Through his research it was identified that least 11 local people and events had links with slavery. An education intern worked on the conceptual framework for the educational resource which was then tested with local schools. Additional funding was used to deliver workshops with Our Lady's Convent High School and Hackney BSix College. Overall four teachers and 45 students participated and ultimately the project partners created a multi-media teaching pack with sufficient material for six lessons complemented by a film with expert interviews and discussion points linked to the content of the pack.

The Local Roots/Global Routes project grew considerably during the delivery timeframe. Additional funding was sought from Arts Council England's Grants for the Arts programme, which enabled the partners to pay for two creative practitioners to work with young people to develop creative responses to the educational resources. The young people then presented their responses at 'Putting the Black in the Union Jack?', a conference about teaching Black history that took place in November 2015 and attracted an audience of 250. The event addressed the marginalisation of Black history in Britain and showcased some of the best of Black British culture. This was followed by an interactive debate on the role of national, global and diasporic histories within education.

While the social justice element of the Peckham Cultural Institute project was perhaps less tangible there are a number of elements of the Local Roots/Global Routes project that address a more explicit social justice agenda. In the first instance, the project was focused on creating educational resources for local schools that address issues of race and identity. Frederickson and Petrides (2008) note that since the 1980s there has been concern about the lower achievement levels of particular minority ethnic groups in Britain and 'consequent exclusion from higher education and employment opportunities'. This is still a big problem across Britain but boroughs like Hackney are proactively trying to address the issue. By working in conjunction with Hackney Museum and Archives and local Hackney schools the Legacies of British Slave-ownership project created educational resources that challenged representations of race and offered young people of all racial backgrounds a more honest appraisal of their heritage. During the project, it became apparent that there was a need for more positive representation of race in the classroom. For instance, the education packs noted that 'Students only encounter African and Caribbean history in the context of slavery'. This affects students' self-esteem and ability to engage with what they are being taught because they don't have access to different histories that allow them to see a broad range of African roles and societies. Feedback from both staff and students was that they wanted to see a wider representation of Black histories in the education packs. Teachers also asked for more contextual information so that they had the confidence to answer students' questions around the subject (Jackson, 2015). It is hoped that the educational resources created by the project will continue to contribute to improving rates of achievement among ethnically diverse students in the borough.

The second element of the Local Roots/Global Routes project to address a social justice agenda was the restoration of hidden or misrepresented histories. It has been argued suppression of narratives which reveal the brutality and pervasiveness of enslavement related activities has worked to the benefit of the slave-owning classes. Hooks (1992) claims that the past has been erased and denied to the extent that we are completely ignorant of our own history. What we see now is a mass media littered with negative or stereotyped representations of race, what Hooks describes as the 'colonising gaze'. Cheddie (2012) argues that museums have particular responsibilities to communities whose history and heritage have been under-represented within collections, institutional structures and modes of address. The Legacies of British Slave-ownership project attempted to disrupt the colonising gaze by uncovering repressed historical narratives. By sharing knowledge of how widespread slave-ownership was and how many businessmen, philanthropists and private individuals made at least a proportion of their income from slavery associated activities the project has encouraged people of all races to reconsider their identity within the narratives of the past.

The project also worked with artists and community consultants who acted as a bridge between the institution and the communities. Toyin Agbetu, the community consultant, played a key role in advising on the project, particularly around issues of language and representation. He argues from his position of a British African social rights activist that in forgetting contentious histories we risk repeating what has gone before. Agbetu believes that racism and its structural forces, many of which have been in place since the days of enslavement, continue to affect us today. He used the Local Roots/Global Routes project to challenge negative representations of African people from a local level, arguing that without local change it is impossible to effect change globally.

Challenges and benefits of collaborative practice

In presenting two such positive case studies it would be easy to pass over or ignore some of the challenges and difficulties associated with collaborative practice between universities and museums. Throughout the Share Academy project, partners expressed frustration at many of the same issues including the different languages used by academia and museums, different timescales (including different financial years) and the bureaucratic and slow moving nature of the universities, particularly in terms of legalities and finance. Seemingly simple things like the payment of freelancers or purchasing of materials can be frustratingly slow. Universities often did not seem to be aware that museums have carefully curated activity programmes, planned years in advance and finely tuned to their audience's wants and needs. On the other hand, museums exhibited a naïve expectation that just having inspiring or unique collections was enough. They vaguely anticipated that a PhD student or researcher would come and work on their collection, little guessing how pressurised academic schedules are, leaving little time for activities outside specific research interests. In terms of collaboration, almost all of the projects that received Share Academy funding underestimated how much time and effort they would have to invest in the partnership to make it successful. Working with students requires training and patient management (particularly where English is not their first language). Making research accessible in a format the public can understand is time consuming and actually co-producing research is much more labour intensive than acting alone. Collaboration turns out not to be the silver bullet that will address resource issues in either the university or museum sectors.

However, good things can and do happen as a result of collaborative practice. Working with new partners can unlock knowledge, lead to greater organisational sustainability and give both project partners new skills and experience. All of the Share Academy funded projects were assessed by an independent evaluator who concluded that participating in cross-sector collaborations brings significant value to those involved, with potential for positive and unforeseen benefits beyond the immediate project including the development of new and wider connections, reaching new audiences and improved visability. A significant number of Share Academy funded projects have developed a sustainable legacy through building new relationships, exploring new opportunities, building on or expanding existing work and having a wider impact on society and communities. A number of the projects funded through Share Academy have lodged joint grant applications to continue and develop their work. Almost all of the partners who received Share Academy funding said they would continue to seek partnerships with other sectors. Many of them still work with their Share Academy partners and a good number have used the frameworks developed through Share Academy to approach other potential collaborators.

Although Share Academy was not explicitly designed to address social justice issues, there was a strong moral imperative behind the projects. The application processes incorporated an insistence on reciprocity and the early identification of shared goals and benefits for both the university and museum partners. Another driving force for Share Academy was the idea of social responsibility, both for universities and museums. As 'beacons of cultural production' and 'key players in cities and communities' (Comunian and Gilmore, 2015), the role of universities in society is increasingly recognised. Similarly, museums have been recognised as institutions which have the capacity to combat disadvantage, racism and other forms of discrimination (Sandell, 2002). The fact that museums (particularly publicly funded museums) are already preoccupied with addressing social equality meant that many of the Share Academy funded projects delivered direct benefits to local communities through co-produced or co-curated activities. From working with LGBT communities to exploring the politics of utopianism through an artist-in-residence programme, many of the Share Academy projects incorporated a strong restorative or egalitarian element that contributed to what has been called the core economy of 'the household, the neighbourhood, the community and civil society' (see Stephens et al, 2008).

Conclusions and next steps

As Jackson (2015) notes, with the progress of the Share Academy programme, there has been a move away from transactional relationships, where, for example, museums see universities as a source of free labour, and universities see museums as a source of practical experience, towards transformational relationships where the skills of the partners are melded to create new products, ideas and relationships. It is this sort of high-impact collaboration that Share Academy wants to foster and encourage in the future. Since 2015 Share Academy has been working with the National-Co-ordinating Centre for Public Engagement to map and codify museum–university partnerships across England and create the space, through networking events and digital support, for new partnerships to be formed. Information about this ongoing work can be found at: https://www.publicengagement.ac.uk/work-with-us/current-projects/museum-university-partnerships-initiative

Acknowledgements

I would like to thank the Share Academy team for their hard work and enthusiasm for the project. I would also like to thank all of the project participants, many of whom went over and above the call of duty to ensure their projects were successful.

FOUR

From poverty to life chances: framing co-produced research in the Productive Margins programme

Sue Cohen, Allan Herbert, Nathan Evans and Tove Samzelius

Introduction

What is it like be a community partner in an ambitious university-led co-produced research programme? Is co-production on equal terms really possible? What is in it for us and why did we get involved in the first place? There are many articles about engagement, co-production and participatory practices written by researchers and mainly for academic audiences. Despite the ambition of many to be inclusive and to 'represent the voices' of community members and organisations, those accounts are rarely written by community organisations themselves. Instead they are often written on our behalf, which in itself poses questions around accessibility, opportunities and the rules that govern research processes. With this chapter, we want to make a contribution to the debate about co-production and participatory practices from a community perspective.

The 'we' in this article are Allan Herbert and Nathan Evans from South Riverside Community Development Centre Ltd (SRCDC), Tove Samzelius previously from Single Parent Action Network (SPAN) and Sue Cohen, a Community Co-investigator. All of us are part of the Productive Margins research initiative, a major five-year co-produced interdisciplinary research programme involving the University of Bristol, Cardiff University and nine community organisations from England and Wales. The programme is seeking to remap the terrain of regulation, by involving the knowledge, passions and creativity of citizens often considered on the margins of politics and policymaking. In doing so the programme aims to 'move away from problematics of participation as simply 'lay' involvement in pre-determined regulatory structures (Newman, 2005; McDermont et al, 2009), to creatively embrace engagement as constitutive of regulation in ways that fundamentally challenge its forms' (McDermont et al, 2012).

It was the ambition to enable ground level rather than top-down perspectives on regulating for engagement that led to SPAN and SRCDC's interest in participating in the process. We were also interested in the quest for ways of designing regulatory regimes that began from the capabilities of communities excluded from the mainstream. Both organisations value participatory research and have been engaged in anti-poverty work for many years with the aim of supporting people experiencing socioeconomic exclusion to empower themselves, while also challenging structures and regulatory frameworks that contribute to processes of marginalisation. The co-produced research ambitions of Productive Margins are, however, a new way forward for both SPAN and SRCDC.

Rather than examining the progress and outcomes of the research project itself in this chapter, which as we write are still on the horizon, we examine the settings and process leading up to the establishment of the research project: the formation of the working group where SPAN and SRCDC explored the theme of poverty; the Research Forum where academics and community partners came together to share knowledge and interdisciplinary ways forward; and the challenges, rewards and learning that took place in formulating our co-produced research project.

Engagement at the margins: a shared history of exclusion, dissent and empowerment

Prior to engaging with the Productive Margins programme, SRCDC and SPAN knew very little about each other and the areas in which we work. However, we soon discovered that we had a lot in common; this rapidly opened up space for establishing confidence and trust, key elements in the co-production process. Both organisations were created by groups of people that had come together to challenge poverty and disadvantage in multicultural inner-city areas of Cardiff and Bristol respectively. SRCDC has been in existence for 40 years and SPAN for 25 years. Both SPAN and SRCDC had matured and sustained themselves over this time as charitable companies with histories of managing in an often difficult multi-funded environment.

SPAN was set up in 1990 under the Third European Poverty Programme of the European Economic Community (EEC). SPAN's driving force came from Bristol One Parent Project (BOPP), a grassroots organisation collectively run by a multi-ethnic group of single parents. Most were living in poverty, many with a history of displacement, domestic violence, childhood poverty and discrimination, in a social activist era. Many activists were influenced, if not directly then indirectly, by the black liberation and women's movements and by the thinking of Paulo Freire on participatory action, praxis and the collective empowerment of the dispossessed (Freire, 2005). BOPP had formed to organise around challenging the council on their poor housing conditions with some success, and went on to develop childcare and collective 'self-help' projects. SPAN built on this history by successfully applying to the Third European Poverty Programme with the purpose of developing a self-help network across the four nations of the UK. An underlying principle was that single parents through collective action could empower themselves and others to improve their life chances. SPAN used empowerment in this context long before the concept became part of an institutionalised community capacity building discourse under the New Labour government (Ledwith, 2011).

Both organisations were adept at moving with the times. SRCDC was also set up as a campaigning organisation, bringing together local activists, community artists and educationalists to address challenging housing conditions in Cardiff, particularly on behalf of the most needy who were in the grip of the worst landlords in the city. SRCDC was soon influenced by the welfare rights movement of its era and went on to establish a welfare rights centre as an anti-poverty strategy, employing over 15 advice workers. In the 1990s the focus changed again – to community development – and, like SPAN, the organisation was inspired by the radical activist movements of the period, with a particular focus on Black and Minority Ethnic (BME) groups, younger and older people and women. More recently, the organisation has been involved in asset transfers, and leasing and managing buildings for local groups to develop their community activities.

SPAN in Bristol and SRCDC in Cardiff both promote education and training at local access points, recognising and responding to barriers experienced by individuals and families from many different backgrounds and cultures. These responses include community, family and child friendly facilities, affordable or free childcare, and low cost or no cost access to meeting and activity spaces. This shared history is an important factor in explaining why we were interested in 'Productive Margins' in the first place and why we felt ourselves to be kindred spirits. Given SPAN and SRCDC's long histories of challenging established views on people living in poverty, both organisations were particularly interested in the sub-theme 'spaces of dissent' within the

Productive Margins programme. As described in the original case for support:

> Spaces of dissent raises questions about how non-mainstream views and voices are positioned within processes of engagement. How might groups whose views that dissent from mainstream politics be engaged to inform how social problems of various kinds are understood and addressed? What are the social, economic, cultural and political barriers and facilitators to creating regulatory mechanisms for engagement? Can legal rights support engagement or do they create barriers? (McDermont et al, 2012)

Sites of experimentation

Productive Margins' methodology of co-production begins with two principles:

1. Academics and community organisations are equal partners in the design and delivery of the research programme.
2. New, innovative understandings of regulating for engagement can arise when communities and academics from different disciplines and fields of experience who had not previously worked together are in dialogue, share their expertise and reflect on their different perspectives.

A primary site for interaction between the different parties is the 'Productive Margins Research Forum'. The original research proposal in the case for support states:

> The Forum is not a conventional advisory board, nor does it follow a familiar model of 'partnership' dominated by powerful actors. Rather it is itself a site of experimentation, acting as a dynamic location for co-producing knowledges, enhancing exchange and dissemination, and developing innovative methods for the social sciences, arts and humanities. Understanding research as a process of co-production between academics and communities rather than as academics doing research on communities raises a host of new questions and dilemmas for research practice. (McDermont et al, 2012)

The Research Forum in practice has indeed become an experimental space, where both academics and community organisations meet in somewhat uncharted waters in a community or academic setting related to one of the partner organisations, grounding what takes place there in the practices of all partners. Each Forum has a different theme and approach. A major objective has been for participants to identify the focus of the seven research projects and to collectively develop research questions and interdisciplinary methodologies that progress the research.

SPAN and SRCDC were the two community organisations to highlight poverty as a key marker in this setting. We spoke about common concerns and of 'systematic neglect' that we could see in our areas. There were also comparisons made with regard to community activism and community approaches on dissent. "SPAN was born out of protest," said Tove. Sue also felt at home with SRCDC.

> 'Certain phrases stood out for me – they resonated with similar struggles I'd experienced. Nathan spoke of the 'unconscious incompetence' of some key city decision makers in the area; Allan of the need for doggedness if change was going to happen.'

The two organisations 'found each other' with reason. In a relatively short space of time, the closeness in approach led to a sense of mutuality, confidence and trust in each other.

We knew that we wanted a research project that focused on poverty, but there were so many different interests and ideas floating around in the Research Forums. When the research theme began its tenuous emergence, Tove and Helen Thomas-Hughes (research assistant on Productive Margins), who already had many years of personal and professional connection, were able (without the time consuming preamble of developing areas of mutual understanding on which these relationships are dependent) to dive straight into a deliberative debate that eventually drove this thread from an idea to a research project. As Helen Thomas-Hughes says,

> 'The spaces for this development were not institutional or 'professional' but, by the necessity of full work schedules, were instead familial, coffee in a kitchen surrounded by the chatterings of small children. We should ask what might have happened without this pre-existing connection. We would postulate that for 'work' to leak into 'life' in this

> way there is a sure demand for either strong relationships or strong topical interest. Luckily, for this project, there were both!'

This conversation sparked the earliest iteration of the research proposal on poverty.

Helen, Tove, Sue, Nathan and Allan began a series of discussions to discuss different ideas of entitlement to welfare from places that people understood, from historical, ideological, ethical, philosophical and spiritual starting points. Both SPAN and SRCDC had previously not had such an open-ended opportunity to put these discourses into our participatory action research writing, even though much of the thinking and values came from these arenas. We became known as the 'Poverty Working Group'.

> 'I think when we came together, the working group, it was just a really coming together and a synergy of like minded people who seemed to just mesh and click.' (Nathan)

A scoping study undertaken on behalf of Productive Margins found smaller group meetings conducive to informed, deliberative dialogue (Noorani, 2013: 8). Certainly, Productive Margins supported us in opening up a space for reflection and iteration, rare for hard pressed community organisations. In many ways the group became a micro, interdisciplinary learning environment with the potential for praxis, and new ways of thinking and acting (Freire, 2005).

Critically, we had the opportunity to consider more radical anti-poverty agendas than were possible under most of the local, national and EU government funding programmes that had directed a good deal of our partnership work in the past. We had freedom to dissent: to create an alternative space that drew on grassroots knowledge and local understandings, explored possibilities, and questioned assumptions.

For example, many assume in these present times that if you are poor in money you are poor in spirit. We considered how this fed into the discourse on sanctions and the notion of the deserving and undeserving poor – have we ever moved away from poor relief? How did welfare come to develop in this way? We talked about children and the 'if you can't afford it don't have children' discourse. Why is there such nastiness about the way in which children can be regarded in the UK? We wanted to look at dissent around these issues.

Given the underlying focus of the research programme was regulation, we considered how these assumptions played out in different regulatory settings. Rather than solving problems defined by a government funding body, Productive Margins gave us the opportunity to consider the problems from the starting point of the families themselves. For example, we thought we might examine how children experienced welfare regulations comparatively in England and Wales, and how these regulations impacted on child poverty. We thought we could also focus on welfare regulations governing 'working families', in particular that adult workers in this context were not treated as parents, a theme that had come out of a number of SPAN's participatory research programmes with single parent families at a local, national and EU level. Some of us told personal stories of the problems faced – raising the personal as political.

We discussed the erosion under austerity of what people were entitled to – what happened to universalism? We made reference to Danny Dorling's (2014) research and why the growth of the wealthy is making the UK a more dangerous place to live. Can we afford the rich? We discussed how the wealthy are kept wealthy. That places with the most wealth attract best services: how those in poverty are kept poor by regulatory controls – forced to attend job centres every day with no room for manoeuvre.

We thought that we could look at the way 'welfare into work' regulations were diverging under the coalition government and the devolved Welsh Assembly. What might this mean for the future? There were different engagement processes for a start. Under the previous Labour government, anti-poverty networks from both England and Wales met with civil servants and ministers at a Westminster level but the coalition government closed these networks down. Poverty was not on their political agenda. Yet there are significant differences in Wales. SRCDC has much closer relationships with Welsh ministers and civil servants than could ever be envisaged at a Westminster level. How does this impact on regulations? In Wales there is a Department of Work and Pensions (DWP) Strategic Board via partnership work with Oxfam and an operational DWP Working Group; the 'Want to Work' programme had also been kept because it proved that it worked.

We talked about time and time poverty as a regulator: use of time as a historical perspective and how hours of unpaid work have increased. We thought we could follow how people's time is being used, countering the rhetoric of scroungers and time wasters. For the first time in our discussions we also began to talk about the future rather than the past, that it was more important to secure the future than the present. Unrestricted by the hegemonic controls of funding regimes that define governmental service delivery needs or indeed the rationale for community engagement in the here and now – community cohesion, active citizenship – we had the freedom to range across different temporalities present, past and future. We thought we could look at the aspirational with regard to different temporalities. (We did not know at this stage that 'aspiration' would become a political hot potato in the 2015 election.) What would it look like if social welfare was transformative, if people had the ability to manage their lives? We agreed we wanted to diversify power and knowledge and not be rigid and target driven, again to break away from the restrictions of bounded funding applications and research projects.

All the initial discussions had taken place without an assigned social science researcher present: discussions were still explorative in nature. We were excited that we could talk about issues that we cared about deeply, without having to think about the restrictions of a one-year research project. However, we reached a stage where we knew we had to focus and decided to tease out the research questions with those who had more experience in the field. A 'fishbowl' exercise at the next Research Forum helped us to progress – as we anticipated, academics queried the breadth of our focus and one academic questioned whether the historical theme was at all original in considering why the welfare state had developed the way that it had in the UK.

By this stage the Poverty Working Group was already moving away from history and into dreams of the future, although we still ranged across temporalities. We discussed the need to politically take account of the dreams of parenthood; what we want for our children; how difficult it was to hold onto the dreams; how ideas of the future affect decisions today. Utopian futures began to be discussed for the first time. The Community Co-investigator, Sue, was influenced by academic readings and the discourses on Utopias and temporalities that she encountered in the Connected Communities programme (Levitas, 2013; Connected Communities Symposium, 2015).

Overall, we acknowledged the increasing fear of the benefit system as an overriding concern for the families we were involved with and that if people did not do as required they would be sanctioned, deepening family poverty. We reached an initial synthesis. We discussed how we might hold participatory workshops on:

- How parents in poverty and job centres as institutions encounter one another.
- How are people's futures imagined in job centres?
- How do we disrupt this?

- If participants could influence job centres, how would futures be reimagined?

We had used seed corn money (small grants provided by Productive Margins supporting initial discussions) to open up conversations with community members from the two organisations on the theme of poverty and how regulatory controls affected them. We only considered testing the more recent ideas that came out of the Poverty Working Group's iterative process once the focus of our research question became clearer. Prior to this we had not been clear – how could we have presented to community participants when we ourselves were not clear of ways forward? Yet, bringing wider community participants in at this later stage felt on reflection something of a contradiction for participatory co-production. Could it have been organised differently? The impact of time and resource pressures on hard pressed communities and community organisations were an overriding concern, as we explore in the next section.

Co-production, equality and time

Co-production inevitably takes time. During the whole process we have reflected on whether it is truly possible to be 'equal partners in the design and the delivery of the research programme' (McDermont et al, 2012), particularly when thinking about the time involved and the different pressures that regulate that time.

> 'There are differences between the daily considerations of partners – "facilities" to those that work in Higher Education are whether the room was booked and the projector is ready; for the third sector it's fixing the roof and paying the business rates; for community members it's often the security that comes with a door key.' (Allan)

As community partners, the time we are able to dedicate to the actual process of co-production will regulate or impact on our ability to influence how and what will be investigated. The principle of equality is a great aspiration and, in furthering this, effort has been made in Productive Margins to allocate funds to pay for community partners' time: Community organisations are paid to release representatives for their time to participate in Research Forums, attend meetings and run events within communities. However, reflection, reading and writing are also paramount to the research process and for us to be able to become equal partners, we need time for academic activities. Is ongoing praxis possible without sufficient time for these pursuits? (That said, this chapter may never have been written without the time and resources allocated by Productive Margins to a writing retreat involving both community partners and academics.)

Working in cash strapped community organisations with people who often have complex lives and needs is time consuming and energy draining. As Tove reflected in relation to her role as Director of SPAN's local work:

> 'I am not only responsible for overseeing all the operational aspects of our frontline service delivery, but also for staff wellbeing, fundraising, finances, and contracts. If there is a crisis with a service user I sometimes have to intervene. This means that without allocated time for the research projects we are part of, however important we feel that they are, it is not a straightforward task. Funding for my job is tied in to different projects and is time limited. Without knowing how much time I will dedicate to the Productive Margins programme on a more long-term basis, it becomes difficult to profile budgets and plan ahead in terms of human resources. As a result, I do not feel able to spend as much time as I would like to, and see as necessary for us to become an equal partner in the co-production process.'

The process of involving community members in the research project held additional challenges. These included communicating the essence and purpose of the research, its intended or possible audiences, and the potential impact of the findings. It was also difficult explaining the notion of co-production and the expectations that were placed upon them as participant research partners/peer researchers. Community based third sector organisations are not geared up for research programmes – they have few systems in place to support the step changes required to manage the research process and keep community participation running at the same speed: "Higher Education and research institutions have the systems in place to accommodate this change of gear" (Allan). Community organisations may have frontline staff who are much better placed than academic institutions to recruit participants and sustain participation but have relatively limited administrative resources compared to universities.

How could parent volunteers become equal partners if they too did not have the sufficient space or time to commit to the research process?

'At SPAN, we often use the concept of "time poverty" when we talk about some of the issues facing single parents. "Time poverty" is not a new concept and it has been used widely in social science research. Although living with time poverty and living in actual poverty is not the same thing, time poverty becomes particularly problematic when you are also experiencing material poverty. People with money can often buy time through paying for dishwashers, cleaners, childcare, transport and other services or products that help to free up time. The families that we work with at SPAN often spend their time to save money. Having children, but lacking commodities such as a car and a washing machine means that people will spend a lot more time on everyday basic activities. All families living in poverty will experience this type of "time poverty", but it will become more acute when there is only one adult with younger children which is often the case in single parent households.' (Tove)

Time poverty is something that also impacts on people's ability to engage with regulatory processes and practices facilitated through neighbourhood forums, political activities or community groups. For example, few parents, particularly single parents, will have the time to go to evening meetings. In some cases, this is because they will not have enough money to pay for a babysitter and in other cases it is because they have been at work all day and feel that they need to prioritise their children over a meeting. To offer childcare can offer a practical solution for some parents, but it is not necessarily taking into account the time parents need to spend with their children.

There is a strong argument to be made that time, for people in poverty, is more regulated by others than it has been for many generations. With changes to the welfare regime and the introduction of stricter conditionality on job seekers and parents on income support, the question of time has become more poignant. For example, if somebody is in receipt of Job Seeker's Allowance (JSA), Job Centre staff and welfare legislation regulates what they are and are not allowed to do with their time. They have to look for work for x amount of hours, they have to go to appointments x times per week, they have to attend training for x number of hours and so on. If they disagree or fail to do what they are told, they are at risk of being sanctioned. Even if they feel that their time would be better spent doing something else, for example attending a course of their choice or being part of a research project such as Productive Margins, they might be told that they cannot spend time doing this because it does not fit with the regulations of the Welfare Act.

The regulation of time imposed by legislation and prevailing power structures has a knock-on effect on people's ability to decide how to use their own time as well as their ability to dissent. If they dissent, they might be punished through sanctions. If they are sanctioned, they have no money to feed their children.

The research process: the impact of co-production across disciplinary boarders

Academic lead

SPAN and SRCDC have been partners in a range of research projects and programmes, but this was our first involvement in an overt attempt at co-produced research, bringing both rewards and challenges. To be involved at an early stage and to be key to the setting of research questions was a new experience as was the involvement in the ethics process. There was the additional experience of working as two separate organisations in different cities with two university partners. All of this is furthering new knowledge, learning and further collaborations between community and academic partners.

The open-ended way in which research questions are worked up in Productive Margins is both a strength and challenge. The programme is interdisciplinary and experimental – we did not know at the outset of the Poverty Working Group which academics would/should work with us to inform and mobilise the research process. The expertise required from an Academic Lead was left largely up to the working group to decide in order to allow space for community partners to work up the direction of the research questions. To do otherwise could in itself have acted as a regulatory force, constraining the focus and ideas developed by the group.

In the first phase the Poverty Working Group moved the goalposts for what we wanted from an Academic Lead. We did not know at this stage what we did not know – we were cocooned in the iterative process. We had identified an historian, but by the time we invited her in we were moving away from history into the future and she rightly did not see how she could come on board. Bringing in new people from outside of the Poverty Working Group or indeed outside of the Research Forum could sometimes prove challenging, given the organic development of the programme, the impact on group dynamics and the initial disconnect new people might feel towards an experimental programme (Bion, 1961; Tuckman, 1965). Sue said at the time, not entirely tongue in cheek, that if we were becoming organic intellectuals (Gramsci, 1978) we would need to become more permeable.

When we became clearer on the direction of the research question, we decided we needed an Academic Lead with experience of multiple methods, and with particular expertise on poverty; but also one who had experience of arts practice given that this was an interdisciplinary programme supported by both the Arts and Humanities and the Economic and Social Research Councils. Perhaps at this stage we needed an Academic Lead who could not only intervene academically but at times go with the flow of the community partners – a difficult balance that not all academics might want to explore. We were lucky to find this balance with our Academic Lead, Debbie Watson who, when she come on board, described how a colleague from her department had introduced her to the possibility of joining the programme with, "It wouldn't be my cup of tea."

Arts practice as research method

Once the focus of the research question had been decided on, the Poverty Working Group thought that we might use participatory art or drama to help us in the research process, a creative way for breaking down barriers. We were still not thinking about arts practice as a research method. We thought we could work with existing history, theatre, art or literature groups, or set up new arts based groups as part of the facilitation process. Arts as an enabler for showcasing outcomes also received focus when we began to think how we might disseminate the work to share with a wider audience. We thought we could have an exhibition in a shop front setting where people would least expect to encounter an installation or event. There could be pop-up workshops that included music, film or theatre. Again these considerations were more with regard to the dissemination process rather than the research methodology – getting the project to wider audience.

> 'At this stage the lack of an academic from the Arts might have started to become an issue. SPAN had a history of using arts practice but as a tool but we did not have the knowledge of it as a research method. We thought we could learn something.' (Tove)

Once we began to collaborate with Angela Piccini, the Productive Margins' Co-Investigator on furthering arts practice as an integral element of research, the Poverty Working Group entered a new interdisciplinary phase. We had already experienced the Research Forum as a site for interdisciplinary investigation; we had considered how art, theatre and poetry could open up spaces of dissent, be used as another language, say unsettling things that are difficult to say otherwise. Some wondered if the division between social sciences and arts may be in the head of academics, how communities may be better represented through the arts, opening up new ways of thinking. "But what questions are they generating?", someone asked at the Forum. We were on a learning curve.

It was not that SPAN and SRCDC had been cocooned from artistic experimentation. Both organisations had worked with artists, musicians, animators, writers and performers. However, the work with creative practitioners had, in the main, been part of an educational activity using a variety of different mediums including crafts and decorative arts. This tended to take place in more recreational settings, sometimes perceived as a break from the usual conventions of classroom learning or training, often as part of the preparation and enactment of cultural celebrations or festivals. The introduction of arts practice as research, exploring issues such as Utopian futures and regulatory systems within the context of making art, provided a whole new set of challenges.

The impact of interdisciplinarity in a time of flux

The Poverty Working Group's previous focus on the regulatory controls inherent in welfare cuts and job centres began to tilt towards arts based concerns. This shift coincided quite separately with major staff, management and governance changes in SPAN, which for a range of reasons was going through a period of instability and flux; during this period, Tove moved back to Sweden to work for Save the Children.

Interdisciplinary tensions and shifts in personnel are not particular to Productive Margins – in many ways we were managing change – but anxiety-making nevertheless for some participants:

> 'I felt this stage coincided with the slipping away of the social science discourse that we were used to representing. At one stage it felt as if the research might become an arts project and sideline the contemporary regulatory structures that were deepening family poverty and low paid employment – sanctions, the benefit caps, JCP requirements. The grip of austerity was tighter than ever. I became anxious that we would lose this discourse.' (Sue)

Whether it was the weakening of organisational knowledge at this stage of the process, or the more exploratory discourse on arts based research that was taking place in the Poverty Working Group or perhaps both – dialogical conversations had become more challenging, particularly around the converging of the arts and social sciences. Were some of us bowing to the mystique of the artist?

> 'Artists will always be treated as the expert coming in unless you can engage them on a certain interdisciplinary knowledge.' (Allan)

At one stage we asked: "Where do the minds meet?" – a throw in line at the time but a loaded question nevertheless given the interdisciplinary ambitions of arts and social sciences in Productive Margins.

Interdisciplinarity in itself is not a panacea for innovative research; it can involve closure – whereas a focused discipline may very well open things up. When it works well interdisciplinarity can be inventive, creating radical epistemological and ontological shifts, and be positioned against top-down governmentality (although then faces the challenge of whether it will be taken up by government; Barry et al, 2008). Further down the line we were able to enter the 'when it works well' stage, developing what was to become a more radically inventive research project than we could have ever anticipated. At this moment in time we were at a watershed, but one from which we were then able to move forward as a collaborative, multi-disciplinary team.

What were the reasons for this progression? Fundamentally, SPAN stabilised enabling the partnership to advance. Moreover, Moestak Hussein, the community development worker at SPAN who came on board to replace Tove and who would be working at a grassroots level with parents participating in the research, had an almost immediate empathy for the project:

> 'I was happy to come across the opportunity. I had been involved in research projects before that were already shaped. This seemed fair – instead of getting ideas from the community and going away and writing about them it's more fair to have the research question produced together particularly in the context of the community being researched all the time. I connected really well – Tove helped – she told me a lot about the project. I have a passion for this work because of my experiences of poverty

and social justice. As a Somali in the community I feel I am able to help and support the community.'

Another turning point was that Tove did remain on board albeit at a distance in another country – she brought new reflections on the global impact of poverty creation in Sweden, especially with regard to new migrant families. Others too came on board to deepen the dialogical process – in particular Eva Elliott from Cardiff University who had long-term interdisciplinary experience in the field of social sciences and the arts. Central too, was Angela Piccini, the Co-Investigator focusing on arts, who stood her ground in the iterative process and held onto informing us about the role of art practice as knowledge-producing research rather than as a facilitation method.

We also began to recognise that as members of the Poverty Working Group we had collectively sidelined our own arts and humanities backgrounds; this became apparent when our work on interdisciplinarity created space for unexplored areas of knowledge and experience to come to the fore. Productive Margins legitimised this knowledge – Sue in literature and history and as a songwriter; Nathan as a poet and songwriter. Allan had an Art degree and had been a community artist, a history that he had kept under wraps for quite a while. He felt an arts background furthered community development:

> 'I'm a firm believer if you have a more creative background you think laterally … it's the creative process. It's the way you think about things. I don't tend to see a barrier immediately. I think how do I get over it, under it.'

He had the most experience of arts practice in community settings where "artists were offered an easy landing strip".

The Poverty Working Group expanded to become more multi-disciplinary and at the same time steadied. Arts and social science methods began to converge. Fundamentally, we held onto the earlier priorities of the Poverty Working Group.

> 'A huge step forward for me and when I breathed a sigh of relief was when the academics and grassroots members were able to synthesise our collective work in reaching out to community members in Bristol and Cardiff. The flyer headed "Low Income Families in Modern Urban Settings: Poverty, Austerity and Participatory Resistance" effectively subverted the Big Society discourse and its

institutionalisation of participatory engagement that controlled voice and resistance.' (Sue)

Nevertheless, once the artists were commissioned to join the research project, the rather long-winded headline title was changed by common consensus yet again, to better reflect the impact of what was to become a new interdisciplinary shift in focus.

Dr Roiyah Saltus-Hendrickson from Cardiff University at the Forum in Cardiff at the beginning of 2015 remarked that when social scientists work with arts practice, it's not enough to bring research alive; that the starting position will not be the same as the ending position. This certainly became the case for the research ambitions of the Poverty Working Group. Close and Remote (www.closeandremote.net), the artists we commissioned to help us research family poverty in urban environments, chosen by both the community volunteer panel and the interview group, brought new discourses and methodologies to the research process. Close and Remote proposed an of-the-moment dimension that would invert the Conservative government's Life Chances Strategy, with its focus on individual 'problem families' and 'worklessness' as central impediments to social mobility and deeply embedded poverty. Indeed, routes out of poverty are not considered by the former prime minister to be structural in nature – for example, via redistribution of wealth/taxation, higher wages and social security, and so on. Cameron (2016) argues rather that 'Families are the best anti-poverty measure ever invented. They are a welfare, education, and counselling system all wrapped up into one'. This begs the question as to why then so many families are living in poverty, including working families, and what these families themselves think of the government's Life Chances agenda (Department for Work and Pensions, 2015).

In interrogating the government's moralistic, top-down, strategies that hone down on the individual when addressing poverty and decreasing social mobility, the research project inverts this thinking, examining the structural power dynamics of regulatory controls as experienced by families in poverty at ground level, while creating space for parents to collectively reimagine their families' life chances. The very notion of 'Life Chances' was appropriated by the Conservative government from Weber, who first framed the concept when expanding on Marx's analysis of the socio/economic factors that inhibit/enable the advancement of different class based groups (Weber, 1978). The inherent irony in this inversion is unravelled in the co-produced research project, now renamed 'Life Chances', exploring individual and collective agency and participatory resistance to regulatory injustices and controls on low income families, from the perspectives of those families involved in the research. This includes as we write, an experimental arts project based on a short novel called Life Chances, authored with the participants on the project; and a jewellery enterprise also called Life Chances that explores one of the contradictions intrinsic to neo-liberal thinking, namely that entrepreneurial activity alleviates poverty. The research project aims to reflect on how socio/economic power dynamics are transacted at both a governmental and community level and consider how shifts in thinking can be enacted to further discourse and expand understandings of different realities. As we write, the progress and impact of these ambitions are still very much in process.

The impact of institutional regulatory systems on co-produced research

Long-term, co-produced research requires organisational stability and the propensity to manage shifts in focus, time and resources. One significant consideration on this co-production journey has been the impact of funding and staff changes; ideally, we need to build in contingencies both in community organisations and within the Academy to address such issues. We accept, however, this can be difficult to plan for in the real world – that the nature of flux and change in funding and human resources, both for community organisations and for researchers, makes this difficult. At the very least, those entering into such collaborative partnerships need to be aware of arrangements that might need to be in place to manage a long-term programme.

This includes the propensity to bring in new and relevant experience into the mix, which means the need for prior arrangements with regard to recruitment procedures agreed between the Academy and community organisations; different sectors have different regulations. For example, the research assistant to be recruited on the research project was a key year-long full-time position, yet university regulations developed with the unions required that this post be first advertised to staff at risk of redundancy within the university, thus limiting the field.

> 'I felt at the time that Equal Opportunity protocols of the voluntary sector to be a more open recruitment process – how was the university "to be turned inside out", one of the overall aims of Productive Margins if we couldn't recruit from a wider constituent group? And yet I later reflected after debates within the team that the university and the

voluntary sector had developed some similar regulatory protections when it came to job security.' Sue

SRCDC highlighted that community organisations themselves had recruitment policies that resonated with those of the Academy: and that these policies could create contradictions in the context of co-produced research.

> 'Third sector also have reemployment policies as part of providing opportunity for staff development and continuity and retention of experienced staff. Opening up recruitment as in co-production is a constant problem for organisations re: putting equalities in the mix and thinking about what you are trying to achieve. There are challenges and it's not about just going with the flow. The important thing is that questions are being asked. We considered the implications. This tipped the balance on recruitment – there are broader people out there including early career researchers from Cardiff who might have wanted to apply.' (Allan)

While there are good arguments for providing some form of stability to workers, and both the voluntary sector and the university have arrangements in place to support people at risk of redundancy, these policies can clash with the principles of co-production where expertise and experience inside and outside the university is recognised as equally valid. Rather than bury the tensions, discussion did take place, a job description targeted on co-production was co-produced, procedures were followed, and the post was eventually advertised externally. We were able to develop an interview process that included a panel of parent volunteers, in addition to the formal interview panel with a combination of members from SPAN, SRCDC and the Academy, leading to the appointment of our research assistant, Marilyn Howard. We went on to use the same co-produced interview process for the recruitment of the artists, Close and Remote, leading to the development of the Life Chances research project.

> 'It was a new approach – the co-production of recruitment. It equalised it out having community representation – key as we're working with communities. The quality was robust. It was an intense process. It shows the value of going into that intensity – it [the decision] was arrived at in a co-produced way – the community and the university. There

were community members on the panel. I would use it again.' (Allan)

Final reflections on the impact and challenges of co-produced research

Reflections on time

The co-production of research, while addressing the levelling of possible hierarchies between university staff and community organisations and creating opportunities for co-design and new practices, does have difficulties for the consistent involvement of their representatives. Life's journey intervenes on many different levels for all participants, academics and community members. Co-production over a period of time inevitably means that most people do not travel the whole journey. In a complex project like Productive Margins they come in at different stages – some at the beginning, others part-way through, and many may not be there by the end of the project. Time is a concern for all those involved.

Is it possible to be 'equal partners' without having 'equal time' in a co-produced research project? How can we ensure that time is not a barrier for engagement? Is this itself a Utopian ambition given the way time is regulated in so many different settings? What can we learn from the different disciplines within the arts and humanities approach to the concept of time? How are praxis and time interrelated? These concerns continue to be unravelled in the ongoing explorations of the Life Chances research project.

If all community participants are to be genuine co-investigators in co-produced research, then time funded by the Productive Margins programme needs to be arranged in such a way that everyone involved is in a position to negotiate how their time is allocated.

> 'When we talk about co-production with communities, we need to take in to account that "time poverty" as well as the "regulation of time" plays a role at a community level and serves as a means to "inclusion" or "exclusion" from participation and engagement. As I was reading through the Productive Margins papers, I noticed that "time" was not highlighted as an important aspect of engagement and/ or disengagement. Yet, I would argue that it is only if we recognise that time can be problematic that we can think about how to create space for co-production between

> academic institutions and community partners on an equal footing.' (Tove)

There is the time community participants have available to commit to research activities, and also the disproportionate and often underestimated amount of time involved compared to other research activities, engaging and retaining community participants. Both of these time related issues potentially inhibit the meaningful involvement of community members in the co-production of research.

Critical to this problematic given the focus of our research with parents interfacing with job centres, are the regulatory controls of welfare to work programmes. Parents on JSA have their time draconically regulated by what are often vacuous, repetitive job search requirements. Surely there could be more productive ways of spending that time – in peer research training for example? If one of the aims of the Productive Margins programme is to challenge how things are 'normally done', we think there is scope for negotiating a different way forward with Jobcentre Plus, allowing single parents on JSA time to be involved with this and other research projects, gaining valuable training and work experience in the process. We are exploring this possibility with the support of the research assistant on the project, given that the overarching aim of Productive Margins is to rethink how regulatory practices might enable, rather than disable, the engagement of marginalised groups in decisions that affect their lives.

The hybrid community researcher

Voluntary sector involvement in co-produced research projects can and should open up new pathways and training opportunities for participants. Productive Margins has been an exemplar in this respect, in the field of research ethics, interview techniques, data analysis and data storage, for example. We could go further in developing model ways of working. Universities and community organisations could in the future work more closely together in developing knowledge sharing environments that further co-production and research and evaluation more generally.

> 'Is there a hybrid function for the future? Are we talking about community workers being equally comfortable with research data as they are working with people in their communities? Demonstrating social impact – community workers need to be prepared for that – people who

can straddle academic and community settings and be comfortable in being productive and purposeful in both.' (Nathan)

We would then be in a stronger position to equip members of smaller community organisations who share the delivery of our work, to also share in data analysis and knowledge exchanges that further alternative arguments and robust evidence bases:

> 'We have found over time working with smaller organisations within the areas that we operate, their need for support in understanding areas of interest, and building evidence of need and influencing policy.' (Nathan)

A way forward could be for the Community Worker to shadow the work of a university-based research assistant. Another would be to have the Community Worker based in the university, with a view to advancing the two-way generation of knowledge: in a position to reflect on the possibilities and constraints of the academic environment, while furthering an understanding within the academic community of the possibilities and constraints experienced by community workers.

Reflections on ethics and interdisciplinarity

Co-production clearly works well when participants identify a closeness in approach and application, leading to a sense of mutuality, confidence and trust that cannot be underestimated in collaborative work of any kind. There can be an assumption in co-produced research that participants in the same sector will bond with one another: that the challenges come between sectors, such as academia and the third sector. But the reality is more complex and contradictory. Community organisations can find it difficult, and in some cases impossible, to work in partnership with one another. Different histories and visions can be part of the challenge; the funding environment too very often puts organisations in competition with each other – making it difficult to be open about difficulties as well as possibilities. SPAN and SRCDC, however, were able to agree sharing the funding transparently and equitably. Most importantly they had a shared ethics and vision, a solidarity that resonated with their histories, both born out of the desire to promote equality and alleviate poverty.

Nik Theodore, Visiting Fellow to the University of Bristol (Theodore, 2015), said on co-production and praxis that in relaxing disciplinary boundaries new and unpredictable insights take place – we 'make the road by walking' but that this does not give us licence to do what we want. Co-production and praxis in the Freirian sense is a 'reciprocal dialogic, …not a set of methods but rather an ethical commitment'. One of the lessons for Productive Margins or indeed for any co-produced research process is the importance of building trust through a shared vision and ethics, the impact of which will add to the institutional understanding of research practice for both organisations. After a session at the Engage Conference (held in Bristol in 2014) Sue wrote:

> 'We (those from different sectors and disciplines) are not as different as we might think. We can frame things differently depending on where we frame it. Our values however are less mutable … Perhaps a lesson I learned in my own interdisciplinary praxis on this journey is "Keep the Vision – Keep the Faith".'

As we write, we are only just beginning the Life Chances research project with community participants. The impact already feels groundbreaking for community development workers, engaged for the first time with a co-produced research project that combines social sciences and arts practice in the same setting. Although we are in the first experimental stages we may even move into transdisciplinarity – the creation of a research project over and above interdisciplinarity (Barry et al, 2008). However, if social science researchers face challenges in affecting transformative changes in the way decision makers regulate for engagement, how will policymakers accustomed to more traditional research methods get their heads around an interdisciplinary/transdisciplinary research project?

Whatever the impact on policymakers, fundamental to university based research of any kind is the principle of academic freedom – that research can be carried out in an environment free from the fear that investigating a particular issue, from a particular perspective or discipline, could generate a backlash – fear of loss of funding, for example. The principle of intellectual freedom extends to community participants involved in co-produced research. Productive Margins gives space for dissent in a current climate of increasing surveillance and control, particularly for people reliant on benefits who can face sanctions that further impoverish their lives and their children, if they are considered to be non-compliant.

Resistance to unjust regulatory systems should include having a vision of how people's lives can be changed for the better:

> 'It's the right time of opportunity for us circumventing central government actions around poverty. At every point we are exploring the opportunity for better futures for the families. It's not about being in where we are now. We are using that energy to propel us to new and imagined spaces. It's an energy it really is. And this is why I like and am committed to a programme like Productive Margins. It really is exciting.' (Nathan)

Productive Margins is opening up spaces for critical reflection, bringing together grassroots groups, academics, artists, communities of interest, in knowledge collectives that explore theory and practice, enmeshing the political, ethical and the human in the furtherance of social justice. Our research is experimental – connects with both the desire and the mobilisation of alternative futures. These co-produced interdisciplinary research experiences and knowledge exchanges represent a nuanced move for us as community development workers in the relationships we build with members of the community, with academics and with artists, an influence that we see as ongoing long after the research project has ended.

FIVE

Methodologically sound? Participatory research at a community radio station

Catherine Wilkinson

Introduction

This chapter is based on a research project that used the case study of KCC Live, a volunteer youth-led community radio station situated in Knowsley, neighbouring Liverpool, UK. The station typically has a 14–25 year old volunteer base, although at the time of conducting this research all volunteers were over the age of 16, and there were a number of volunteers over the age of 25. I conducted this research using a mixed methods approach, employed through a participatory design. I drew on a range of qualitative and quantitative methods, namely: 18 months of observant participation at KCC Live; interviews with management at KCC Live and Knowsley Community College; interviews and focus groups with volunteers; a listener survey; listener diaries; and follow-up interviews with listeners. I chose the above methods as they enabled engagement with the broad range of communities involved in KCC Live, including the listening audience, as well as the volunteer body and staff. In addition, these methods were well suited to the ethnographic nature of the research, allowing for in-depth exploration of the research topic. In this chapter, I reflexively detail how the methods evolved within the field, owing to the participatory design of the project. I problematise the alleged emancipatory potential of participatory research and, in detailing the co-production of audio artefacts in this project, I argue that the meaning of 'participatory' in participatory research should be determined in communication with study participants. Only then can research be considered truly participatory.

Youth-led participatory research

Since the 1990s, research with children and young people has witnessed significant changes that have stood to challenge traditional research methods (Weller, 2006), and have endeavoured to dismantle conceptions of children as mindless and deviant (see Pain, 2003). Consequently, the literature has witnessed a surge in children-centred, and less so young people-centred, research methods. Such methods endeavour to remedy power inequities by supporting participants to choose their own methods of communication (Valentine, 1999; Weller, 2006). This is in line with the emphasis on young people's agency in children's geographies (for example, Holloway and Valentine, 2000). Pain and Kindon (2007: 2807) argue that, owing to the 'inherently spatial' nature of participation, geographers have major contributions to make to participatory theory. Participatory geographies have increasingly gained credibility, heralded as creating 'a more vibrant research agenda' (Cahill, 2007: 4), and opening up new theoretical possibilities, particularly regarding working with young people (Fox, 2013). As Pain and Francis (2003) note, at its best, participatory research works with participants to produce change. When people are involved in research they have greater opportunity to influence decisions that concern their lives (Swantz, 1996). At its most basic, participatory research involves those conventionally 'researched' in the different phases of study: for instance, in the construction of data (Gallagher, 2008); presentation of research findings and dissemination (Pain, 2004); and the pursuit of follow-up action (Cahill et al, 2007). Though ostensibly related to ethnographic research, participatory methods are positioned as less invasive than traditional ethnographies, as participants assume an active role in the research process. While ethnography involves 'telling the story of how people … create the ongoing character of particular social places and practice' (Katz, 1997: 414), participatory research allows the people in the study to do the 'telling'.

It has been argued that participatory methodologies provide opportunities for young people to present their experiences and knowledge that is less likely to be mired by researcher concerns (Dentith et al, 2009). Participatory research attempts to minimalise the 'us and them' dichotomy between academic researcher and participants (Pain, 2004: 656), or rather between 'expert and other' (Mohan, 1999: 44), accepting that participants are 'the real source of knowledge' (Ho, 2013: 6). However, owing to the collaborative nature of the participatory process, power dynamics can be difficult to negotiate (Cooke, 2001).

DeLemos (2006) recognises the problems associated with renouncing total control of the research. The author highlights the shifting power scales from research *on* communities to research *with* and *for* communities. By researching *with* KCC Live volunteers, I endeavoured to break down the hierarchies of knowledge and democratise the research process. As Cahill (2007: 16) eloquently puts it, I attempted to move beyond the 'privileged perspectives of the ivory tower'.

As a part of this research, I recruited twelve volunteers at KCC Live: six students from Knowsley Community College and six members of the broader community. The 'young' participants taught me skills in audio recording, editing and production, required to produce audio artefacts. It is fruitful here to turn to Chávez and Soep's (2005) exploration of the collaboration among young people and adult participants. The authors introduce the concept of 'pedagogy of collegiality' to describe how young people and adults are mutually dependent on one another's abilities, viewpoints, and combined efforts to engender original, multitextual, professional quality work. The point I make here is that being taught and learning new skills and knowledge does not equate to being non-agentic; rather, it is an everyday practice.

Observant participation

I undertook extensive observant participation based at KCC Live for 18 months, during which time I participated as a volunteer and overtly observed the multi-layered everyday lifeworlds (see Habermas, 1987) of the station volunteers and staff. My decision to use the term 'observant participation' over 'participant observation' is largely due to how much weight I gave to each role, that is 'participant' and 'observer'. Monti (1992) notes that, in any fieldwork, there is a battle between the role of observer and participant and, though there is no written rule, the role of observer should take precedence. However, while I observed, I intentionally positioned myself as very much more of a participant (see Wilkinson, 2017). As Moeran (2007) argues, observant participation should be the ideal to which all researchers aspire when conducting fieldwork.

To ensure my participation was equal to that of other volunteers, I completed broadcast training, both internally within KCC Live and externally, via the National Broadcasting School at Liverpool-based commercial station Radio City. Referring to Dunbar-Hester's (2008: 212) study of 'Geek Group', a group of individuals who build radio hardware, the researcher notes that it was a 'hindrance' that she was 'not more versed in the skills of the group', believing that if she possessed such skills she could have contributed to projects more fully. By ensuring technical ability, I was making possible my active participation in the station; this quickly led to me co-presenting a weekly show on KCC Live, and eventually presenting my own four-hour weekly show. This was beneficial in enabling first-hand communication with the listening community. I thus join Moeran (2007) in positioning observant participation as marking an important rite of passage in my fieldwork, affecting the richness of data I was able to gather. The shift from participant observation to observant participation is concerned with the ability to see beyond the social front that informants present to strangers in their everyday lives (Moeran, 2007); that is, to know that there is a difference between their frontstage and backstage behaviour (Goffman, 1959; Wilkinson, 2017), and to have ready access to both those front and back stages.

Participatory focus groups

I held two focus group sessions with volunteers; both focus groups contained seven participants. The focus groups were conducted within empty classrooms at Knowsley Community College. Each focus group lasted approximately one hour. I obtained written consent from all participants prior to conducting the focus groups. I read a statement aloud explaining the format and nature of the sessions and I created an enjoyable atmosphere for participants by providing refreshments (food is seen as a popular incentive, Vromen and Collin, 2010), and emphasising the informality of the sessions.

I initially planned my role to be facilitator and to probe for explanation, yet during the first focus group, I noticed that certain young people were keen to adopt a more key role in leading the discussions. I did not see this as problematic. See the following excerpt from the focus group session:

ROBBIE: You can still have community though because, okay maybe it is mainly older generations but when they live in a close [a residential street], and it's, I think it's sometimes people's reluctance to go and knock on a door and say "hello", I think that if you knocked on, yeah, if you knocked on most people's doors and said "hiya I'm so and so from down the street", they'd be like "oh hiya how are you?"

BRUCE:	Do you think the media has anything to do with that? Making us scared of strangers?
ROBBIE:	You see, when you said you used to play out, I think that like, stuff like with Jamie Bulger,[1] made people not want to let their kids out. Like when I was little my parents would use to say "just go and play, just don't go over the line".
	(Robbie, 26, and Bruce, 25, focus group)

Having noted young people's desire to take the lead in asking questions in this focus group, I implemented a participatory design into the second focus group through adopting a peer-led dimension, allowing the young people to ask the questions. I trained the young people, through informal role-play, in asking questions to elicit rich data and in effective listening skills. One area of training that young people found useful was discussion of non-verbal cues (such as smiling and nodding to acknowledge awareness of what is being said). Since young people's interviews with artists and bands often occurred via recorded telephone discussions, many young people were not conscious of non-verbal cues they were conveying or receiving. Thus, the young people became 'learner researchers' (Byrne et al, 2009: 71) through this process. Below, I provide an excerpt from the second focus group session to demonstrate an instance of the success of this participatory approach:

HARRY:	That's where the Liverpool–Manchester rivalry comes from, like we have the docks, and that's where we built all our money, and then Manchester built the Manchester shipping canal to steal some of our trade, err – it also comes from religion a little bit as well. Things like the Liverpool and Everton rivalry as well, that's where that comes from, one's Protestant and one's Catholic.
ROBBIE:	Do you not think also though that we've lost this sense of community too because funding's been cut for everything?
HARRY:	I think community's actually getting a little bit stronger because of that, like do you remember when the libraries started shutting and people, people rallied. People rallied because like that's when communities get together when they actually started to think, wait a minute, we actually live

here, this affects us, and it not only affects me but it affects my neighbour, and that's when community happens I think, like, lately community has felt a lot stronger and I actually believe that.
(Harry, 24, and Robbie, 26, participatory focus group)

I term this a participatory focus group as, dissimilarly to the peer-led focus groups that Murray (2006) discusses, I remained present during the focus group. This was under the request of participants who asked that I monitored the session in case they went 'off track'. I was a silent observer and only interjected to ensure an equilibrium of power within the group, or when asked to by the young people. I believe that my presence in this situation had no more of an impact than it did during my observant participations and, in line with Murray (2006), I found that the young people's conversations during the focus group were of the same nature as those that I typically observed. Again, I recorded the focus group sessions using my mobile phone, aiming for an unobtrusive presence.

Map-labelling exercise

Within a focus group setting, I held a map-labelling exercise of a Merseyrail map. A popular Liverpool social media account 'Scouse Bird Problems' previously posted a labelled Merseyrail network 'map of the local area'. I used the same map (unlabelled) and asked the young people to help me to label it. Although certain studies have used map drawing with young people (Literat, 2013; Ravn and Duff, 2015), I position map-labelling as a less onerous activity. This was particularly suited to my project as I was curious about young people's thoughts on locations that were geographically mapped. My intention with this activity was to gauge young people's conceptualisations of neighbouring towns and districts. Because the young people in my study were not concentrating their efforts on drawing, I found they engaged in lively debates. Within this task, I used 'word association' (Sanderson and Thomas, 2014: 1170), whereby I read out the names of different areas on the map, in turn, and asked the volunteers to discuss among themselves words that they associated with these places. I then asked the young people to work together to decide one key word that they associated with this place, which I then used to label the map.

Listener survey

Professional audience measurement as conducted by public service and commercial radio broadcasters, such as RAJAR,[2] is not suitable for community radio (Hallett, 2012). There is the issue of high costs that are not appropriate for a voluntary and non-profit sector. Also at issue is whether such approaches are somewhat 'granular', with a propensity towards inaccuracy when measuring smaller services (Hallett, 2012: 377). The young people and I therefore co-produced a bespoke listener survey.

The conducted survey was participatory in the sense that the young people were actively engaged in suggesting questions to be included, and they revised different drafts of the survey before a final version was created. Chris reflects on the skills he gained through his role as a co-researcher in the construction of this survey:

> 'I learnt like how to make up proper questions, to sort of get the right answers. So you can't just ask anything, you have to word them right. That will help me if I get a job at the Council and that.' (Chris, 18, interview)

Similarly, Wright and Mahiri (2012) tell how, through youth-led participatory action research, young people in their study were supported in the attainment of academic literacy skills.

The participants and I decided to produce the survey digitally. SelectSurvey.NET, web-based survey software, was used to create and administer the survey. We released the survey online on 21 October 2013 and left it active for 12 months before closing it, pending analysis. The young people and I worked to produce a short 'Live Read' script:

> Do you have something to say about KCC Live? We're hosting a listener survey and we want your thoughts about the station. If you want to take part visit the KCC Live Facebook page 'KCC Live Official' or on Twitter '@KCCLive'. If you have something to say about KCC Live then we want to hear it!

This was read out on KCC Live at different times during the day, several times a day and five days a week initially, encouraging response to the survey. We also created a user-friendly link that was shared on KCC Live's Facebook and Twitter accounts. As Hallett (2012) tells, if kept reasonably short, it is realistic to expect high completion rates. The final

Internet-based survey consisted of 29 items, a number deemed large enough to acquire the necessary information, yet not too large to be off-putting to potential respondents. The survey included quantitative Likert-type scale items, close-ended and open-ended response formats. From trialling the survey, I learnt that it would take approximately 10 minutes for respondents to complete. The total number of responses was 318. There was no minimum or maximum age threshold for participating in the survey; rather, the survey was aimed broadly at radio listeners. It should be borne in mind that those people who contribute to online surveys are a self-selecting group, and thus may not be illustrative of KCC Live's listenership.

Acknowledging that an online survey alone was not enough to garner the desired response rates, the volunteers and I also conducted street surveying. In order to obtain the most representative sample, we conducted surveying on weekdays, as well as on weekends. The total number of responses to the paper-based surveys was 143. The young people identified key locations within KCC Live's broadcast remit to deploy the survey: Huyton, Prescot, Kirkby and Stockbridge Village. We opted to survey outside supermarkets and shopping centres, at community events, and we approached people working in local businesses. We surveyed a broad range of respondents based on age and gender and we asked those we approached if they were radio listeners before proceeding. Below, Kurt reflects on the skills he gained through in-person surveying:

> 'It was good like, when we were asking people the questions and I was just stood there, and you like showed me how to approach people. Because to begin with I was like "no, I don't want to do it, what if they say no?" type thing, but then I saw you do it, and I'm like it's not the end of the world if they say no, they're probably just err busy and stuff. Even though I speak on the radio to loads of people, I didn't have the like confidence to approach people, but after that training with you I do now, like I will ask someone the time if my phone's run out and stuff' (Kurt, 17, interview)

Kurt recalls an occasion when a group of volunteers and I were distributing listener surveys in Huyton town centre. Although Kurt had been eager to participate, he was reluctant when approaching people. With my coaching, Kurt overcame this, and he mentions that he is now able to approach strangers to ask them for the time.

Audio artefacts

> ...radio is like a modern railroad system. Its freight trains may get everywhere but they serve no purpose unless the freight gets collected at the other end. (Siepmann and Reisberg, 1948: 649)

This historic observation from communications scholars Siepmann and Reisberg (1948) has resonance with the dissemination of findings in this study via audio content. As Makagon and Neumann (2009: 26) recognise, such audio content adds 'sensorial depth' to qualitative studies, which is missing from solely written accounts. Typically, dissemination practices consist of publishing articles in academic journals and writing books that sit unread by the wider public in university libraries (Richardson, 2000).

In this project, the youth-led participatory research involved the co-production of an audio documentary and three-part radio series, broadcast on KCC Live. The documentary, titled 'Community to me is...', is a compilation of the young people's conceptualisations of community. The three-part series, titled 'What we found', focuses on the results of the research. Regarding the latter, the young people and I broadcast one show per month over a period of three months. Part 1 focused on the findings in relation to youth voice; Part 2 on the findings in relation to community; and Part 3 concerned findings regarding skills and development. The documentary and radio series contain the same participatory elements in the co-selection of audio; discussions surrounding what precisely the young people would like to include; and how the shows should be edited into a final package

Through the production of the two aforementioned audio artefacts, I privileged verbal expression in order to facilitate the presentation of 'youth voice', something which Fleetwood (2005) describes as a distinct yet much wanted outcome. This is crucial, as enabling young people to communicate and be listened to is indispensable for improving their lives (see Grover, 2004). Aware of the potentially manipulative and exploitive editing process, accurately representing the young people was something which I aimed for. I therefore encouraged the young people to inform me of any sections they wished to be edited, or if there was anything else they would like adding in. I was surprised that the very rare occasions that young people requested the deletion of an audio clip was because they had made a slip of the tongue or stuttered over speech, and were embarrassed by this being broadcast. In other words, editing was only requested for issues surrounding delivery, as opposed to content. I found that my desire for the young people to have autonomy over their representations was greater than (or at least different to) theirs, as I now go on to detail.

Methodologically sound?

Herein, I respond to the call of scholars (such as Darbyshire et al, 2005 and Skelton, 2008) for greater reflexivity on the success and failures of research approaches. In preparing for the audio documentary and radio series, conjuring up key themes, and thinking about songs and particular lyrics to be included, the young people were eager to participate. They were also forthcoming in volunteering their time to be interviewed, and assisting me with use of the recording equipment. However, when it came to editing the audio clips, the participants seemed reluctant. Chris said: "it's probably best if you do the editing, it's your documentary" (Author's field diary, 01/08/14). Bruce told me "I don't want to cut anything out because it's your work" (Author's field diary, 03/08/14). Part of me felt like I was lazy for 'offloading' my work onto the young people. I was convinced that they thought participatory research was some sort of farce to help researchers divide their time between the office and the field. In contradistinction to work which has positioned participatory research as emancipatory, and the cure-all to unequal power relations (for example, Merriam and Simpson, 2000), my research offers insight that, at least for some young people, co-producing research can be burdensome and an undesirable task. It is worth reiterating that I was working alongside predominantly NEET (not in education, employment or training) young people, many of whom have disengaged with formal learning; therefore participating in a university project may not have been distinctly appealing to them. In addition to this, KCC Live is to a certain extent an 'over-researched community', as geographers at the University of Liverpool, where this research project was undertaken, have conducted a previous participatory research project at the station. Further, during my fieldwork, volunteers and management were conducting their own research at/into KCC Live for their college and university courses. These research projects included use of similar methods such as interviewing and producing audio recordings. In this sense, it is reasonable to assume that young people at KCC Live may have been experiencing what certain authors (Clark, 2008; Mandel, 2003) have described as 'research fatigue'.

After recognising this reluctance to edit, I regrouped the young people and again explained the nature of participatory research. I told them "this is just as much your documentary as it is mine" (Author's field diary, 04/08/14). I reminded them of their right to withdraw from the project at any time; all of the young people were adamant that they wished to continue as co-researchers on the project. We agreed to meet the following week and I was pleased that the young people appeared to have a clearer sense of what participatory research is. This excerpt from my field diary explains what happened when we next met:

> Today I met with the young people again in order to edit the documentary. I hoped that their renewed understanding would lead to a more smoothly running session. Unfortunately, this wasn't the case. Bruce pointed me towards the chair in the studio, when I offered him the chair he said "no, I'll just stand and tell you what to do". Bruce showed me how to edit the audio clip and then left the studio. When I went to look for him, I found him sat in Studio 2 editing his own show. I asked him if he would like to come into the studio to help in the editing process and he said "I'm sure you've got the hang of it". (Author's field diary, 04/08/14)

At this point, I realised that I had been looking at participatory research through rose-tinted glasses. It was not a straightforward case of everybody working together, dividing the production of the documentary into equal portions, and everyone spending the same amount of time on their section. I explore this further through the following field diary excerpt:

> I felt like I had hit a hurdle as I had desired the documentary to be a participatory product, but this didn't seem to be working. When I asked Chris, he told me that this felt like "group work that you did at school", and felt like him and the other young people were "too old to all sit around and work together". I began to consider whether participatory research was uncool, or whether I was uncool as a researcher. I spoke to the young people about what would work best with them. They all clearly emphasised that they would like a part in shaping the documentary. The young people came up with a new type of structure for the participatory work. They suggested that I could make progress with editing the documentary and then they would call me in for a 'snoop'. (Author's field diary, 11/08/14)

A snoop is a type of meeting in radio where presenters receive feedback on their work, listening back to clips of audio. The young people chose to work in this style as it is familiar to them. The means of using a 'snoop' to critique the documentary content reversed typical power relations, putting the young people in the superior position. In industry, usually the station manager conducts these snoops. I welcomed this approach, particularly considering the resistance of the young people to be involved in more seemingly juvenile approaches to co-production. Appreciation of the reversed power relations can be seen through the excerpt from Calvin below:

> 'It was good to tell you which bits sounded good and which bits didn't, because then I developed like me leadership skills, so like I was the boss, I was like "that sounds shit", nah I'm kidding, but it was good to be in charge of you because like you're a bit older.' (Calvin, 20, interview)

Discussing the snoop format for commenting on the 'Community to me is…' audio documentary, Calvin proclaims: "I was the boss", telling that he developed leadership skills through 'being in charge' of someone who is older. Desirably, as discussed by Pain and Francis (2003), this shifted the typical hierarchies that position the researcher as expert and the co-researchers as informants.

Thinking reflexively, I realise that I had a vision and hoped to make the research participatory but, ironically, in the process I had failed to allow the young people to shape the meaning of 'participatory' in the participatory research. This relates to a point made by Smith (1999: 40):

> Idealistic ideas about community collaboration and active participation need to be tempered with realistic assessments of a community's resources and capabilities, even if there is enthusiasm and goodwill. Similarly, the involvement of community resource people also needs to be considered before putting an additional responsibility on individuals already carrying heavy burdens of duty.

In sum, I learnt that the meaning of participatory in 'participatory' research should be determined in communication with the people in one's study. Only then can research be considered truly participatory.

Concluding remarks

This study has a number of methodological contributions for both the children's geographies literature and the participatory geographies literature. First, through the co-production of the audio documentary and three-part radio series, my research stands to encourage new ways of disseminating research back to the community of study in 'culturally appropriate ways' (Smith, 1999: 15). By promoting young people's active engagement in the research, I valorised their competencies, conferring on them the status of experts in their own lives. By uniting personal testimonies with music and sound, the young people and I co-produced high quality audio artefacts that have been broadcast on KCC Live as an 'offering' from the research to the community, and remain accessible to them. This form of dissemination is participatory in nature, and was useful for relinquishing control of the research and handing research findings over to the community (see also Van Blerk and Ansell, 2007). My research therefore highlights the importance in going against 'doing research that ends up not being read and not making a difference to anything but the author's career' (Richardson, 2000: 924). Further, the co-production of this audio content sits in line with Smith's (1999) argument that this does not prohibit writing for publication; rather, it is part of an ethical and respectful approach. It is in this vein that young people's voices in my research move beyond dialogue with the researcher, and enter into the public realm.

Second, I problematised the alleged emancipatory potential of participatory research. I assumed the young people, as proficient creators of audio content, would desire a hands-on role in editing the audio documentary. However, I found that not all young people wished to occupy such a role. I therefore allowed the young people to dictate to me how this would work, and they suggested a snoop style format that reversed typical power relations. This reflexive tale contributes to work on the 'promise and perils' (Luke et al, 2004: 11) of a participatory research approach, in highlighting that the meaning of 'participatory' in participatory research should be determined in communication with study participants. Only then can research be considered truly participatory. My research offers insight that, at least for some young people, co-producing research can be a burdensome and undesirable task. This stands in contradiction to research (for example, Merriam and Simpson, 2000) that has positioned participatory research as emancipatory, and the cure-all to unequal power relations.

Notes

[1] James Patrick Bulger (known in the media as Jamie Bulger) was a two-year-old boy who disappeared from the New Strand Shopping Centre in Bootle, while accompanying his mother. It was found that Bulger had been abducted, tortured and murdered by two ten-year-old boys.

[2] RAJAR, Radio Joint Audience Research, is the official body in charge of measuring radio audiences in the UK.

SIX

The regulatory aesthetics of co-production

Penny Evans and Angela Piccini

Introduction

In co-production, the arts have been situated as mediating praxes that translate and transmit knowledge between 'researchers' and 'communities'. The sciences engage art in order to engage communities claiming that 'art releases the visionary impulse, bringing an innovative dimension to problem-solving' (Wyman, 2004: 6, quoted in Cox et al, 2009: 1472). At the same time, art engages with communities in a belief that art 'rehumanises society rendered numb and fragmented by the repressive instrumentality of capitalist production' (Bishop, 2012: 11). Artists and arts researchers thus align themselves with the 'pedagogic state' (Newman, 2010; O'Neill and Wilson, 2010), in which the citizen is somehow empowered to take responsibility for all forms of production and transformation. Despite all this interdisciplinary engagement, art remains at the margins of power. As Cox et al remark (2009: 119), there is 'no consensus on how to balance scientific research requirements (e.g. for rigour) with the aesthetic dimensions of arts-based inquiry'. Science is research, rigour and rationalism while art is inquiry, aesthetics and emotion. Yet, we know that 'we have never been modern' (Latour, 1993), that science is entangled with aesthetics, emotion and hunches while art involves empiricism, rigour and research.

In this chapter, we will discuss three projects on which we have worked closely together over the past decade in order to question some of the assumptions made about art's relationships with knowledge production and the ways in which the aesthetics of co-production can regulate the possibilities of artistic practices. The 'we' here are Penny Evans from Knowle West Media Centre (KWMC) and Angela Piccini from University of Bristol. KWMC is a purpose-built media arts organisation based in a community in Bristol, UK, and is housed in the largest straw bale building in the South West. KWMC and the University of Bristol have been collaborating across a number of research projects over the past decade. KWMC works with media artists to engage citizens often excluded from decision making and research through exploring local, national and international issues in order to co-produce and co-design the testing of ideas, products and technologies. Examples of these activities include creating data visualisations; documentation and engagement strategies; a comprehensive young people's programme teaching skills in media; coding; and 'making'. KWMC's three core ambitions are: building tools, skills and places, with people, which support positive social change and opportunities to experiment with 'making and producing'; shaping the way we live in the future through experimentation and sharing ideas with people; and making visible, celebrating and building on the cultural and creative wealth of communities, extending opportunities for those who have had least opportunity to engage, participate in and enjoy excellent arts and culture.

This chapter is also a chronicle of a journey from colleague to friend. We are interested in the role of chemistry in collaboration: why some relationships work and some do not and how, despite not always agreeing on directions and actions, we are able to work together effectively and also have fun. This chemistry is also part of the aesthetics of co-production. The projects on which we have worked together are linked by their focus on collaboration and participation.

The projects are also linked through their positioning of arts practices as knowledge producing, rather than as instrumental or facilitative. That is, where the arts have popularly been mobilised for the purposes of public engagement and social change across a number of fields (Bishop, 2012), KWMC and University of Bristol are also interested in the ways in which art raises its own research questions and generates contributions to knowledge in its own terms. It is for this reason that in this paper we use the term 'arts praxes', where art is a critical-creative practice. In this way we use praxis in the context of Hannah Arendt's theory of action (1998); Gramsci's sense of embodied, practised theory (2005); and Paolo Freire's sense, outlined in his *Pedagogy of the Oppressed* (2001), of praxis as transformative. Within the context of academic knowledge production through critical-creative practice, the other key reference is practice as research across performance, the moving image and contemporary art (see Allegue et al, 2009). In other words, we are interested in how the formal qualities of arts practices – not just their subject matter – can raise and investigate research questions that are rigorous, original and significant.

Research questions

The core question we ask is: what are the aesthetics of the regulatory frameworks that shape co-production? We ask this question in order to think about the ways in which co-production, as a material-discursive practice in the contemporary academy, impacts on the media arts practices that KWMC fosters within partnership projects with the university. The shift in institutional language and funding contexts from collaboration and social practice to co-production is a regulatory shift. It impacts on contractual relationships, access to funding and commissioning strands. Given the infrastructural and bureaucratic regulatory impact of co-production, to what extent can arts praxes within co-production models generate new knowledge and social justice outcomes? What is the potential for art to move beyond ameliorating the symptoms of structural inequalities in order to transform regulatory structures? What are the aesthetics of co-production and what is the value of such practice as art? Moreover, what is the value of these art praxes *as* research?

In order to address our research questions, we need to map a number of distinct, if overlapping, discourses across the arts and academy. This chapter necessarily responds to debates around collaboration, participation and co-production in terms of how they overlap and diverge. How do those different nomenclatures impact on the practice of KWMC itself, on the scholarship possible within community–university partnerships and on the arts practices that emerge out of these partnerships? While it is beyond the scope of this chapter to provide an in-depth overview of participatory, community-based or socially engaged arts practice (see Bishop, 2012; Carpentier, 2011) we need to address some of the key issues around both collaboration and regulation. How are collaboration, participation and co-production framed by regulatory structures? How do organisations such as KWMC and University of Bristol enact their practices through institutional regulation? How are the arts-based projects on which they collaborate shaped through the intersection of their institutional regulatory structures? And how do the regulatory frameworks of funding – from the local of the city to the national of Arts Council England and Research Councils UK through to European funding initiatives – produce different kinds of practices?

Context

Co-production frames an encounter between 'communities' and 'researchers', with the arts situated as mediating praxes that translate and transmit knowledge across fields. The sciences – social, medical, engineering, health – have engaged with art to engage with communities claiming that 'art synthesizes the rational and the emotional, the imaginative and the intuitive. It releases the visionary impulse, bringing an innovative dimension to problem-solving' (Wyman, 2004: 6, quoted in Cox et al, 2009: 1472). At the same time, art has itself turned to engagement and participation in the belief that art 'rehumanises society rendered numb and fragmented by the repressive instrumentality of capitalist production' and that rather than art revolving around the making of objects for consumption it must now be 'an art of action, interfacing with reality, taking steps – however small – to repair the social bond' (Bishop, 2012: 11). Where the disciplines beyond art see it as a form of pure creativity that drives visionary innovation – problematically echoing Richard Florida's liberal renderings (2002; 2005) of the 'creative class' and urban regeneration – within art there is a desire to co-produce real social change through participation. In this way, artists and arts researchers align themselves with a much broader turn towards the 'pedagogic state' (Newman, 2010): from welfare to education to planning and now even to art, the citizen must be empowered to take responsibility for all forms of production and transformation (O'Neill and Wilson, 2010).

Beyond complicating disciplinary boundary-making practices, the aesthetics of co-production that we discuss here engage with what Jacques Rancière describes as the 'distribution of the sensible' (2006). Rancière's influential text, *The Politics of Aesthetics*, responds to Walter Benjamin's discussion of the radical political potential of art in the age of mechanical reproduction (1936), which sought to discuss the ways in which the fascist politics of 1930s Europe was itself 'art'. Rancière's focus is on how aesthetics – what is possible to say, to show and to recognise – is always already political. The possible here is what is permissible. This is the space of regulation. Rancière (2006: 19) suggests that the arts

> only ever lend to projects of domination or emancipation what they are able to lend to them, that is to say, quite simply, what they have in common with them: bodily positions and movements, functions of speech, the parcelling out of the visible and the invisible.

Whereas Claire Bishop critiques social practice art for failing to take aesthetics seriously and for abandoning that which is unique about art in favour of a loose social justice agenda (2012), Rancière's position is a more complex one that helps collaborative projects like ours beyond the unhelpful impasse of good versus bad, elite versus populist, socially engaged versus for-its-own-sake art. Instead, the regulation of the sensible suggests that the relationship between art and emancipatory social and political projects is itself a co-production, an entangled relation of commonality. The art that is possible to make with communities is already regulated by the aesthetics of those communities' politics at the same time that those politics are already aesthetic.

KWMC creative, regulatory and evaluation contexts

KWMC's practices are inspired by a range of local, national and global collaborative contexts. KWMC works across a diverse range of art practices using performance in the context of citizen sensing, database models for thinking about mapping and shops, performance to facilitate and connect knowledges and film to envision possible pasts and futures. During the course of developing this chapter, Penny Evans brought a selection of publications and grey literature (such as reports, leaflets, web copy, evaluation documents) to a writing residential weekend in the autumn of 2015. She chose the books as indicative of KWMC's ethos, aspirations and methods. As an organisation that relies on grant capture, KWMC has to be agile, nimble and able to respond to multiple agendas emerging out of creative economy contexts but also to community, young people's agendas and employability and skills development. For example, a V&A Digital Design weekend in which KWMC participated generated a publication (Rogers et al, 2014) cataloguing a rich diversity of open collaborative digital design projects spanning higher education, large organisations such as the BBC and smaller start-ups. The focus on maker cultures, hackathons and the internet of things illustrates KWMC's interests in staying at the leading edges of media arts and digital technologies.

KWMC is also inspired by methods of collaboration developed across the arts sector. For example, Situations, the Bristol-based international public art producing and curatorial organisation led by Claire Doherty, has developed a series of key texts about situational and site-specific art in the public realm. Situations was commissioned as part of the Arts Council's Creative People and Places programme to produce an 'incomplete glossary of quality' toolkit for use in the development, implementation and evaluation of collaborative and participatory arts projects (www.creativepeopleplaces.org.uk/our-learning/taking-bearings). KWMC was particularly inspired by its approach to 'route planning' that asked: where you are heading and how you would define what the destination looks like; why are you going; what do you want from collaborators and what do you think they might want from you; and what obstacles do you think you might find and how will you overcome them together? 'Packing' involves the skills and knowledges that each person takes along with themselves; what each person seeks out; who each person might rely on to be active and what the limits of collaboration might be; and the pitfalls that each person might be looking out for based on past experience. 'Re-routing' involves investigating whether obstacles are due to disagreements about directions; looking at problems from other perspectives; identifying people who can help; and devising other actions. 'Arriving' invites participants to consider whether this is where people expected to be; what got lost along the way; what things will be taken away; and what will be left behind. In short, KWMC responds to and adopts innovative ways of thinking and doing that are evident across the sector. They are not constrained by academic knowledge production and instead focus on appropriation, transformation and implementation.

KWMC's *Approach to Community Development and Measuring Impact* report (Knowle West Media Centre, 2014) articulates its approach to working with communities as one of practice-led, action research. That is, KWMC does not simply work with local people to find answers to predefined questions. Instead, it works with local people to identify pertinent questions that demand interrogation. In this way research focus is defined through exchange with local communities and therefore co-design of research is at the heart of all they do. Evaluation processes and activities are developed alongside project planning, allowing reflection to be built into the creative process itself. This enables an ongoing monitoring of the aims and ensures clarity.

For KWMC, indicators of success through evaluation are the aims of specific projects and how far they have been met. The reasons for having this approach are threefold. First, KWMC aims to avoid questionnaires as people do not always have time or take the time to consider in-depth and reflexive answers. The aim is to create evaluation contexts that create enough time to realise the value of what people have experienced, and how much has been achieved as participants, audiences, facilitators, artists, project managers. Second, using creative processes to produce knowledge rather just gather evidence makes explicit the learning that has taken place and the difference this has made for people. Third, evidence is also generated by making the value of the 'impact' of the work explicit. Evidence is then reflected on by the team who can use the process to determine the best ways forward and take it forward for further community involvement in the process. This is how KWMC defines its action research approach to projects.

The KWMC planning form is another aspect of the regulatory context in which it works. It was developed to ensure activities are planned on the basis of aims and intended outcomes. Evaluation is planned into the process, designed at the same time as the project. All activity flows out of the planning form and no project is undertaken without one. Central to this is the identification of the 'so what?' factor. Where a large number of projects may be seen to be exciting and innovative and contribute to the knowledge and understanding of the Knowle West community, the business of the charity must speak to its mission statement and aims, articulated annually. KWMC does not have the same constraints or freedoms as the higher education institution. All projects must address the vision of the centre.

Data is another key regulatory framework within the organisation. The KWMC database records both quantitative and qualitative data so that project participants and the KWMC team can reflect iteratively on the differences that projects are making so as to develop future projects in an informed and evidence-based way. Key Performance Indicators (KPIs) are listed on the database and can be assigned to project sessions or individuals and that relate to the organisation's overarching aims and ambitions. The KPIs include building tools, skills and places; shaping the way we live in the future; and making visible the cultural and creative wealth of communities.

Commissioned projects, evaluative frameworks, planning forms and the organisation of the production and storage of data are all regulatory features of KWMC's work. They also have their own aesthetics. Evaluation within KWMC tends to take the form of face-to-face and one-to-one conversations, often accompanied by clipboards and cameras, as though the thinking is always already about how to stage evaluation within an annual report. Planning forms shape projects into deliverables and organise knowledge into a generic document-based template into which all proposals must fit. Similarly, data is envisioned as sitting within form-field databases and are distributed across KWMC's servers and standalone desktops and laptops. That is, there is an aesthetic gap between the digital and computational participatory artworks that take place at KWMC and the conceptualisation of evaluation and strategic forward planning. As in universities, innovative practices at KWMC are contextualised by the administrative systems that enable and constrain them.

Projects

Beyond the regulatory aspects of data recording and analysis at KWMC, which have their own specific aesthetics, there are questions, too, about how specific participatory, co-produced work regulates aesthetic possibilities. It is within this regulatory context that University of Bristol and KWMC collaborations take place. There are three case study projects that we discuss in this chapter:

1. the University of Local Knowledge (ULK) as an interdisciplinary partnership project with discrete but interlinked activities across arts and computer science;
2. Know your Bristol on the Move, which used co-production as a core method with focused research activity around a clearly defined set of 'objects'; and
3. Productive Margins, which takes a radically open approach that seeks to put organisations and people into the room to co-develop research questions, research design, research implementation and research evaluation on the topic of regulating *for* engagement.

These three projects produce very different aesthetics. To what extent are those aesthetics shaped by the modes of working or by their production contexts or intended audiences? Moreover, how do aesthetics matter in the production, circulation and reception of participatory artworks? On which institutional terms do they need to succeed and who decides? In what ways do these projects respond to, extend or complicate Rancière's politics of aesthetics that are grounded in a 'distribution of the sensible'? For KWMC project outcomes mean jobs, training, grant capture, connecting diverse/new practices, working to produce artworks with potential national/international significance and impact. KWMC aims to show the value of art through engagement in different ways to innovate, experiment and play. Social justice and social impact are aims that sit within that. For collaborations with University of Bristol, however, everything depends on the collaborating department and individual. Where collaborations take place in the humanities, social sciences or sciences, participation in the production of arts-based projects is about social impact. Where collaborations emerge with arts-based disciplines, the aim is to produce rigorous, interesting artworks that engage with form and the critical-creative aspects of the work. How does the artwork extend, complicate or say something new about media arts? In programmes where the collaborative teams are multidisciplinary, the challenge is around the need or desire to work in inter- or transdisciplinary modes. To what end do we produce these artworks? And who judges their value? It is at these points that our collaborations come against the work of Claire Bishop, but also the important work of Eleanora Belfiore and Oliver Bennett on the autonomy of arts practices (2008).

University of Local Knowledge

The University of Local Knowledge (ULK) is a durational (2008 to date), socially engaged artwork devised through complex collaborations between US artist Suzanne Lacy, Knowle West Media Centre (KWMC Directors Carolyn Hassan and Penny Evans, and Simon Poulter, lead artist/curator for KWMC's 2008 Keys Commissions), the residents of Knowle West in South Bristol, and Arnolfini Gallery (Tom Trevor and Nav Haq). It has been developed with University of Bristol and Arnolfini, and supported by Bristol City Council (Art in the Public Realm), the BBC, National Co-ordinating Centre for Public Engagement (NCCPE), and the University of the West of England. ULK aims to uncover, share and celebrate the skills, talents and expertise within Knowle West and the surrounding areas. By referencing this academic system of categorising 'knowledge', the initial idea developed for ULK by the team aimed to challenge perceptions of how we gain, use and value it. ULK also aims to promote the value of community-led learning alongside more traditional academic understandings of knowledge.

Since 2011, residents of Knowle West have been sharing their specific expertise with the filmmaking team at KWMC. Suzanne Lacy and KWMC worked with Knowle West residents to stage open conversations to shape the initial stages of the project. The project used a deliberately corporate Steering Group model, to generate the pedagogical aims of the alternative university and to begin to design its curriculum and 'administrative' structures. Lacy's participatory practice often uses corporate and/or industrial structures as a way of valuing people's participation and to critique the assumed logics of such structures that so often exclude communities from power and decision making (Irish, 2010). The university was chosen as a deliberately contentious metaphor to provoke debate around what constitutes knowledge and why values are placed on different spheres of expertise. Historically, Knowle West has been subject to an official culture of low aspiration, reproduced through city policies and education provision, which has been internalised by community members. KWMC and Lacy have been committed to supporting community members to recognise and value the considerable knowledges generated and passed through the community. Knowledge spans a range of diverse areas, including engineering, care, science, food growing, crafts and technology.

Filming of local experts resulted in some 970 films, all produced with a commitment to professional production values. In Spring 2011, Lacy returned to Knowle West to collaborate on a series of seminars, which took the form of group conversations between University of Bristol, University of the West of England academics and community experts arranged in local sites, including shops, car parks and homes. For example, a seminar on Animal Husbandry from ULK's Department of Veterinary Science took place in the Fur and Feathers local pet shop. Local horse experts Darren Nash, Gail Rawlings and Leanne Stutt and veterinary scientist Becky Whay (University of Bristol) spent an afternoon discussing horses, their care and the transformative role of horse owning in the community. Lacy and the KWMC team 'dressed' Fur and Feathers as a performance space for the conversations, with hay bales and film lighting. The filmed conversation was 'witnessed' by a small group inside and members of the community watched the conversation through the cinema screen-like window. Other seminars included conversations about informal education and youth exclusion, which connected Gail Bevan with Ros Sutherland (Graduate School of Education); grandparent carers, which linked Patricia Lucas (School for Policy Studies) and residents, including Denise Britt; and engineering, which put resident car restorers Ted Crockrell, Phil Leonard, Etienne de Coensel and Terry de Coensel in conversation with engineer John Piper (University of the West of England). These filmed seminars were produced as an additional, performance-focused outcome of the ULK durational artwork.

In early 2012, a further iteration of ULK was led by Professor Mike Fraser (Computer Science, University of Bristol). Funded through the Research Council UK's 'Into the Wild' programme, this stage of the project brought partners together to explore physical and virtual relationships across live performance and web-delivered media. We wished to develop technologies and techniques to scale up and study community skill and praxis. We studied the deployment and use of technologies and techniques to collaboratively develop knowledge to enhance our understanding of the relationships between physical and digital community. We used ULK's university-like structure to teach and publicise to others within and beyond the community; individual 'classes' were assembled into programmes of 'study' that were housed in 'departments' and 'faculties'. We built systems through which further 'classes' were added and pedagogic structures could be changed by contributors. These 'classes' are the videos of Knowle West residents describing how to do something that they are an expert at. Users are invited to add their own knowledge and create their own courses by grouping related films together. After various iterations, the current ULK website (https://www.ulk.org.uk/) has been designed by Yoke, a Bristol-based ethical design company, with support from a University of Bristol Impact Accelerator grant (Principal Investigator [PI], Angela Piccini) and the Arts and Humanities Research Council's Connected Communities Showcase funding (PI, Angela Piccini). Both the original and the current websites are powered by Knowle West residents, who have devoted many hours to co-designing and testing.

In the ULK project, various regulatory frameworks shaped the project. The curatorial vision of Arnolfini at the time, led by former director Tom Trevor and curator Nav Haq, focused on the emergence of relational aesthetics and socially engaged work. The opportunity to bring Suzanne Lacy to Bristol was an exciting opening for Arnolfini to enter this space with an international project. In a higher education context, the funding structure of the Engineering and Physical Sciences Research Council Into the Wild call determined the direction of research questions such that what might be needed or desired by the community and artist had to be shaped in ways that would demonstrate a contribution to knowledge in the field of computer science. More locally, the institutional organisation at University of Bristol shaped Fraser's and Piccini's collaboration across Faculties, which involved hiring procedures and defining the skillsets needed by the project research assistant (RA) and also the management interface between the university and KWMC and between KWMC's project coordinator, Martha Crean, and the university researchers. What was permissible on the project was also shaped by Suzanne Lacy's designs for this participatory practice and how this became juxtaposed with KWMC's systems, networks and file organisation, its existing community social networks, KWMC staffing structures and their collaborator-producer model. At the same time, KWMC's history of digital arts practice did not always sit easily with the research enquiry demands of computer science, despite the seeming close fit of their remits and interests.

Expectation is also a regulatory force. KWMC had expectations that this would be a co-produced project. They understood the project as wanting to go beyond gatekeepers, to challenge hierarchies of knowledge, scale and value and that computer science would take those concepts and present new ways of looking at them and challenge institutional ways of knowing through different technologies. KWMC did not have an understanding of the university research model whereby the RA performs most of the on-the-ground work while the principal academics take on more of a management role. KWMC also expected a tangible output that would have recognisable value as a public-facing website. The academics involved in the research project had expectations that KWMC would provide a complete and full dataset with which they could experiment. The researchers had expected to be able to take the 900+ video files and create interfaces both online and in the real world, with a specific focus on producing significant and original contributions to computer science knowledge. KWMC was interested in the same thing but with a design and community-learning agenda. This is where the distribution of the sensible becomes an acute issue and resolving different valuing systems such a challenge. All of these diverse regulatory frameworks – both formal/institutional and informal/habitual – shape outcomes. The need for effective communications systems is clear, certainly, but colliding values and the politics of aesthetic disposition are not easily resolved through language and sharing. The human and other-than-human regulatory forces circulating through the complex artwork become resolved through the different website manifestations.

Know your Bristol on the Move

Know your Bristol and Know your Bristol on the Move were two AHRC-funded Connected Communities projects (PI, Professor Robert Bickers). They were based on the Know Your Place web-based planning tool, which was launched in March 2011 by the City of Bristol and which presents place-based data via a browser-based tool. The web service is a GIS-based resource that layers historic maps of Bristol and modern Ordnance Survey Mastermap digital mapping as a planning tool for developers and planners during the preplanning application processes (http://maps.bristol.gov.uk/kyp/?edition=). Historic maps include 19th century plans by George Ashmead, 19th century parish tithe maps and 1881–83 and 1902–03 Ordnance Survey maps. Added to this are images from Bristol City's Museums and Archives, including images from the Braikenridge Collection, which show the city and its buildings in the 1820s. The web service is further augmented by data from the Bristol Historic Environment Record (HER). Know Your Place enables users to contribute written commentary, photographs and a range of digital files to a unique 'community layer'. Personal and informal archival materials are thus incorporated into a formal planning process and, at a statutory level, inform decisions taken by the city, community and developers.

The two projects were a collaboration between University of Bristol and local communities, which worked together to digitise and make accessible personal archive material via the Know Your Place website. The Know your Bristol (Bickers et al, 2015; Insole and Piccini, 2013) workshops visited seven different parts of the city where attendees contributed oral histories (which were added as audio files to the community layer) and were able to have their family photographs scanned and objects digitally photographed and, where appropriate, added to Know Your Place. Ownership of digitised images and film remains with individuals, with permissions and release agreements for the deposit of materials in the Bristol Record Office the responsibility of Bristol City Council. One strand of the project sought specifically to explore the potential for people's home movies and videos to enter into the HER, and this centred on a day workshop at KWMC, involving the Filwood Chase Historical Society, Brislington Community Archaeology Project and the archaeology subgroup of Greater Bedminster Neighbourhood Partnership. As an emerging feature of the archaeological record, people's family photographs, home movies and oral histories complicate formal histories and can become important elements of the archaeological understandings of place-making and lifeworlds through time.

The two Know your Bristol projects have worked with members of the Knowle West community to explore how moving image archives enact multiple historical and archaeological narratives and provide new information about specific everyday spatial and material practices. Scholarship on family photographs and home movies has tended to focus on the home mode as documenting the everyday, as materialising the impact of camera technologies on domestic life, as expressing cultural norms, and as documents of the ongoing social reproduction of ideology (Chalfen, 1987; Hirsch, 1981; Zimmerman, 1995). The constructed image has been understood as recording kinship, material culture and aesthetic preference and this has been seen to be essential to the home movie mode rather than technologically contingent (Chalfen, 1987; Moran, 2002: 35). That is, home movies have been understood as signifying underlying sociocultural norms and their photographic representation is argued to directly index how the subjects featured in these films see themselves. In other words, home movie images are seen, ultimately, to be constrained by historically specific ideologies that determine what can be represented and shown. In Know your Bristol on the Move, we were interested in exploring how communities can use film and video archives to tell their own histories of place. Film and video can show people how landscapes have changed over time. In the moving image what appear are buildings that no longer exist, shops that are now houses, and ways of inhabiting neighbourhoods that may no longer be recognisable.

The core activity of the Know your Bristol on the Move project involved the digitisation of some 20 hours of 1" IVC video tape from Peter Lewis's pioneering Bristol Channel community cable TV experiment which was broadcast from 1973 to 1975. Inspired by the National Film Board of Canada's Challenge for Change programme, which put early Sony Portapak video cameras into the hands of marginalised and vulnerable communities to enable their self-representation, Bristol Channel also adopted a community access approach to programming. Its aims to democratise media production were somewhat at odds with the commercial motivation which led Rediffusion, at the time the UK's largest cable company, to launch the service on its Bristol network (Lewis, 1976). As such, community television became the test bed for the installation of Bristol's cable communication infrastructure, which now carries the city's most advanced networking links. As part of Bristol Channel, Knowle West TV (KWTV) was developed to test the decentralised media model and 40 hours of broadcast were produced and transmitted by the community itself.

In this project, we aimed to work with people in Knowle West who participated in KWTV or who had lived in the community for long enough to recognise participants and locations. The video digitised by the British Film Institute (BFI) in Berkhamsted is now archived by the City of Bristol and KWMC makes this material accessible to the community. We organised three workshops over the year. Workshop 1 brought Peter Lewis to Bristol to work with community members to investigate the paper video log of KWTV in order to identify tapes for digitisation. Spreadsheet entries provided basic information about content and timing. The BFI then digitised the material and sent it to Bristol. Workshop 2 brought community elders to KWMC to watch the raw video footage with an aim to add cataloguing information. KWMC was particularly interested in identifying the people that KWTV showed whereas Piccini's research focus was on the changing landscape of Knowle West over time. This information was to feed into the emerging website and mobile app being developed by the larger Know your Bristol on the Move project (https://www.mapyourbristol.org.uk/). The final workshop was KWTV week in May 2015 with students editing video in situ, public drop-ins to crowdsource metadata, an installation and the screening of Know your Bristol on the Move artist-in-residence David Hopkinson's films. Hopkinson worked with the digitised KWTV collections to produce eight short films that explore the formal qualities of the material and some of their conceptual themes. Utilising humour and musicality, Hopkinson worked with KWMC to finalise the films for online distribution and large-scale projection (https://www.youtube.com/playlist?list=PLmWCEpa3waUCmWKBEMXmBMQZ399GkZdEB). The films were screened as part of the 2015 Floating Cinema tour from London to Bristol.

During the week-long May 2015 workshop at KWMC, we installed video in a 1970s living room set and set up individual viewing stations, thematically organised, in the KWMC training room. Widespread publicity on local BBC radio, the 15,000 views of BBC Radio Bristol's Breakfast Show Facebook page posts (at time of publication now up to 50,000) and transmission on the new community cable channel, Made in Bristol, drew significant attention. Local women Barbara Hooper, Enid Woodford and Pat Dallimore began their transformative moves from being housewives to becoming professional media producers through their work on KWTV and their humorous sketches on the channel proved particularly popular in the 2015 public screenings. As word of the event spread, other community members came through the KWMC doors to view the footage. One of these visitors had an emotional reconnection with his family through seeing footage of his band, Circle, and his grandfather that he had never before seen. The affective power of the home movie like raw footage was clear and served to make new links between the Knowle West community and KWMC.

Where ULK had a strong socially engaged arts aesthetic at its core, which at times collided with a computer science research agenda, the Knowle West TV activities within Know your Bristol on the Move had a coherence informed by the single research object: the video archive. Using archival footage to drive community workshops, to shape a relatively autonomous artist residency and to provide the grounding for student practice-based learning allowed diverse aesthetic registers to co-exist with no requirement for a single formal response. Rather than being a large-scale collaborative project, the Knowle West TV workpackage within Know your Bristol on the Move was a focused co-produced research project between KWMC and Piccini, with expertise from KWTV founder Peter Lewis. It generated a number of linked but conceptually and aesthetically distinct practical outputs that gave artist and students freedom to experiment and focus on developing their practice while it also provided opportunities for community members to gather and reminisce and to contribute practically to the sustainable security of an important, if little-known, aspect of their heritage.

Productive Margins

Finally, Productive Margins is a five-year Connected Communities programme led by Morag McDermont of the University of Bristol. It is a collaboration among seven community organisations across England and Wales and the Universities of Bristol and Cardiff. Productive Margins seeks to co-produce research into regulation for engagement. That is, we are exploring how we might question, intervene in and rework regulation in order to better support communities at the margins to participate in meaningful decision making. KWMC is one of the community partners. Piccini is Deputy Principal Investigator and oversees the arts and humanities research activities across the programme. Arts and humanities research in this context spans conventional historical scholarship through to practice as research, whereby those working in higher education across contemporary art, dance, film, music and performance produce art works as research outputs (Allegue et al, 2009).

The community organisations and social science researchers involved in Productive Margins have longstanding histories of working in collaboration with professional artists. Researchers across the social sciences have adopted arts practices as methods (such as Leavy, 2015). This work can be focused on engaging participants in research, on eliciting new data from participants and also on the emancipatory aspects of involving research participants in art projects. Community organisations are also involved in a very wide range of projects with artists, spanning the commissioning of community-based arts that have a therapeutic focus through to developing computational art residencies whose main purpose is to add value to communities through the production of high-profile artworks.

In Productive Margins, the seven individual projects that are taking place within the programme are co-produced from inception through to planning, delivery and evaluation. The programme has adopted a Forum model as a site of experimentation and collective project development. In the early stages of the programme, these Forum meetings of all participants were organised around different modes and practices of collaboration. We engaged in object-based exercises, collective mapping, food sharing, brain-storming, values exercises, fishbowl discussions and critical feedback. KWMC has been involved as a programme partner and has hosted two of the programme Forums.

The first, held in 2013, involved a brief artist commission from Matt Olden who developed a series of computational artworks using Productive Margins documentation, minutes and transcripts as source material in order to investigate how the programme as a whole is self-regulating. Olden's work also engaged with the Productive Margins themes of Dissent and Digital Spaces in so far as it aimed to show how digitally distributed material-discursive texts are both regulatory and can be reconfigured in multiple ways to perform an auto-critique of the notion of co-production and engagement. Reflecting on Rancière's discussion of the politics of aesthetics as centred on that which is recognisable, on what is permitted to be seen, the resistance of the Forum to Olden's work as alienating and elite suggests that his practice was not seen as commensurate with the aims of the community-based arts in which most Productive Margins participants have engaged. Moreover, despite frequent and often-heated discussions about the regulatory aspects of management structures within the programme, transforming that conversation into an art practice was seen to be an irrelevant distraction.

KWMC has been involved in a number of the individual projects within the programme. The most notable of these has been 'Who decides what's in my fridge?', which explored how people experience the regulation of their food habits in their community. The project's academic lead was Naomi Millner (Geography, University of Bristol) and the RA was Kitty Webster. The project drew together Co-exist, Single Parents Action Network and KWMC. In Knowle West, the emphasis was on gathering quantitative and qualitative data through surveying the local community, organising events and holding focus groups. The co-producers in this project were the working group team, KWMC, the Junior Digital Producers (JDPs), traditional cooks in the community who want to share, people cooking on restricted budgets, the Health Association, Inns Court, Square Food Foundation, the allotment community, young parents and women in their late teens and early 20s. KWMC JDPs investigated what influences people's food choices, from the location of shops and the price of goods to the amount of time they have available to cook. They developed an interactive survey using a life-size fridge filled with food and questions. The research indicated that the location of shops and availability of food are key considerations for many people in Knowle West.

The project also involved an artist commission. The development of the commissioning process was conducted independently within the project rather than in close communication with the Productive Margins programme. However, towards the end of the process the project engaged with other projects on the programme to develop the final stages of the outline commission. Specifically, the idea behind an arts commission on this project was initially to disseminate findings from the project and to engage community members in this research. However, in Productive Margins there is a responsibility to ensure that arts practices themselves generate and respond to research questions, that they constitute significant and original contributions to knowledge in themselves. In the end, Anne-Marie Culhane was commissioned to work with project participants to explore and re-imagine community food spaces to improve access to affordable, nutritious food. As part of the commission, Culhane brought a 'Shed on Wheels' to Bristol to act as a hub for food-based activities and workshops. Culhane designed and curated two days of events in Knowle West called a 'Taste of Knowle'. In Easton, participants worked with the artist to organise a pop-up 'Somali Kitchen'. In total, more than 750 people attended these events that focused on sharing food as a framing context for discussing the provision of food within marginalised communities.

Where the ULK project manifested competing academic and community agendas around the constitution of original research, 'Who decides what's in my fridge' faced issues concerning the differences in scale and culture across the three neighbourhoods that the community organisations represented. Moreover, Co-exist, Single Parents Action Network and KWMC have different visions, mission statements, governance structures, politics and stakeholder groups. The way in which they model the world is diverse and not necessarily in concert with one another. Moreover, all three organisations need to engage in projects that further their community remits. This meant that ideas about what was needed within the communities and what was needed as a flagship project for the organisations were very different. Culhane's commission and the research of the JDPs at KWMC represent a compromise solution that generated some useful information and created a generous space for community sharing if not change. While food preparation and sharing is not a new practice in contemporary or community-based art, connecting this with the regulatory focus of Productive Margins was significant. The shared food space adopted the craft aesthetic of so many similar participatory works but it was a successful compromise in terms of bringing three organisations together that would not normally collaborate.

Conclusion

Jo Freeman (1970) wrote powerfully about the 'tyranny of structurelessness'. In this influential paper, Freeman described how the lack of structure, which looks like a flattened democratic approach, can mask vertical power relations. Without a clearly articulated and shared structure, power concentrates in the hands of the few who internalise rules and regulation. In the long history of our collaborations across a number of co-production projects, it is clear that projects with the most obvious structures, such as Know your Bristol on the Move, provide the most innovative artistic outputs. Complex, distributed co-production projects that aim to resolve multiple research agendas and desires are exhilarating and valuable projects from a social perspective but without a clear structure they can become regulated by unspoken rules and a lack of clarity around the aims of the artwork to be produced. There is no singular aesthetic of co-production. Co-production as a regulating practice does, however, produce a range of aesthetic responses.

A key regulatory force within all three projects discussed above is that which governs the flow of money and the shape of contracts. In ULK, KWMC was contracted as a project partner on the Research Council UK's Into the Wild project and directly invoiced University of Bristol for its time and resources. KWMC participated in the KWTV strand of Know your Bristol on the Move through direct invoicing for time and resources, without a formal contract in place. As such, KWMC participated in the project as a community host. In Productive Margins, KWMC and the rest of the co-production working group operate with a clear sense of budget going in to the relationship. Allocated budgets are distributed across community organisations in the most appropriate way that the organisations themselves negotiate and agree. Keri Facer and Bryony Enright's *Creating Living Knowledge* (2016: 5, 95, 106–19) specifically discusses the regulatory force of the interface between university administration systems and effective co-production. The way in which labour and input from academics and community organisations is costed sits alongside the other regulatory forces in these collaborative projects and therefore shapes their aesthetics.

Our work together across differently co-produced projects is also significantly informed by the development of our own personal relationship. In shaping this chapter out of the initial presentation that we delivered in absentia in 2014 at the Royal Geographical Society (with IBG) Conference, we spent some time thinking about what makes us 'tick'. Over the past decade we have developed a close professional working relationship and, importantly, a real friendship.

We have fun together and have similar values and interests and we think that this is perhaps an overlooked aspect to successful partnership working. Friendship means that disagreements about work can be held positively as there is a core of trust and respect that runs through our activities. Rather than friendship inhibiting critical distance, it frees us to be more honest with one another and to question one another's activities and motives. We have tried to pin this down a little more specifically and during our writing residential weekend we worked through the qualities that we feel we bring to our collaborations and which shape our diverse projects. Our personal keyword exercise focused on commitments to: positive opportunism, copyleft, collectivity, authenticity, integrity, being catalysers, injecting energy into situations, a desire to respect the integrity of arts practice, long-term commitment, sustainability, heritage, art as an investment in the community's future, faith in people's abilities, 'reluctant' and sometimes ambivalent activism, political action, socialist-feminist practice that insists on being awkward and … resisting labels.

What have we learned across ten years of working together? From these projects it is abundantly clear that shared languages and being open about what all parties expect from a project are both necessary and impossible to achieve. We have a shared aesthetic that is informed by both our educational and professional lives. We share a similar sense of the value of art within communities and a commitment to the belief that all communities deserve to access, host and participate in the making of great art. Our collaborations are connected by a sense that community organisations and universities share a responsibility to provide the facilitating contexts through which the sensible is distributed (Rancière, 2006). Clearly, our own abilities to recognise the aesthetic values in one another's practices is itself political and points to the political emphasis of our work. The prevalence, visibility and elevation of co-production in transdisciplinary settings has put collaboration and participation – particularly in the arts – on the agendas of policymakers. While in itself not a new suite of practices in the arts, what is new is the validation of collaborative work and the new expectations that this is how all university–community partnerships will operate in future, with research and arts practice agendas developed collaboratively.

SEVEN

Participatory mapping and engagement with urban water communities

Özlem Edizel and Graeme Evans

Introduction

The use of interdisciplinary methods has been a key approach to better capture and analyse complex relationships and address 'wicked problems' in urban environments (Harrison, 2000). Exploring issues and conflicts around the sustainability and ecosystems agendas by deploying multi-partner, arts and humanities-centred interdisciplinary research promises to untangle some of the complexities in the different layers of urban governance and experience. Water is a fundamental necessity for sustainable communities, economies and biodiversity. It also forms an intrinsic, but complex and contested, part of our cultural landscape and heritage. By investigating how local communities relate to and engage with urban water environments using arts and humanities methodologies, this can help to explore and develop notions and practice of community resilience in eco-social and cultural terms.

The research approach in question uses a combination of in situ methods, such as Participatory Action Research (Pain et al, 2012), practice-based art research, cultural geography and cultural mapping, as vehicles for engaging communities and reflecting existing understandings, and for engineering new affective relations and possibilities. Cultural ecosystems mapping in particular draws from Participatory Geographic Information Systems (PGIS) and is considered a useful tool for imagining and visualising the sociocultural realities and aspirations of communities and their local landscapes in place and time. This chapter therefore focuses on the application of cultural ecosystems mapping as a participatory, co-produced visualisation and engagement method, based on a case study of the Lee Valley – London's second or 'hidden river' stretching 26 miles from the home counties through north and east London to the Thames and with a flood catchment of over 1,000km². Engaging people with issues around cultural ecosystem services through the interaction with large scale maps of the local area helps to ground the more abstract issues of identity, connectivity, sense of place, emotional attachment and spirituality, as well as overcome the traditional barriers to participation and inclusion at various spatial scales. Cultural mapping in particular helps to articulate the spatial and historical relationships and triggers debate over connectivity, governance, environmental justice and both environmental and social change.

Towards sustainability and culture-led sustainable development

Sustainability is a complex term that has been defined and applied in various ways by different disciplines. Although sustainable development is a fairly abstract and broad 'meta' subject, it has caught the attention of policymakers and citizens worldwide, not least in the context of climate change and everyday environmental concerns and practice. One of the most remarkable challenges of the term sustainable development is that it seeks to explain different things to so many different people and organisations. Therefore, it is no surprise that the concept of sustainable development usually reflects the political and philosophical position of those proposing the definition rather than any clear-cut scientific view (Mebratu, 1998).

The emergence of the sustainability concept has developed from a global geopolitical perspective, which searches for solutions to the most powerful needs of the anthropocene era, namely the need to balance and in many senses, reconcile, economic development/ growth, environmental protection, social justice and cultural diversity. Sustainability does not therefore simply refer to achievements in the environmental arena, but also social and economic development. Sustainable development necessitates policy changes in many sectors and greater coherence between them; as Dalal-Clayton and Bass state, sustainable development requires 'integration of objectives where possible; and making trade-offs between objectives where integration is not possible' (2002: 7). These objectives act in different ways and scales – at global, national and local levels, but should be consistent between these levels (Evans, 2013). There are a wide range of sustainable development approaches which reveal different challenges faced by individual countries and regions and their response to these. Hence, although sustainable development is a global challenge, it can only be operationalised through a national framework and local practice (Dalal-Clayton and Bass, 2002).

The sustainability discourse is not surprisingly dominated by the economic, social and environmental impacts of growth, while the cultural dimension to sustainability has been lacking (Evans, 2013). However, culture in various forms now appears as an emerging component of regeneration and development (Evans, 2005) in both economic and symbolic ways: from revitalising decaying centres with iconic buildings and public spaces, to bringing communities together around cultural events, as well as being promoted in both Agenda 21 and UNESCO Culture and Sustainable Development initiatives (2009). The role of culture in sustainable development has been key in more progressive urban policy and planning. In particular, cultural planning, which is 'a process of inclusive community consultation and decision-making that helps local government identify cultural resources and think strategically about how these resources can help a community to achieve its civic goals' (Stewart, 2007: 1), is a novel way to integrate the cultural values of a community into otherwise abstract and bureaucratic local and regional planning initiatives and processes (Evans and Foord, 2008). Culture in this respect can be viewed as a 'fourth pillar of sustainability' (Hawkes, 2001) but this concept has been more prevalent in developing countries where the separation between heritage, culture and everyday life is not felt. Universally, however, the area of human behaviour within governance systems is where culture, governmentality and sustainable development offer the possibility for notions of eco-citizenship to emerge and solidify.

There have been several important initiatives to encourage a balance between development and sustainability. For example, the Millennium Ecosystem Assessment (MEA) was carried out between 2001 and 2005 to assess the role of ecosystem change for human quality of life, and to establish the scientific basis for actions needed to enhance the sustainable use of ecosystems and their contribution to human wellbeing (Plieninger et al, 2013). Ecosystem services are the benefits that people obtain from nature, and the MEA identifies (2005) four ecosystem services: *provisioning, supporting, regulating*, and *cultural services*. In order to evaluate how the changes in ecosystems affect wellbeing, the following dimensions have been determined: *security, basic material for good life, health, good social relations* and *freedom of choice and action*. Cultural services differ in various aspects from other ecosystem services since they are difficult to quantify and their economic evaluation is usually controversial. They are contributions that 'ecosystems are deemed to make to the non-material benefits (e.g. capabilities and experiences) that arise from human-ecosystems relationships' (Chan et al, 2012: 9). They are less directly linked to human wellbeing than, say, provisioning and regulating services, but their potential for mediation is low (MEA, 2005).

Potentially, therefore, cultural mapping can be considered as a useful tool for articulating the sociocultural realities of communities in relation to their landscapes and ecosystems (Ryan, 2011), particularly in light of the physical and economic bias of environmental sustainability and ecosystems analysis. The initial *UK National Ecosystem Assessment* had for instance lacked an arts and humanities dimension – or input from arts and cultural organisations and practitioners. Ecoystem cultural services (DEFRA, 2011, Chapter 16) have been largely rationalised in terms of externalities – health, recreation, tourism – and as cultural 'goods' ('human benefits from nature') arising from 'environmental settings' – and these are dominated by natural settings, green space/parks, recreation and tourism, rather than urban settlements. Little recognition is given for example to the established work in environmental art (Lacy et al, 1995), art and regeneration, or the role of community arts groups (an exception is Commonground's 'Parish Maps') in ecosystem, urban and sustainable development. This national ecosystem review drew mainly on environmental and ecosystem studies in the treatment of cultural services, and did acknowledge that 'this approach to cultural services struggled to find a consistent theoretical and methodological framework to match that underpinning other areas of the NEA' (DEFRA, 2011: 639). The NEA also highlights knowledge gaps related to ecosystem cultural services, specifically in 'data collection and the uneven monitoring of change in different environmental settings' (DEFRA, 2011: 638) – and spatial data generated through cultural mapping methods will hopefully contribute to meeting this gap.

In response to this deficit, the *UK National Ecosystem Assessment Follow-on* report (DEFRA, 2014) offers new approaches and tools to help decision makers across all sectors to understand the wider value of ecosystems and cultural services. This includes recognition of the value of mapping in different forms including Geographic Information Systems (GIS), participatory/creative mapping (Church et al, 2014) and digital data analysis:

> Mapping is fundamentally about meaning and the environment, about what we care about in place, space, site, landscape and physical setting, and how these overlapping entities can be disclosed and represented. As a form of modelling, mapping is both metaphorical and material.

Maps can combine and display a range of multi-layered information, past, present and projected, textual as well as pictorial. They can encompass cultural memory and possible scenarios (Read, 2012). Maps are a metric, indeed often technically sophisticated, whether on paper or in digital form. They are a form of practice, both scientific and artistic.' (Coates et al, 2014: 39)

Participatory creative methods

A number of creative methods have been developed especially from the 1990s to include communities in the decision making process of development and the design and use of local neighbourhoods and public spaces. Depending on the goals of public participation, methods can be varied. For example, Beierle (2002) identifies educating and informing the public, incorporating public values into decision making, improving the sustentative quality of decisions, increasing trust in institutions, and reducing conflicts as the main aims of public participation. Cultural mapping is considered as a practical, participatory planning and development tool and an emerging mode of research (Duxbury et al, 2015; Longley and Duxbury, 2016). It is potentially a linking methodology for interdisciplinary projects, especially 'to bridge forms of artistic inquiry with research based in other disciplines' (Longley and Duxbury, 2016: 1). Consulting communities to identify the needs assessment for planning by using the mapping and visualisation of physical/environmental and human activity can lead to a broader approach to development in general and notably to local environmental improvements and relationships (Evans, 2013).

Stewart (2007: 8) defines cultural mapping as 'a process of collecting, recording, analysing and synthesizing information in order to describe the cultural resources, networks, links and patterns of usage of a given community or group'. Therefore, the mapping process usually helps to reveal unexpected resources, values and problems in an area and can also build new cross-community connections (Longley and Duxbury, 2016). Cultural resources incorporate both tangible and intangible cultural assets that 'fuel local cultural vitality and contribute to defining the unique local cultural identity and sense of place' (Ontario-MCP, 2010: 51). Cultural mapping can be enabled in different ways, and using GIS – which has been considered as a driver for technical development around geographic representation since the 1960s (Goodchild, 1992) – is one of the most promising ways. While there are a variety of approaches to engage with communities and get them involved in the decision making process within their local neighbourhoods, techniques of PGIS used for community mapping have been considered as particularly reassuring for participants (Crawhill, 2008; Smeets and Yoshida, 2005).

PGIS in particular facilitates the representation of local people's spatial and site-specific knowledge with maps, which can subsequently be used in decision making processes, as well as supporting communication and community advocacy (Corbett et al, 2006). It seeks to contribute to the enhancement of methods appropriate for use with the general public. Cinderby, for instance, has applied PGIS in England to urban renewal projects, air quality and accessibility assessments (2010, 1999). The relatively informal setting of the approach allows for wider inclusion of normally excluded participants – so-called 'hard-to-reach' communities, while Rambaldi et al (2006) define PGIS as a practice with a special emphasis on empowerment and communications.

PGIS projects can also take many forms, depending on the way they are conducted and which GIS features are used. While using online and interactive methods are possible, the least technologically demanding method is using paper maps, which was implemented early on in the development of PGIS. PGIS approaches often involve significantly less sophisticated techniques; using topographic maps or satellite images. For example, Cinderby's (2010) hard-to-reach methodology used an aerial photography-based map to examine urban design (such as streets, squares or transport) with participants. They were invited to apply comments directly on the map using flags, thus taking part in the collection of knowledge. Paper-based maps were seen to be widely accessible and eliminated possible technology and language barriers as well as fieldwork based limitations. The application of PGIS-based cultural mapping in urban water environments has therefore been developed in our case study river system.

Engaging with water communities

Water is one of the most essential elements for sustainable communities, economies and biodiversity, as well as a key part of cultural landscapes and heritage. There are multiple water-related challenges in urban environments as a result of climate change, population growth/density, including increased flood risk, drought/scarcity risk, pollution and degradation of aquatic ecosystems, which are all embedded in numerous social, cultural, political and economic contexts. Confronting these water-related risks generates different forms of conflict in communities that need to be negotiated both within and across wider networks and geographic areas (for example, upstream, downstream). Governance processes at local, national and transborder scales all over the world need to negotiate and manage these issues through collaborative dialogues both at the local community and riparian community levels. Cultural mapping in particular is a stimulating method to generate conversations within and between communities around water spaces and urban waterfront areas. For Longley and Duxbury (2016: 1), cultural mapping is a method that 'aims to advance our conceptualization and understanding of diverse approaches to mapping intangible dimensions of culture, and to synthesize some insights from these approaches to advance methodological practice in this area'. Therefore, it can bring non-human and ecological materialities into creative conversation within social and community concerns. Approaching water as a connecting element in urban environments and landscapes and developing narratives around them, helps in the understanding of the ecological and social production of the places where people live. In our case study, cultural mapping has been practised in focus group meetings and arts and community festivals along the River Lee by the authors, as part of the Hydrocitizenship project research team. The project has been funded for three years under the Arts & Humanities Research Council Connected Communities programme with a particular emphasis on co-design and co-production. The cultural mapping method has been used to collect data about spatial and sociocultural issues derived from cultural ecosystem services within this urban river environment and to visualise these perceptions and experiences on both a site-specific and iterative basis. The Cultural Ecosystem Services Framework (Figure 7.1) first makes a distinction between cultural values, environmental spaces, cultural practices and cultural benefits (Church et al, 2014). In order to assess cultural services (as established in the UK NEAFO: DEFRA, 2014) the following indicators have been created: *Use* (sense of place, activities, and recreational use), *Cultural Value* (recreation, social relations, and cultural heritage values), *Problems* (accessibility, safety, unpleasant) and *Community Cohesion* (diversity, involvement). Cultural mapping in this situation is used to better understand the issues around the access to, and use of water spaces, and to engage with the general public through the use of these indicators. The following sections therefore focus on some of the results of the cultural ecosystems mapping undertaken in the Lee Valley,[1] including discussion of this participatory method and issues arising.

Figure 7.1: The cultural ecosystem services framework

Cultural Values
Norms and expectations **influencing and influenced by** services, benefits and their biophysical context

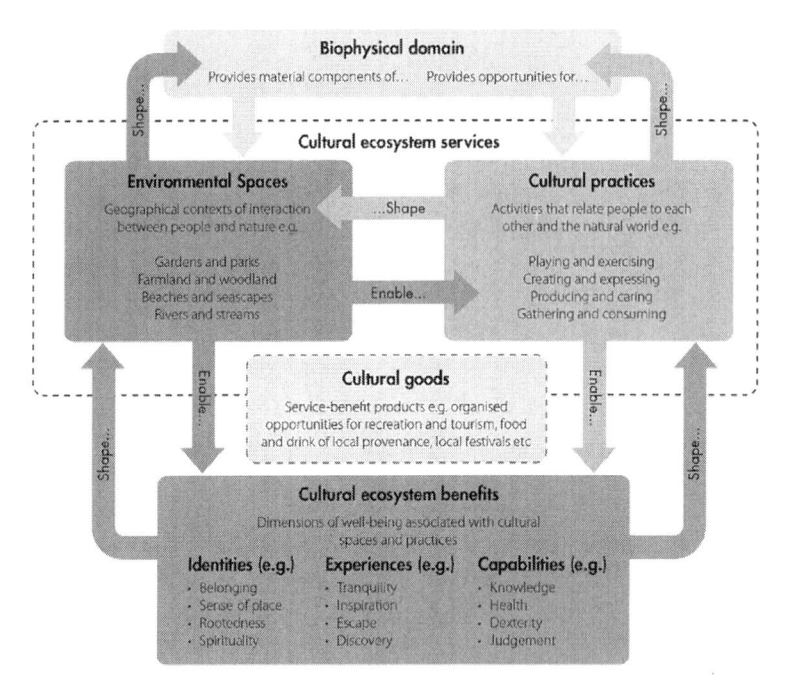

Biophysical domain
Provides material components of... Provides opportunities for...

Cultural ecosystem services

Environmental Spaces
Geographical contexts of interaction between people and nature e.g.

Gardens and parks
Farmland and woodland
Beaches and seascapes
Rivers and streams

...Shape

Enable...

Cultural practices
Activities that relate people to each other and the natural world e.g.

Playing and exercising
Creating and expressing
Producing and caring
Gathering and consuming

Cultural goods
Service-benefit products e.g. organised opportunities for recreation and tourism, food and drink of local provenance, local festivals etc

Cultural ecosystem benefits
Dimensions of well-being associated with cultural spaces and practices

Identities (e.g.)	Experiences (e.g.)	Capabilities (e.g.)
• Belonging	• Tranquility	• Knowledge
• Sense of place	• Inspiration	• Health
• Rootedness	• Escape	• Dexterity
• Spirituality	• Discovery	• Judgement

Source: Fish and Church (2013)

Cultural ecosystems mapping in focus groups

At the outset of the cultural mapping sessions, a set of sociodemographic questions are asked of participants in order to start the conversation. This captures information such as gender, age, home postcode and familiarity with the study area. This information is useful for subsequent analysis, representation and locating participants in relation to the study area. Since this is an iterative process the mapping exercise can be carried out in the same location but with different participants as well as in different locations. Participants are then asked to identify recreational uses, cultural uses and problem areas with the use of a large aerial view map. Using colour-coded sticker dots and sticky notes for locating sites on the map, participants were also asked to mark areas with landscape values and special places. The data on the maps and questionnaires are then transferred onto a digital database and entered onto GIS. Cultural mapping in particular helps to articulate the spatial relationships and stimulate discussion over 'accuracy', sense of place, history, connectivity, governance and change in different parts of the study area.

Focus groups are an effective method to explore the ways in which people perceive their local environments and reflect on each other's approaches about the same issues and areas. This method is a form of group 'interview' and workshop, which involves several participants and a facilitator/moderator, and there is an emphasis in the questioning on a particular topic where the focus is on interaction within the group (Bryman, 2008), in this case over a map. During cultural ecosystems mapping, participants usually reveal a wide range of views across a broad section of social experience and, while this does not claim to identify public opinion in any definitive sense, it does provide good qualitative evidence based on participant experience and interaction. Undertaking the cultural mapping activity through a focus group format also offers the chance of letting people explore and challenge each other's reasons for holding a certain view (Bryman, 2008), while in a one-to-one exchange, interviewees are rarely challenged.

As a first pilot, perspectives on local cultural ecosystems values were collected from a focus group meeting held in Hackney Wick (adjoining the Lee Navigation Canal) at the Cre8 Lifestyle Community Centre and analysed collectively to derive local community values. Several techniques can be used in order to represent landscape values and special places when creating the map such as defining sites and routes through use of pencils or markers, using colour-coded stickers for locating sites and identifying and numbering special sites and annotating them on the map (Plieninger et al, 2013) – see Figure 7.2.

Figure 7.2: Cultural ecosystems mapping in the Hackney Wick focus group

By the nature of focus groups, the method helps to gather in-depth information about the area in an interactive way. Participants discuss each other's points of view and their knowledge of the history of the river and waterfront areas, and map anecdotes about certain locations and experiences, which helps to explore the intangible features that create the identity and perceptions of the area and water resources.

This process can lead to bringing creative solutions for conflict sites and issues as well as 'benefit from the direct involvement of artists, crafts and designer-makers, whether as interpreters, catalysts or visionaries' (Evans, 2013: 231) in visualising and animating the physical landscape, human activity and aspirations, which became clear in the case of Hackney Wick. Annotated cultural maps, which can be layered with the results of other mapping exercises, or revisited with the same cohort of participants, can also be analysed with other spatial data once digitised. This can add layers of different information on, say, demography, housing, land use, environmental quality (such as air, noise, water), crime incidents, flooding/flood risk, and so on, providing a rich canvas which can be the basis for artistic interventions (such as drawing/painting, sculpture – Read, 2012) and for feedback to participants. This can also reveal divergence between lived experience and official data, and provide stakeholders and stewards of the water system with important local knowledge (Geertz, 1983) which can inform policy, planning and operational practice.

Cultural ecosystems mapping in arts and community festivals

As well as the more closed group meeting, arts and community festivals can bring local residents and users of a neighbourhood together in a friendly, relaxed and animated way. People can also have the opportunity to hear about the latest developments, events and concerns such as safety/crime, new building developments/changes of use. Here, the conversation through the cultural map helps to identify not only tangible aspects of the area but also the intangibles. The intangible elements of a place such as stories, histories, values are 'the aspects that provide a "sense of place" and identity to specific locales, and the ways in which those meanings and values may be grounded in embodied experiences' (Longley and Duxbury, 2016: 2). The dialogue developed around the map captures features that are not easy to quantify but are important to truly understand a place and its value to its residents and visitors. People's interactions in their community as well as personal and collective memory help to build up the narratives. The activity itself helps to create a community-driven 'visual' of values and place-based meanings which are evidently different from official plans and maps (Cauchi-Santoro, 2016) and even of official history, narratives and 'worldviews'. This is in contrast to the masterplanning process that dominates the design and development of major regeneration sites, as experienced by these communities as a result of the major redevelopment of the Lower Lee Valley during and following the nearby London 2012 Olympics (Evans, 2015).

Mapping at open festival environments also brings together locals and visitors who may have differing perspectives and experiences, while mapping as part of a wider festival provides the opportunity for participatory arts activities, installations and performances to allow cultural expression, exchange of ideas and complement the responses to the cultural map, and vice versa. In the Hackney Wick Festival, alongside artists open studios, street performance and design exhibitions, open debates were held on topics such as community land trusts, while a derelict site was occupied along the canal to build a temporary DEN-City from recycled materials and rubble where residents and visitors could explore the waterside environment in the context of urban change and sustainability with a group of independent artists, whose installations, artworks and performances reflected and responded these concerns (Figure 7.3). Cultural ecosystems mapping has therefore been undertaken during several community events along the River Lee such as the Hackney Wicked Connected Communities Festival 2015 (above), Love the Lea Festival 2015, the National Mills Weekend at Three Mills 2016 and Firs Farm Wetlands Festival 2016.

From these iterations it is possible to identify three types of interaction around the mapping exercises during these festivals. The first form of interaction is the conversation that takes place between the participant and the researcher, which is mainly about understanding their use of space and values in the area. The participants are asked several

Figure 7.3: DEN-City, Hackney Wick Connected Communities Festival

questions that draw on the Cultural Ecosystems Assessment approach. Also, this sometimes evolves into a form of knowledge exchange between researcher and participant. While having the meeting places and heritage locations being clustered around the same areas is not a surprise, the findings also reveal interesting and unexpected results, which can help in the further planning, development and priority setting for the area. For example, the findings of the National Mills Weekend cultural mapping revealed that Victoria Park, the House Mill and Olympic Park are indicated as meeting places where people get together to have a drink/meal or enjoy the natural environment and also considered as a part of local and regional heritage. This shows that people like to spend their time around locations that they value as part of their cultural heritage. On the other hand, there are some conflicting locations in terms of their use and how they are perceived by local people. The results of the Love the Lea Festival cultural mapping show that participants value being around the river path and marina most, and raise safety issues (such as lighting at night and muggings) in these same locations (see Figure 7.4). While green spaces such as Springfield and Markfield Parks are acknowledged as pleasant and peaceful as well as hubs of meeting places for locals and have heritage value such as the Beam Engine (Grade II listed), they can still be neglected at times with rubbish, littering and antisocial behaviour. Therefore, cultural

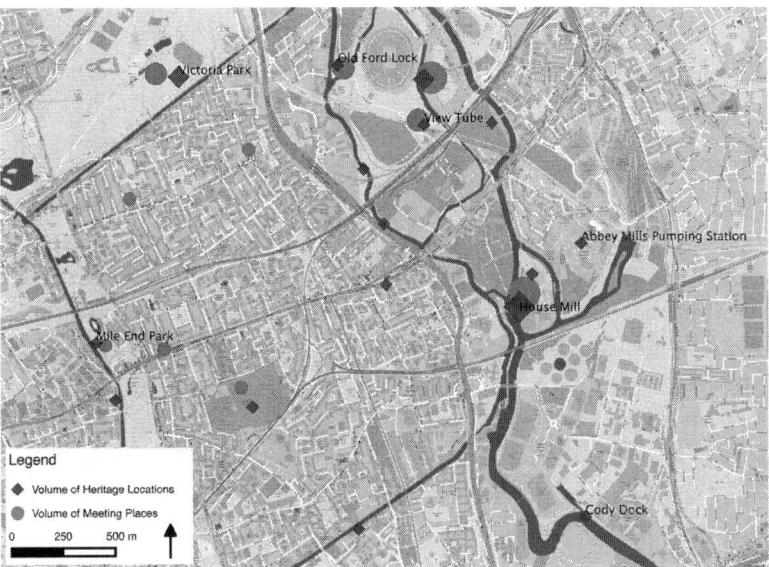

Figure 7.4: Cultural mapping findings from Love the Lea Festival (volume of likes and dislikes)

mapping was able to uncover the fact that sometimes the problem areas are the same as the culturally and aesthetically valued areas, but that these are experienced differently by different users, and at different times (Lefebvre, 1974).

The second type of interaction takes place between participants while contributing to the research. Sharing knowledge, experiences and memories in certain locations on the map is most of the time a conversation starter, which leads to exploring some of the perceived qualities and recent history of the area. While this is a key feature in more intensive focus groups, the interaction between participants also takes place at more open community festival exchanges.

The final type is the interaction of participants with the marks and textual responses that other participants leave on the map. People usually start with analysing the map themselves and trying to understand why others chose certain locations to identify certain feelings and activities. While this process may end with agreement with other participants, sometimes complete opposition comes across. During the mapping at the Three Mills, National Mills Weekend, after one of the participants put a sticker on Cody Dock as a valuable asset in the area, the others also considered and acknowledged this and the local community organisation based there (Figure 7.5). The Gasworks Dock Partnership based in Cody Dock is a charity for community-led regeneration and encourages public engagement in the revitalisation of waterways. Its vision is to rehabilitate Cody Dock, create a creative industries quarter with new workspace, visitor facilities and public space, and to foster a stronger sense of place and civic pride by celebrating the area's waterways and rich industrial heritage through increased participation in the arts and improved access to the River Lee. Seeing the mark that one of the participants had put on Cody Dock led the others to question the value and importance of this location. Eventually, some others of the group who did not think about it immediately or had not heard about it before, ended up learning about and appreciating this emerging creative quarter as a result of the cultural mapping activity.

This map-based activity in particular helps to remove the limitations of the structured and solely text-based survey questionnaire, and brings engagement and participation to the process in a more interactive way. Some of the participants leave the cultural ecosystems map acknowledging that they have found out more about the area and feel more ownership of it, sometimes mentioning that taking part in this activity inspired them to get more involved in the decision making for the development and usage of their water environment. Here engagement included campaigning on issues such as tow path safety,

Figure 7.5: Cultural mapping findings from Three Mills, National Mills Weekend (volume of meeting and heritage places)

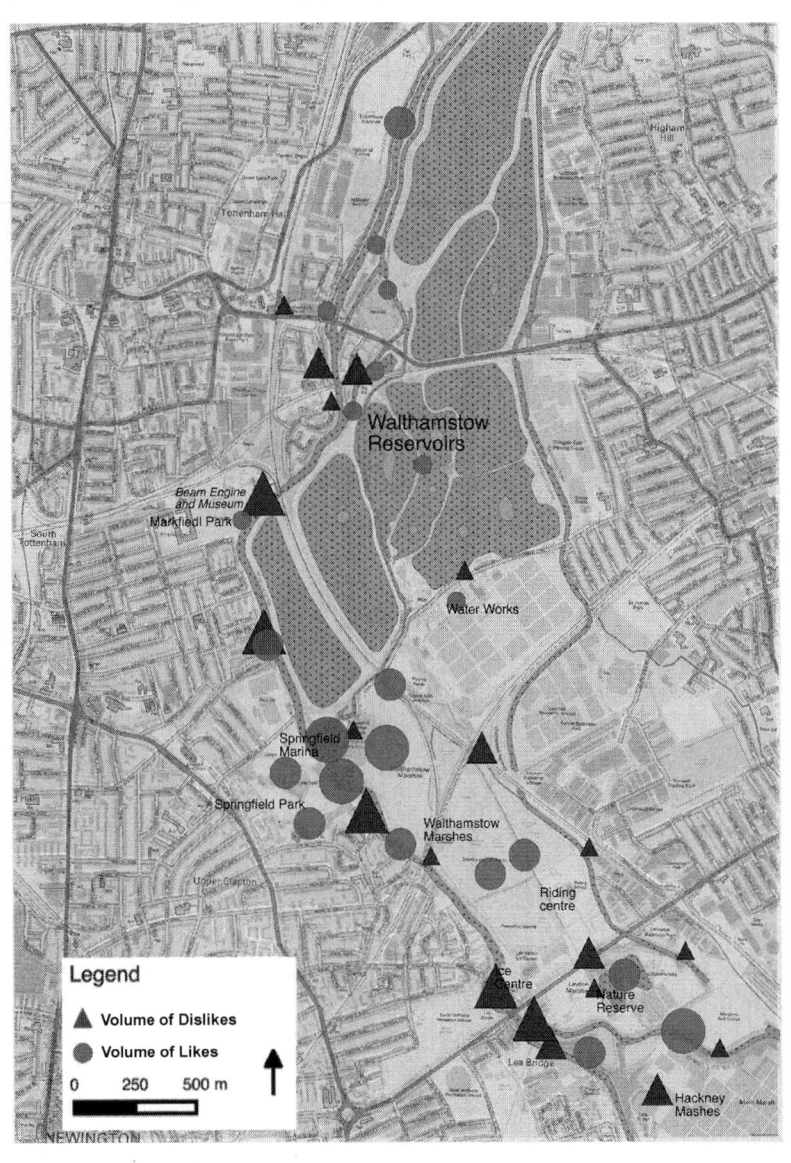

improved but sensitive lighting, clean-up of waterside areas, retaining community facilities and raised awareness around new developments such as restoration of heritage buildings, redevelopment of industrial sites and new housing.

Conclusion

It is evident that 'the symbolic marking of places, the preservation of symbols of recognition, the expression of collective memory in actual practices of communication' (Castells, 1991: 351) are very important in order to recognise and, if necessary, protect the identities of places. However, the cultural assets that communities value are not always the same as those that local authorities consider as 'culturally' or environmentally 'significant' (Cauchi-Santoro, 2016). In the Lee Valley, for example, Cody Dock has been acknowledged on the one hand as a cultural heritage asset for the area not just because of its history but more for its contribution to the values and sense of place; on the other hand, this is not mentioned in either official policy documents or promotional literature. This suggests that cultural mapping can be considered as a useful tool to make some of the intangible amenities and less obvious heritage more valued and recognised, particularly where they are absent from official documents and narratives.

Besides making some of intangible heritage visible to officials and communities themselves, cultural mapping also helps to bring public awareness of developments in the local neighbourhood and river. Public awareness of changes and developments are usually controlled by the efforts of local government and other planning authorities – in the case of water resources this includes a plethora of intermediary agencies such as the Canals & Rivers Trust and Environment Agency who are distant and not democratically governed locally, but who can override local governance systems. Some of the information presented on the cultural maps, or provided verbally by the researcher/facilitator, can help the participants understand the impact and scope of developments in their area, as well as visualise future scenarios, and encourage participants to get involved in the planning and design consultation process. In the case of the Love the Lea Festival for example, the aerial map included the Greenway initiative between otherwise disconnected Walthamstow and Woodberry Down Reservoirs, which caught the attention of the participants and helped them learn more about this 'green' cycle route which otherwise was not widely publicised. Moreover, some of the participants acknowledged that contributing to the cultural ecosystems mapping of their neighbourhood was the start of more active involvement in the changes and developments underway in their local area and waterfront environment.

While organisations like the Chartered Institute of Water & Environmental Management (*Arts and Environment Network*) and Canals & Rivers Trust (*Arts on the Waterways*, *Humans of the Waterways*), have been developing initiatives that promote more cultural forms of engagement with communities, the Hydrocitizenship project has used participatory cultural mapping in order to bring a better understanding of the physical, social and environmental connectivity and characteristics of these urban water spaces and systems – both natural and anthropogenic. Overall, cultural ecosystems mapping helps to approach water-related issues in a more holistic way rather than a single dimension by generating public interest in wider water and ecological issues. Cultural maps (printed and digital) provide a practical resource and legacy – the maps do not seek to 'make physical spaces static, to connote ownership, or to articulate territory' but to demonstrate the 'dynamic lives of places in their complexity, diversity, and richness' (Longley and Duxbury, 2016: 6).

To conclude, our research indicates that cultural ecosystems mapping can be a valuable tool to articulate community perspectives, experience and aspirations and thereby to inform local agencies and other policymakers about the values, concerns and knowledge that people have of their environment. It can also serve as a grounding for socially engaged arts practice that can benefit from the co-design and co-production of knowledge and visualisation of community visions. For example, following the cultural mapping undertaken at Three Mills, an artist-led citizen's science project will construct and install a live water wheel at this heritage venue, to oxygenate the water in order to encourage fish life and demonstrate the power of the water ('Active Energy'), working with a group of local pensioners who were former dock workers. Here cultural ecosystems mapping has combined with practice-based art and engineering science to engage local communities in co-production. Interdisciplinary working in this sense has helped develop collaboration and methodological innovation. In turn it is hoped that this will also lead to more sustainable and resilient planning and usage of the water resource, as well as empowering residents and other users to co-create and link this embedded knowledge with official narratives and day-to-day usage and management.

Note

[1] See www.leevalley.org for fuller results and maps.

EIGHT

Hacking into the Science Museum: young trans people disrupt the power balance of gender 'norms' in the museum's 'Who Am I?' gallery

Kayte McSweeney and Jay Stewart

Introduction

Concerns for inclusion, diversity, representation, social justice and a broader understanding of what knowledge can be have moved cultural institutions (in the case of this chapter – museums, galleries, heritage sites) in the last decade to reassess and rework how and why it works with its audiences. Many have adapted working practices that might be termed 'participatory' or 'co-creative', which seek to involve visitors, non-visitors, community and interest groups with diverse forms of expertise and perspective in their activities. In parallel, members of the public, particularly those who have felt excluded, overlooked or unfairly represented in our nation's museums and galleries, have sought to form alliances with institutions to challenge the traditional models of representation (or non-representation) and gain access and exposure to new audiences and alternatives platforms for dialogue, debate and advocacy. This paper will reflect on one such partnership; that between Gendered Intelligence and the Science Museum, London and a project they developed together in 2013–14 as part of the Arts and Humanities Research Council's 'Connected Communities' and the Heritage Lottery Fund's 'All Our Stories' programmes.

The Science Museum, London, is the largest museum in the UK dedicated to the history of science, technology, medicine and innovation. It has a long history of including the public in its development to ensure its outputs are accessible, audience focused and responsive to the needs of those coming through its doors and those they hope to serve. In the past ten years this has included inviting groups (young people, artists, communities of interest, amateur historians, user groups, teachers and so on) in to the museum in order to conceive, develop, research and deliver exhibitions and programmes collaboratively with them (Boon et al, 2014; Bunning et al, 2015). The 2013–14 'All Our Stories' project instigated one such partnership with Gendered Intelligence (GI) and sought to investigate how, through sharing decision making and deeply embedding a group of young adults in exhibition development processes, to readdress a problematic representation of gender in the museum's 'Who Am I?' gallery.

GI is a not-for-profit Community Interest Company, established in 2008. Working predominantly with young trans or gender questioning people from the ages of 8 to 25, GI's aims are to increase understandings of gender diversity. Some of the ways it hopes to achieve this are by empowering young trans people and platforming the voices of young trans people through creative projects. GI is committed to the idea that everyone can become more intelligent about gender and come to understand gender identity and gender diversity as a rich and interesting subject, which plays a huge part in shaping and knowing who we are.

Through a partnership that initially focused on the co-production of a small temporary exhibition and a public event, it became rapidly apparent that the learning and research emerging from the collaboration substantially transcended its impact on both organisations– for the museum, by developing displays with particular members of the public and for GI, by working collaboratively with large cultural institutions to raise questions and conversations around the ways in which museums (as particular producers of knowledge) posit particular values and 'norms' around gender identity.

This chapter will not only outline the 'Hacking In' project and the impact it had on the partners involved, but will also reflect on and explore the potential within collaborative projects to redress and acknowledge the power imbalances that exist within the narratives of cultural institutions. It is a chapter about empowerment and the social responsibility to include, listen to and work with those whose histories, stories and identities have been marginalised, excluded or communicated with little, if any, involvement from those communities. Going further it advocates and champions a *sharing* of power, and also considers the democratisation of knowledge creation with a direct input by those with the greatest stake in how future narratives, histories and collections are carried out and represented.

To start with, this chapter will outline the project and its multifarious outcomes. Not only will it reflect on the impact and value it has had on both the Science Museum and GI but, most importantly, it will also explore the workings of power and empowerment that takes place when gender variance is on display: the power to tell one's story, the power to influence and change national institutions, and the power to (co)create knowledge. We ask:

How can knowledge be (co)created? What is the value of breaking with traditions and delivering on multidisciplinary collaborations?

Establishing the partnership

GI and the Science Museum first collaborated in 2012 on the 'i-Trans' project. 'i-Trans: Constructing Identities through Technology' was a project funded by the Arts Council England and explored how science and technology shape our gender identities.[1] A natural progression from this short-term project was to continue to explore and critically review the Science Museum's gender-related collections (including their medical collections). In the first instance GI imagined such an exploration and critiquing as a 'hacking'. For the museum project, hacking was described as an intervention, to upset or trouble the conditions and understandings of the spaces, objects and scenes around us. Hacking is about taking found objects and adapting, redesigning them, reinventing them. Hacking is subversive, creative and productive. Hacking involves a rethinking in order to reinvent and create new meanings around gender. This interventionist approach was initially favoured by GI.[2]

Members of GI's youth group felt that the portrayal of gender in the Who Am I? gallery is overly simplistic, binary and problematic. For example, one of the display cases encourages visitors to consider how their biological sex and gender plays a part in their identity yet frames this within the binary parameters of the question 'Boy or Girl?'. Interactive exhibits also challenge visitors to think about the gender of their brain and their identity, yet again offer only a dual approach to choosing. Staff from the Science Museum acknowledged this overly binary approach to portraying gender and saw the potential of working closer with GI and its young people. The aim here was to move beyond a short-term intervention to a more embedded critical examination of both the gallery and the collection though a collaborative project. Indeed, for the museum the upcoming redevelopment of its medical galleries (due to open in 2019) meant that this project enabled staff to start considering how gender identity and gender diversity could be displayed and narrated at the museum. The museum was also keen to experiment with how it can co-create experiences and displays with people who have personal experiences of and complex relationships with science and medicine.

GI's mission is about making the world more intelligent about gender and so is committed to engaging with the wider general public through educative opportunities. A display that was going to be created and curated by young trans people and be part of the exhibition for a 6-month period provided an excellent opportunity to engage with the Science Museum and its visitors (typically over 3 million people per year), and to begin to open up discussions and debate around how gender identity manifests in society and specifically here in the arena of science and medicine. What people in wider society *know* about gender matters to the ways in which people can be *or do* their gender.

A very common way people come to know about what it means to be trans is through popular culture such as TV, newspapers and mainstream media. However, despite massive reach and serving an educational purpose, museums and heritage centres typically and historically do not tend to figure gender as something that is diverse, nor feature the stories of trans and non-binary people. Certainly understanding of trans lives is limited and raising awareness across the general public is imperative. The creative and cultural sectors are starting to engage with trans inclusion and gender diversity as, like other minority groups, trans people make up part of their visitors' demographic and so their/our stories should also be represented. Such representations, meanings and messages that are made through the displaying of objects consequently have a positive impact on trans lives. In this vein the Science Museum, like other museums, has tried to diversify its audience, be more inclusive, introduce new narratives and embrace this idea of collaboratively working with the public (both current visitors and those they would like to reach).

In addition, the field of science – and medical science in particular – is a very important knowledge field that affects transgender lives. In particularly over the last 60 years the development of the genome project, understandings of the brain, neurology, endocrinology and biochemistry are all scientific discourses that are highly relevant to understandings of gender as innate, genetic, and/or socially brought about. In addition, a history of medical and technological achievements, as well as cultural understandings and social attitudes of why or how we become gendered beings, is also key (Hausman, 1995).

Such examples include how sex hormones have come to be understood by scientists since the mid-1950s, and where scientific achievements include the extraction of natural sex hormones and the production of synthetic sex hormones in the laboratory. In addition, surgical procedures have become more sophisticated over time, including gender reassignment surgery. Yet science and medicine have also played their part in pathologising transgender lives, and historically and currently trans people are involved in a socio-politic of mental health and treatments. Historically, these include Electric Shock Therapy, as well as drugs and treatment programmes such as chemical castration.

From the perspective of GI, the Science Museum has the potential to reach a substantive audience in which to engage with these topics and to unpack the relationship between science and gender. Moreover, the 'Who Am I?' exhibition was an ideal location to pose questions around how gender makes us who we are, or how who we are (and what we do) is gendered. From the perspective of the Science Museum and its embracing of the concepts of participation and co-creation with the public, particularly those whose lived experiences bring an alternative, nuanced understanding of the collections and gallery themes, this meant that the Science Museum was looking for collaboration partners. Though the display was relatively small scale in terms of its production output, it sought to embed the participation project team deeper into the conceptualisation and delivery of displays than had been done before.

The project

In the summer of 2013 the new partnership project was underway. It sought to achieve the following objectives:

1. To explore transgender heritage in relation to the world of medical science through engaging with and critically reflecting on the museum's collection.
2. To create tangible outputs that could enable the research and learning of the project to be showcased and shared to a wider public: (i) a display in the Who Am I? gallery; (ii) oral histories of memories and experiences from 'older' members of the trans community; and (iii) a blog style website to serve as a digital legacy of the project.

Working with a group of 17 young trans people, the project was formulated as seven half-day sessions. These included sessions at the museum itself; a visit to the stores where we considered some of the archived objects that offered a gender-related story; and a series of oral history workshops. Following these workshops the young people were also involved in the installation period and finally the launch of the display case.

The workshops consisted of a range of training and skills sharing sessions that introduced the young people to museum exhibition development tools like content hierarchy generation, oral history production and object selection. In addition, these sessions offered a series of reflections and knowledge exchanges about how the museum was currently 'talking about gender' and how the group would like to present their story to the museum's audiences. The workshops were co-facilitated by staff from GI and the Science Museum. A collaborative approach ensured that the activities ran smoothly and that the project was aligned with GI's own organisational procedures and best practice. Crucially GI was also the support network for both the museum staff who were inexperienced with working with young trans people and the young trans people looking for support in the workshops and outside. Without this co-planning and facilitation, the project could not have happened.

The group were given full licence to generate ideas, display themes and avenues for research, and presented these to the exhibitions team members and curators at the sessions. Iterative and frustrating for the young people at times the group was essentially initiated into an exhibitions process world, stepping through the stages any 'professional' team at the museum would need to. This included concept and theme development, object research and selection, design idea generations, source collections, label writing, audience consideration and event planning.

Accompanied by one of the Science Museum's medical curators, a trip to its objects stores proved to be a turning point in the project. Walking around the vast stores (though it should be pointed out the museum does not have a gender specific collection), objects were identified that were thought to be of potential relevance to the display theme and the young people themselves. Examples include Barbie dolls, toy cars and coloured crayons used in experiments that monitored the gender behaviour of children and babies. Such experiments aimed to 'scientifically prove' the innate behaviours of each of us as people assigned *either* 'male' *or* 'female'. The young people were less than positive in their responses and were disappointed with the limited number of objects directly linked to non-normative ideas of gender and sexuality identities and expression. Carrying out a project that centred on the telling of 'Our Stories' seemed to be rather difficult given that none of the museum's objects would work. With the museum's items unrepresentative and unappealing, the project initiated an alternative display of a small but significant trans-specific collection borrowed mainly from the young people themselves. These newly brought in objects and the stories they wanted to tell merged more succinctly to represent the identities and the politics of this group of trans youth.

In addition to the object display that the group wanted to showcase, another dimension of the project was to hear stories from older trans people about their experiences and ideas in relation to the medical world and the role of science in transgender heritage. The life experiences of trans people differ across generations and the stories of people reaching their older years risk getting lost. There are also no long-term scientific studies of medical intervention on trans people and we know little about what the medical treatments were and how they differ today.

Listening to the medical related experiences of older members of the trans community were crucial to contextualising the display case theme. Key people were identified and invited to provide their testimony for the project. The young people attended an oral history training workshop that focused on a range of interviewing techniques they could use when exploring the older trans people's memories. By developing and conducting the interviews themselves, the young participants were able to reflect on these stories and consider the cultural and medical changes over time for trans people. Edited versions of the three interviews were then displayed in audio form in the Who Am I? gallery when the case was installed. Alongside the display case and the audio clips from the oral histories, the series of seven workshops also worked towards a finished website. The website hoped to share learnings gained by the participants, including the medical collection and served as an archive for the project itself.

Collectively these key outputs sought to demonstrate a shift from seeing gender no longer as a binary of boy/girl but moving towards viewing gender as something much more dynamic. The group also wanted to communicate the idea of how we *all* have experiences of conforming and not conforming to societal expectations of being a 'boy' or a 'girl' and so showcased a rich, varied and surprising set of objects and audio exhibits in the case. The contents sought to show how each of our gender identities emerge and indeed are always emerging. Conceived through the perspectives of the young trans participants it asked the visitor to consider 'What makes up your gender?' and to think about what objects they use to express their gender identity. Working with an artist facilitator they envisioned a closet full of every day but important things that trans people use. The closet has become a pertinent metaphor for LGBT people who 'come out' and share something about ourselves to the public world. Michael Warner tells us: 'We blame people for being closeted. But the closet is better understood as the culture's problem, not the individual's' (Warner 2005: 52). People come out as lesbian or gay because the assumption is that everyone is straight. People come out as transgender because there is an assumption that everyone identifies with the gender that they were assigned at birth. This metaphor appealed to the group and formed the design concept for the case.

Objects on display: capturing otherness

Having described in some detail the project itself and offered some context to the ways in which this work was able to take place, it is important to position this within a wider context around object displays that bring information, knowledge and meaning about a particular community or culture to another – the anticipated visitor. For instance, historically, museums have typically displayed objects found from lands far away, other cultures and phenomena belonging to people who are 'different' and 'other' to our own – the Western viewer. Such a mode of 'othering' produces knowledge through and around these objects in a way that adopts the standpoint that the 'nature' of the object studied (mostly indigenous peoples) sits outside and separate from the identity, viewpoint and cultural framing of the museum. What appears (in the form of visual materials and the written labels) is the impression of a particular objectivity, neutrality and distance from the subject matter, while the Western lens through which the museum curators see, records and writes bears a particular set of cultural values that go unnoticed. Visually and linguistically we see and read how such approaches have certain voyeuristic characteristics, evoking a sense of being the outsider looking in on this exotic and different world. Through the use of certain technologies, methodologies and clever performances, the identity, values and culture belonging to 'The Museum' is rendered invisible and the object of study appears to sit alone in and of itself.

Such notions of objectivity have been challenged in postcolonial discourse. Edward Said's book *Orientalism* has been instrumental to a critical thinking of, not only Western imperialism, but the ways in which an epistemology or systems of knowledge production has Othered the 'orient' through its 'aesthetic, scholarly, economic, sociological, historical and philological texts' (Said, 1978: 12). Here Said argues that the 'Orient' holds the 'Occident' in place, which, while remaining central, thrusts the 'Orient' to the margins becoming the 'constitutive outside' (Ahmed, 2006: 114). Ahmed also tells us:

'Most important, the making of "the Orient" is an exercise of power: the Orient is made oriental as a submission to the authority of the Occident'.

In addition, when Gayatri Spivak so notably asked 'Can The Subaltern Speak?', her thinking centred around how power is situated within the position of the academic or intellectual rather than the 'subaltern' who is most often in, and of, the focus of study but not permitted to occupy the author's position (Spivak, 2010). While those who are marginalised are rarely in a position of being writer/speaker/curator (maker of meanings), any such stories and perceptions that make their way through to a public platform come about through a very particular Western hegemonic framing. As a consequence of these critical race and postcolonial interrogations, the field of anthropology and the practice of museology have taken a postmodern turn, creating considerable debate, not least because of it bearing such colonial legacies (Clifford and Marcus, 1986, 1988, 1997; Geertz, 1973).

While such discourse rests within critical race theory, there is certainly something to be learnt here that we can map onto other 'minority' communities such as trans ones. That is to consider not only those voices on the margins, but also the antagonistic, messy and complex power play through various scenes of such representations. Additionally the work of feminism has also endeavoured to expose the identity of the authors of knowledge, and to question the authority in which one speaks (Skeggs, 1997). 'The point', Haraway (1988) famously noted, 'is not just to read the webs of knowledge production; the point is to reconfigure what counts as knowledge'. From this, both politically and theoretically, the 'concept of experience gained validity for feminists' as this became a route to achieving another kind of epistemology (Skeggs, 1997).

> To challenge the power of normative masculinity, feminists established a popular and research agenda through the sharing of experiences (often through the method of 'consciousness raising'). (Skeggs et al, 2002: 356)

Sharing and writing about 'women's' experiences validated both 'woman-ness', as the object of study, and the position of women as writers and researchers (producers of knowledge). Similarly for lesbian and gay activists, the endeavour to gather stories and speak experiences became central to a (re)historicising of the lives of non-heterosexual people and their practices. Such projects of gathering experiences and (re)telling the stories of minorities raised new concerns about the politics of representation. Among such communities and subcultures there were, and still are, debates and arguments around whether those products that represented their own lives were deemed 'positive' or 'negative'.[3] In addition, 'Queer' writing commits itself not only to the critical attention of queer subjectivities, but to consideration of the productive possibilities of challenging and reframing heteronormative knowledge productions (Foucault, 1976; Warner, 1994; Sedgwick, 1994).

Authorities often esteem scientific knowledge with its Galilean imperatives to *prove* a statement or to formulate a grand universal law. Still today as members of the public peruse the museums they expect to be informed of scientific accuracies. Foucault has been imperative in thinking about a heteronormativity at play in modes of knowledge production such as museums (Foucault, 1995). He tells us how disciplines and knowledge fields do not simply describe the distinctions between *what is known* (categories) and *how it comes to be known* (methodology), but are themselves technologies of power that position knowledge within elite bodies of specialist expertise (Halberstam, 2011: 7; Foucault, 1976, 2003; Sedgwick, 1994). Knowledge is not power itself, as Sedgwick (1994) explains, but power clings to knowledge like a magnet and thus gives purchase to the knowledge; it produces value, status and power. Within this historical context considerations of how power works within a display of 'otherness' we turn now to a reflection and exploration of partnerships and their potential to 'hack in', trouble or upset the power structures of knowledge creation and representation.

Partnership: power at work

Some of the common criticisms of co-creation, and indeed community engagement, are that its impact is limited, its reach short (rarely stretching beyond those directly involved in the engagement and almost never to senior levels of organisations) and the power leveraged by partnership working is not utilised to its full capacity (Lynch, 2011, 2015). Reasons for this might be around not deeming such projects of co-creation as 'serious' or 'proper' compared to the works of those 'experts' in museology, archaeology, curatorial professions and such like, all of which are more highly esteemed. Community collaboration projects are usually exhibited (if at all) as temporary displays – on the sidelines, the margins, rather than the 'heart' of the institute. They are a 'nice addition', but do very little to alter or contribute to *the way things are done* at the institutes themselves. The consideration that any democratic co-creation as limited has been noted. These projects are often pre-determined by the museum but driven by the community partners. Consequently, they can feel one sided and even exploitative. The quest to define partnership working and qualifying the balance of authority within them has been debated by many and there seems to be little consensus. For Nina Simon (2010) co-creative projects by definition ask 'institutional goals to take a backseat to community goals' but is this always possible within the governance and strategies of large cultural institutions? Govier (2010) advocates for co-creation to be something more open that would see the project outcomes and outputs being more freeform, a 'journey' that all participants take and see where it takes them.

While diverse opinions such as these are important, building relationships based on trust and respect is vital for partnership working. This is especially so when collaborating with those whose identity is not widely understood across society, and where current representations on the whole are not productive and arguably not even accurate. Consequently, such representations render trans people 'vulnerable' and fearful to potential hostility. Trans people participating in co-creation projects need respectful, safe partnership conditions. Contributors from 'communities' want their involvement to be valued, their voices listened to and for these inclusion initiatives to feel genuine in their intention to instigate change and influence transformations. Tokenistic gestures are transparent and only compound exclusionary feelings and practices, delaying the trust that is so necessary to build. With this in mind, and aiming to overcome some of the known barriers, central to the project's planning was that it should not be tokenistic or limited within the traditional model of community engagement, but have instead a legitimate legacy.

Recognising the 'All Our Stories' project was a short-term initiative and the exhibition small in scale and only on display for six months, the ambitions for longer-term impact were articulated from the beginning. Dialogue sessions exploring trans heritage in relation to science and medicine were as important to informing and sharing knowledge with the museum as was the production of the display case. The embedded way the young people worked with the curatorial and exhibitions team also ensured that the knowledge and experiences created would be captured for prosperity and be both transferable and scalable on future projects. An ethnographic research approach was applied to the project where a participant observer was present at all sessions and spent time interviewing the participants and staff involved at various points of the project. The principal objectives of this research were to explore how co-creation focused public engagement could be valuable for an institution such as the Science Museum and how collaboration could challenge patriarchal, heteronormative, racist assumptions often engrained in 'Western' science collections. The research also explored how an understanding of research might empower community groups and how working in this way could raise new questions about the collection (Iervolino, 2014) It was important for those involved that the research generated, though led by the Science Museum, would be useful and useable in the future to aid in the development and improvement of subsequent project and was shared with all involved in the project. It was a transparent open process, which was hoped to serve as a knowledge based legacy and the moving of this relatively short-term project (approximately six months) into a long-term impact.

Borrowing from Sandell and Nightingale's 2012 publication *Museums, Equality and Social Justice*, we also use the term 'social justice' here to refer to

> the ways in which museums, galleries and heritage organisations might acknowledge and act upon inequalities within and outside of the cultural domain … a belief in the constructive, generative character of museums, their capacity to shape as well as reflect social and political relations and to positively impact lived experience of those who experience discrimination and prejudice (Sandell and Nightingale, 2012).

The partnership between the Science Museum and GI was a co-creative endeavour. It was designed to produce a set of mutually beneficial outcomes and envisioned as an opportunity to expose the particular gender- and heteronormative operations and approaches used by the Science Museum in its displaying and describing of its objects. The project, however, proved to be far more than an engagement initiative. It started to push the boundaries of how museums, as representations of authoritative public funded institutions, can become platforms for social and inequality justice, narrowing the divide and broadening the narrative, between those who traditionally have the right, power and platform to speak about science and medicine (the scientists, experts, academics) and those with lived experiences (in this case the young trans people).

As previously stated, GI wants to play its part in encouraging the cultural shift needed to gain understandings of trans and gender variant lives.[4] As work and projects with young trans people have been undertaken at GI, what can be noted among the team is that, on the whole, the young trans people have extraordinarily high level of intelligence when thinking about gender. Experiencing the world as a person who does not conform to gender norms requires great thought. Trans people are intelligent about gender because they need to be. In many ways, the *need* of young trans people to know about gender in ways that are perhaps more rich and nuanced challenges the notions of the 'expert' who can deem gender in more simple and albeit normative ways. GI as an organisation places centrally a calling to apply an intelligence when it comes to thinking about gender. Intelligence is about an aptitude; it demands a labour around processing and thinking. Moreover, when it comes to gender, intelligence can be a process of learning, but it can also be an un-learning of the norms that are so deeply embedded (Halberstam, 2011).

By collaborating with community partners, in such embedded ways as outlined here – through shared decision making, sharing the ownership and authority of knowledge creation and redistributing the responsibility for telling the stories of others – the arts and heritage world can start to assist (and become better networked with) those seeking to rebalance the inequality and prejudice in society. Museums have a responsibility to make better efforts to build in the flexibility and openness necessary when working with community partners. This can affect how inclusion work can be jettisoned beyond the realm of 'community engagement' or 'new audience development' and start to strategically effect change in how institutions move beyond their comfort zones and champion transformative or even radical shifts in how they develop, create and showcase knowledge and information.

This particular approach or experience to producing such knowledge bears its own value and we might note how power (and empowerment) within such knowledge production might shift and be shared (or even handed over!) through the encounter. No doubt, however, as practitioners from within the fields of heritage, cultural, academic and grassroots communities, such experiences expose challenges and opportunities, not least in terms of dealing with a potentially sensitive subject (the medical world and trans identity) and balancing out the emotional consequences of a historical void where trans people have often felt (and potentially still do feel) silenced or excluded from the official narrative of science and medicine.

Such a legacy of working on the project is to note the very effects of the collaborations on both the young people from GI and the Science Museum; how the experience of this project allowed for a breakthrough in formal requirements and norms in heritage sector collaboration projects and how the stories of trans youth can be told by trans youth in a way that more fully empowers them as individuals who can articulate *who they are* through a newly formed understanding of the medium of museum curation. The feelings of empowerment for the participants through the opportunity to disrupt the portrayal of gender in Science Museum displays was a valuable outcome but empowerment could also be located in the legacies of the project and through some of the unexpected outcomes.

Legacy

Perhaps one of the most transformative outcomes and indeed outputs of the partnership for the Science Museum was the acquisition of new participant chosen objects for the permanent collection. There had been few community-led collections projects done at the museum previously and certainly not around the experiences of gender. The objects donated were different and more modern than many things the museum already owned and came entrenched with rich personalised histories. For example, one young trans woman donated a pair of worn, much used breast enhancers and her first ever hormone pill packet. For her, her donation was a chance to immortalise in a national collection a pivotal moment in her transition and a hope that those who accessed them in the future could hear her story and thus have a greater understanding of what it means and what is involved in transitioning in 2014. Captured in an audio recording, the participant states:

> 'Hormone therapy was incredibly important for me. It marked the turning point in my health and happiness. Having the wrong hormones in my body was incredibly painful both physically and mentally. Getting the right ones gave me the relief I needed to live a fulfilling life.'

While interest in these objects was high from the outset, it was on seeing the finished display, engaging with the rationale behind why these objects were chosen by the group and hearing about how the visitors responded to them, that the museum more fully recognised the value of accessioning them into the collection. The objects, in truth, could have been sourced from elsewhere but what was most critical about *these* specific objects were the stories attached to them – genuine and personal stories that would allow future researchers and museum staff to access and use a far more meaningful interpretation of them in the future. It also meant that the stories and experiences of the young trans people who donated these objects were turned into an official record – a forever more protected and accessible testament to their contribution to the nation's understanding of trans heritage in relation to science and medicine. These objects are the 'legitimate legacy' the project aspired to achieve as they can now offer new ways into discourse about trans histories in the scientific context. This also represents a moving towards the democratisation of a national collection where 'the public' actively contribute to what should and will be preserved for the future. During interviews, the donors also commented on their joy of a more representative collection being started at the museum (remembering they had been disappointed by their initial explore) and, though a small step, the collection of 'their' objects meant the Science Museum was giving recognition and validation to trans identities.

A second example around the legacy of the project is an event was planned for the February 2014 Science Museum's LATE programme – a monthly over 18s late night opening of the museum. This event coincided with both the launch of the case and LGBT History Month and offered tours and discussion sessions delivered by facilitators and participants enabling them to celebrate, share their experience of the project and explore what they learnt with a wide range of people.

GI heavily promoted the event and brought in a substantial volume of people (many new to the museum) who were keen to hear more about the endeavours the museum was making to showcase more inclusive and representative narratives from trans people, about the project itself and to contribute to the discussions had around the display case. In addition, a performance by renowned cabaret singer Ms Kimberly (who contributed to the oral histories element of the project) was also planned for the LATEs. With a large and dedicated fan base, her performance, a wonderful addition to the event, brought many first time visitors, trans and non-trans people, to the museum – many of whom had not been aware of the trans youth project. However, it was some of the more unfortunate occurrences of that night where a few guests experienced both explicit transphobic behaviour and more general ignorance was experienced. The visibility of trans and gender non-conforming visitors in a large cultural heritage space asks questions around the responsibility on the side of the institute to ensure such visitors are free from discrimination and can feel safe. The consequences of this night led to an awareness from the museum that change and inclusion cannot be solely collections based but most go to the heart of the organisation. To claim an institution welcomes diversity and encourages inclusion of all, then change, awareness building and training need to be provided. On the back of this event LGTBIQ training was commissioned for the museum's public engagement staff and GI provided best practice guidelines and resources to ensure the experiences of others in the future would be more welcoming. Such work is of course is in a constant mode of mindfulness and forms part of the everyday practices of staff working day to day in and for the organisation.

Conclusion

Working in close partnership with non-museum groups, such as GI, can be deemed risky and difficult by museums. The potential for influence and change can be limited within the current structures of organisation and power. Museums are often slow to invite people in out of fear they will either expose these limitations or the participants will be disappointed by what they can realistically achieve. External groups too can be slow to partner with large, seemingly immovable institutions, and have, through past experiences and unfulfilled ambitions, become disillusioned with the potential impact of their investment. But being brave, being willing to take the risk can pay huge dividends. Ambition can be mutually beneficial as was seen in 'Hacking In' – both the outcomes for the museums and GI were far greater than originally expected.

To offset the old balances of who gets to create and tell the stories of others in cultural institutions, partners need to push beyond the 'safe' and acceptable (perhaps even traditional) deliverables of collaboration projects and be more demanding of what it expects out of these projects. Engagement for engagements sake is not always sufficient and real agency only comes from jointly led initiatives that lead to real impact. The old models of once-off or light touch community engagement do not shift the culture of engagement away from a patriarchal delivery of services or reach out to those deemed to be in need of something the museum can offer. This new model recognises the value of what others can bring – the expertise, experiences, knowledge – and acknowledges the rights of others to be involved in the telling of their stories. An openness and willingness is needed and shared ambitions can move these partnerships towards making cultural institutions sites or platforms for greater social inclusion. These new more embedded practices, with a clear rationale for why the partnership was formed and what the ambitions are will allow cultural institutions to build new relationships with partners who, like GI, are more invested in and willing to input into the changes many museums are now striving to achieve.

While physical outputs like displays, exhibitions or events are engaging ways to showcase and share the work done on projects (particularly with the public), emphasis should also focus on more long-term and embedded outcomes. Collaboration projects need to create opportunities for more permanent change if their legacies are to be effective and future proofed, for example, through the collection of more representative objects, the changing or adding to official records, and the adding of new histories and stories to the databases of museum information systems. In addition, it is necessary to consider what it means to include trans people through its systems and its practices, and how an organisation thinks about embracing gender diversity not solely in its collection and storytelling but in its visitors and workforce across the institute.

Notes

1. See https://itransblog.wordpress.com
2. See https://itransblog.wordpress.com
3. Endeavours such as Black History Month, or LGBT History Month, which take a month of the year to platform and celebrate famous and 'successful' people from these histories, continue to grapple with these politics. Such agendas, driven mainly through school programmes across the UK, Europe and the United States, are honourable in that they look to tackle bullying and poor behaviour and they celebrate diversity. Nevertheless, one critical response has been around the normative processing of this kind of (re)canonisation and how such lives are read through a Western, heteronormative and capitalistic value system that perpetuates its own values. What constitutes 'good' or positive citizenship is determined by deeming certain acts as 'positive' contributions to society and identifying 'success' within these specific frameworks. Crucially these systems themselves go uninterrogated. See Halberstam (2011).
4. The logic for our company name came from thinking through Howard Gardner's notion of 'Multiple Intelligence', which argues that intelligence is not linear, but rather people can be intelligent in multiple ways – he specifically argues seven different ways (Gardner, 2006).

NINE

Mapping in, on, towards Aboriginal space: trading routes and an ethics of artistic inquiry

Glen Lowry and Mimi Gellman

Introduction

> Unlike Cartesian maps which are largely projections of conceptual territory and the power relations that they imply, these map-works explore a lived experience and an alternative reality, both materially and metaphysically. These maps offer an opportunity to investigate and visually manifest the gap between what is deeply known about a place and what is merely drawn on a common map. (Gellman 'TerritoReality' didactic for Exhibition in Red Plains Gallery, University of Regina)

> The resulting real and imagined geographies, the material, symbolic, and hierarchically organized spaces of colonial occupation along with the processes that produce them, contextualize enclosure, exclusion, domination, disciplinary control. (Soja, 2005: 37)

As a settler colony, the historical development of Canada reflects a will to map, and geography continues to influence on public discourse across the arts and sciences. Confederation (1867), which set the terms for the continued expansion of the Canadian nation throughout the 19th and 20th centuries, is connected to a techno-political ability to imagine and map a social space of unprecedented size and complexity. We might say that the possibility of Canada required and refined cartographic representations that were capable of suturing together disparate territories, terrains, and sociopolitical entities into a contiguous grid of regions and provinces, spanning the North American continent and connecting three oceans. How the map of Canada – the ongoing process of mapping various geopolitical interests – is taken up across academic disciplines and by creative practitioners (visual artists, filmmakers, performers, curators and critics) remains central to debates about present and future of Canada. More particularly, as we discuss in this chapter, different maps and mapping differences are vital to discussions of relations among Indigenous and non-Indigenous peoples. In courtrooms, boardrooms, and classrooms, as well as *out on the land* the legacy of maps impacts understanding and interpretations of Indigenous sovereignty and self-governance within and across our national borders. As the quote from geographer Edward Soja suggests, colonial geographies continue to 'contextualize enclosure, exclusion, domination, disciplinary control' (2005: 37). Whether one approaches the map of Canada through the lens of new economic zones, the imperatives of global warming, or 'forging a new relationship between Aboriginal peoples and other Canadians' as the federal government's 2008 'Statement of Apology to former students of Indian Residential Schools' puts it, significant changes to geopolitical contexts require renewed interest in the land and discussions of how it is represented. Differences between colonial and Indigenous mapping and ways of knowing fissure the singular map Canada. Travelling through Indigenous territories, being out on the land, listening to the chiefs and elders alters our ability to see Canada as a stable political; instead we see gaps or cracks in the representational artifice of the nation. Coming to terms with these differences is crucial to developing a more nuanced understanding of the spatial dynamics underwriting a colonial will to power as well as the means of resisting that will.

Geographer Cole Harris argues that Canada develops out of a drive to unite massive tracts of land that were beyond the conceptual powers of early settlers. Settlers had no way of picturing, remembering or experiences geography on the scale and across the geopolitical terrains what would become Canada: 'there was endless complexity across the lands and peoples on which, eventually, Confederation was superimposed' (Harris, 2008: 454). 'Canada has been a reluctant creation,' Harris writes. 'No European country has anything like its past, nor does its neighbour, the United States' (2008: XVI). In contrast to the expansion of the US, which is based on an 'American past [that] has to do with extension and abundance,' he argues that the Canadian past was:

> slowly worked out near or beyond the northern continental limit of agriculture, with discontinuity, paradox, and limitations – with boundaries at almost every turn. There

have been no a prioris, no master plans, no first principles. There has been an evolving patchwork of settlements, and in each of them an accumulating experience with the land and peoples nearby that eventually would be combined into a country. (Harris, 2008: XVI)

The process that Harris describes is inherently culturing nature. As exemplified in the map of a similar name, 'Cultured Nature' by Métis artist and scholar David Garneau, Garneau demonstrates that his peoples' lands have been spatially and temporally compromised through the imposition of the cartographic grid upon the landscape of the Prairie Métis settlements. In this map-work, the natural rivers along which settlements were established are juxtaposed against the British/Canadian property grid and the pre-existing long and narrow lots of the French/Métis property system creating profound consequences for traditional Métis ways of life, access to natural resources and spatial justice.

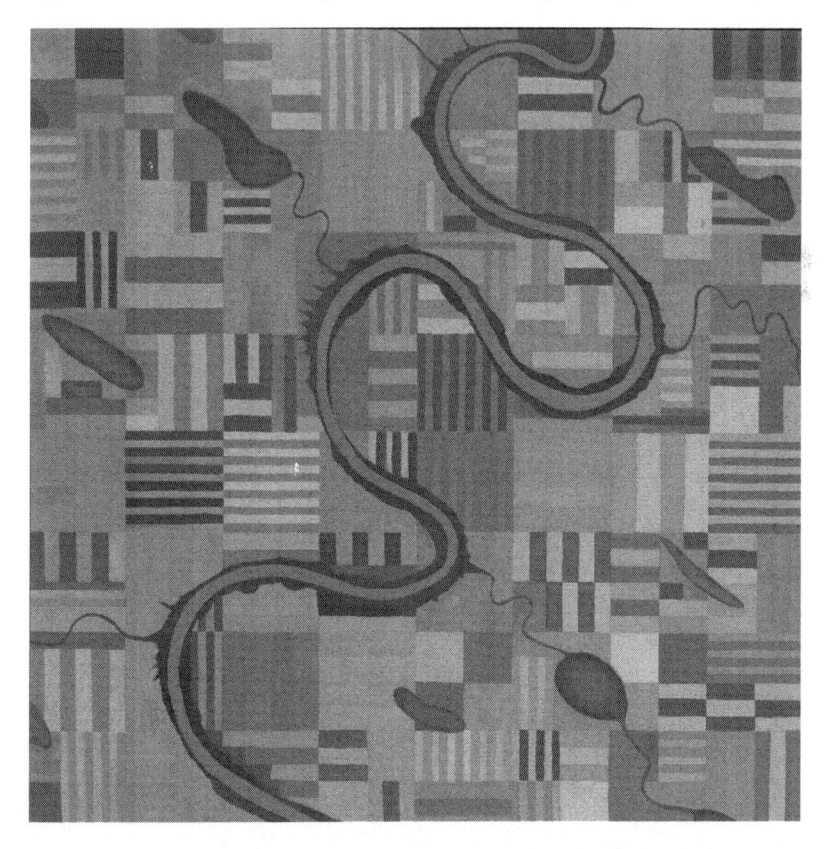

Figure 9.1: 'Cultured Nature', by David Garneau, 2012 (Courtesy of the artist)

Arguably the Royal Proclamations underwriting this expansion provided key 'first principles,' and as examples from Mimi Gellman's research on Indigenous maps demonstrates, Indigenous approaches challenge this lack of 'a prioris'. Nevertheless, the initial fragmentation Harris's analysis posits is instructive. To the extent that these 'patchwork settlements' would be subsumed in a concept of confederation 'that superseded the rock-bound limits of particular colonies and was commensurate with the scale and opportunities of the steam age and the capacity of science to digest and order the land' (Harris, 2008: 468), they are suggestive of ongoing challenges to the edifice of nation. Figuratively and functionally, the map of Canada as a single geographic space helped to unify Lower Canada (Quebec) and Upper Canada (Ontario) with an emerging network of provinces and treaty negotiations. The idea that Canada might chart a contiguous border, separating it from the United States provided a political focus that was able to

> break the political stalemate in the union of the Canadas by giving the French (as Lord Durham and others tended to call French Canadians) their own province and local powers while giving the British the other provinces and a central government in which they would constitute the majority (Harris, 2008: 468).

A unified confederation – represented in a contiguous, single map of Canada – has not however addressed the complex relations among the First Nations, Métis and Inuit who still maintain sovereign rights to massive tracts of land within the boundaries of the nation. As tenuous as confederation was and as contested the difference between Francophone and Anglophone interests might be, the basic outline of the nation remains intact. However, what is missing from this narrative and what is currently demanding the attention of politicians and academics (legal scholars, cultural theorists, historians, geographers), Aboriginal and non-Aboriginal, is the internal and intra-national relations that are submerged beneath the surface of European maps, including the map of Canada. For many decades, Indigenous-led court challenges and negotiations with Federal and Provincial governments have resulted in radically altering the map of Canada, contesting its representational validity and dislodging landforms on scale larger than many European nations.

Collaborative approach

This chapter evolves from a co-presentation that developed under the auspices of 'Trading Routes', a four-year SSHRC-funded Research-Creation project that is based at Emily Carr University of Art + Design in Vancouver. This hybrid art project/research venture was developed on the unseeded lands of the Musqueam, Squamish, Sto:lo and Tseilwa'teuth nations and has sought to engage with the contested geographies in northern British Columbia and Alberta and relations among Indigenous and non-Indigenous ways of knowing. The initial goal of the 'Trading Routes' project was to bring together artists, academics and curators to investigate the intersections of distinct historical forces and geographical mappings. This ambitious creative-critical collaboration hinged on the notion that the proposal Gateway pipeline from the oil fields of Alberta to the coast of British Columbia traces some of the routes of the ancient 'grease trails' or ancestral trading routes between the people of the coast and the peoples of the plains. However, from the outset we recognised that in setting out to fix or ascribe these two potentially opposing flows – the east to west flow of sweet light crude and west to east flow of eulachon oil – to a map, the same map, risks flattening important cultural differences and eliding ongoing struggles around Aboriginal justice and sovereignty. As a point of departure, this chapter and the sharing of research it instigates set out to explore differences between Indigenous notions of mapping and a critical analysis of the social space of the nation. From shared and at times contradictory approaches, we look at the hypothetical map/mapping of Trading Routes – the overlapping of the proposed pipeline route and sacred trade routes – as a highly contested space or convergent set of practices. The map itself, as it is understood across creative and critical disciplines, is a way of doing things, and as such, this tool, techné and technology (map as verb and noun), has historically separated Indigenous from non-Indigenous territories and peoples. In Canada and beyond, the exclusionary politics of mapping is deeply entangled in a politics of exclusion and marginalisation or what the Report from the Truth and Reconciliation Commission of Canada (2015) has called 'cultural genocide'. With this difficult history in mind, we come to the question of mapping in, on and across Indigenous lands as a vital questions of social justice.

It is important to recognise that both authors come to this project from very different perspectives and backgrounds: Gellman from Anishinaabe/Métis and Jewish ancestry, and Lowry Scots-Irish/English. As colleagues at Emily Carr University of Art + Design, one of Canada's four internationally recognised specialised post-secondary Art and Design institutions, we are working together around an broader indigenising platform. One key element of our friendship and collaboration is a shared professional interest in and personal fascination with the representation of space and place in relation to political, social and cultural power paradigms, particularly as this both informs and is challenged by contemporary art practice. The careful reader will recognise that this chapter weaves together distinct bodies of research and very different academic interests. The scholarship relating to Indigenous mapping and its aesthetics is derived from Masters and PhD research conducted by Gellman for her theses on the aesthetics of walking and the metaphysics of Indigenous mapping respectively. It is important to note that Gellman's work as an artist/scholar situates her academic research alongside her creative practice (design/ exhibition) and participation in Indigenous community engagement and Midewiwin ceremony. This research is situated here within and alongside Lowry's studies on cultural mapping, mobility studies and contemporary Canadian culture. As a collaborator, or embedded cultural theorist, Lowry's work is connected to many years' experience as an editor, poet and cultural producer. Maraya – a contemporary art project he co-led with artists Henry Tsang and M. Simon Levin – has produced both creative installations and theoretical essays on which this text draws. The transdisciplinary dialogue represented by this chapter is necessarily speculative and often draws language and discourses that will sound strange to trained geographers. We apologise for this conceptual dissonance but recognise too that terminological discord is an inevitable by-product of the cultural and disciplinary divides we seek to transgress. We hope that these linguistic breaks, and the inevitable leaps in logic they mark, might stand as invitation for others to take up key points of discussion – particularly, around ideas of maps and mapping, which may sound somewhat eccentric, or imprecise to some ears.

Indigenous worldviews: where do we begin? When or where are we now?

> Indigenous Knowing is a vision of the world that encompasses both the heart and the head, the soul and the spirit. It could no more deal with matter in isolation than the theory of relativity could fragment space from time. (David Peat, quantum physicist, 1996, p 8)

For Indigenous peoples 'where we have been' is the necessary question in establishing our beginning point of reference. In considering where we have been, we invoke our family, ancestors, nation, clan, history, stories, worldviews, values and our sense of place, as both a spiritual realm and a physical one. In the latter case, I am referring to the specific land base that one's family hails from. It is from these myriad cosmological interrelationships with the wind, water, earth, sun and stars, animals, plants, rocks and spiritual energies that the wealth of Indigenous knowledge plays itself out.

In Cree/Métis artist Amy Malbeuf's map-work 'Mealy Mountains', Malbeuf employs the Indigenous arts of beading and caribou hair tufting to signal Indigenous presence on the landscape. The organic flow of trajectories countermapped onto a Settler Canadian map charts a powerful embodied experience of witnessing and navigating Indigenous territory.

Figure 9.2. 'Mealy Mountains', by Amy Malbeuf, detail, 2013; caribou hair tufting and glass beads on map (Courtesy of the artist)

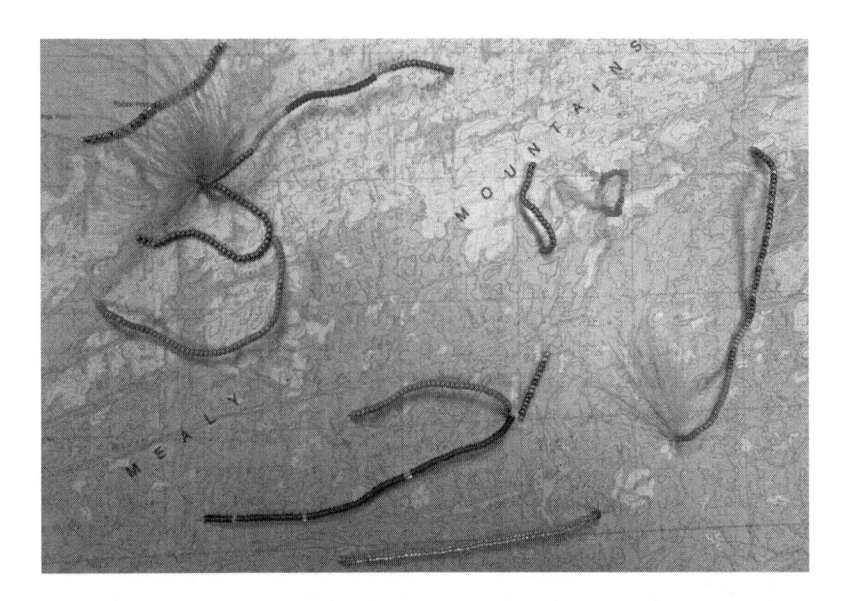

The establishment of our beginning point is a place intrinsically connected to context and that context is intrinsically connected to a specific land base. As Laguna Pueblo Native, Leslie Marmon Silko describes in her book, *Yellow Woman and a Beauty of the Spirit: Essays on Native American Life Today*:

> So long as the human consciousness remains *within* the hills, canyons and cliffs, and the plants, clouds, and the sky, the term landscape, as it has entered the English language is misleading. 'A portion of the territory that the eye can comprehend in a single view', does not correctly describe the relationship between the human being and his or her surroundings. This assumes the viewer is somehow *outside* or *separate from* the territory she or he surveys. Viewers are as much a part of the landscape as the boulder they stand on. (Silko, 1996: 27)

At the heart of many Indigenous ways of knowing is the understanding that being in the world is a phenomenological reality and a co-creation. For example, in Rebecca Solnit's book, *A Field Guide to Getting Lost*, she refers to the Wintu, a Native American tribe of Northern California who do not use left and right to describe their own bodies but rather use the cardinal directions:

> When the Wintu goes up the river, the hills are to the west, the rivers to the east: and a mosquito bites him on the west arm. When he returns, the hills are still to the west, but when he scratches his mosquito bite, he scratches his east arm. In their language the self is never lost. In Wintu, it's the world that is stable, yourself that is contingent. Nothing is apart from its surrounding. Their consciousness is directional and imbedded in their language. (Solnit, 2005: 17)

Solnit's interpretation of Wintu experiences of space and time recalls, Merleau-Ponty's conception of phenomenology of the body in space as being inherently focused on the contingent nature of being in the world; the fact that we live on the world as much as in it. Merleau-Ponty writes,

> I am not in space and time, nor do I conceive space and time: I belong to them, my body combines with them and includes them … Our bodily experience of movement is not a particular case of knowledge: it provides us with a way of access to the world and object, which has to be recognized as original and perhaps as primary (Merleau-Ponty, 1962: 162).

On a map, Indigenous 'being' can be metaphorically represented as a multidimensional, multifaceted system of relational coordinates that reflect the complexity of an Indigenous identity. Imagine that we are positioning ourselves on a four dimensional map that is represented by a complex web of vertical and horizontal layers. On this map, we move from layer to layer and ultimately include those positions that are not visually seen, since they are not on the physical plane but remain rather within the spiritual realm. Indigenous thinking by its very nature is not binary, there is no separation between body and mind. It is rather by nature, circular, organic, relational, contextual, non-hierarchical and fluid. It is inclusive and encompasses alternative attitudes and 'ways of knowing'.

The key to an Indigenous worldview is the understanding that process and context are infinitely more relevant and significant than product. Indigenous thinking perceives the acquisition of knowledge as an exploratory journey and not as a destination. Education is implemented as a transformative process. We play with ideas, surround, envelop or encircle them attempting to explore the interrelationships between disparate things while trying to ultimately come closer to the 'spirit' of the element that we wish to understand or discover. According to Gregory Cajete, a Native American Studies specialist and social theorist, 'Indigenous thinking' incorporates the consideration of multiple aspects or physically changing/embodied points of view:

> The idea of moving around to look from a different perspective, from the north, the south, the east, and the west, and sometimes from above or below, or from within, is contained in the creative process. Everything is like a hologram; you have to look from different vantage points to understand something. In the Indigenous causal paradigm, movement is relational in contrast to Western Sciences linearity (A to B to C and so on). Indigenous logic moves between relationships, revisiting, moving to where it is necessary to learn or to bring understandings together (Cajete, 2000: 210)

In contrast to dominant modes of Western thinking, particularly those related to scientific rationalism and based on linear, deductive and logical ideals, Indigenous thinking is interwoven, additive and outside time. To the extent that scientific rationalism tries to eliminate or explain the unknown through empirical proof, Indigenous thinking seeks to embrace it. European paradigms of academic study, from the

Renaissance forward, have generally privileged knowledge that can be encoded textually. Producing written and formalised canons of knowledge, Eurocentric research and knowledge has been protected historically by disciplinary boundaries and elite institutions, while Indigenous scholarship and education tends to privilege personal experience, perception and intuition and interpersonal exchange. As many writers and speakers have argued, Indigenous teaching and learning generally acknowledge elders as knowledge keepers. Although they are not 'scholars' and 'academics' as formally recognised by the power structures of the 'university,' they nonetheless perform the very real function of an academy. Within the paradigm of Indigenous knowledge, it is understood that knowledge is gained through many portals, and this is where dreams, revelation, ceremony, visual art and other forms of arts and metaphorical thinking come into play. Indigeneity involves the ability to make an infinite network of connections, both real and metaphorical between disparate concepts. It is the capacity to remember a broad array of stories with their relational interpretations that gives Indigenous peoples a richness of material and access to leaps in thinking and creativity. Metaphorical thinking, perhaps especially through the arts, constructs a web of connections and interrelationships. It reflects the ability to express oneself allegorically through story or image, symbolically conveying deeper, often spiritual, ethical, or political meanings. Another means of looking at the concept of the metaphorical mind involves the method of connotation as an alternative to the Western linear method of denotation. Denoting would be the scientific method that stipulates meanings. Connotative, or metaphorical thinking is a comparative and more inclusive method that invites many meanings. The Western worldview points to a tree and defines it as 'tree' while the Indigenous perspective calls it a spirit taking the 'form' of a tree. Cajete distinguishes Indigenous thinking as a holistic cognitive and phenomenological mode of apprehension:

> The ability to transform and metamorphose, to think metaphorically, comes with practice, and the development of meaning and understanding comes with increasing knowledge. Language is more than a code; it is a way of participating with each other and the natural world. At one level language is the symbolic code for representing the world that we perceive with our senses. At a deeper psychological level, language is sensuous, evocative and filled with emotion, meaning and spirit. Meanings are not

solely connected to intellectual definition but to the life of the body and spirit of the speaker. (Cajete, 2000: 72)

In Maps and Dreams, anthropologist Hugh Brody engages with the Dane-zaa peoples of Northeastern B.C. and their community land-use maps. These maps chronicle individual and collective concentrations of hunting activity, the extent, breadth and overlapping nature of their hunting territories, and the divergences and discord that exist between their worldviews (their respectful and reciprocal relationship to their lands) versus the settler exploitation of these lands for resource extraction. Of particular note are his references to the dream hunting of the Dane-zaa which marked their spiritual and metaphysical relationship with their land and their animal relatives. In one of his encounters a Dane-zaa hunter related a dream of hunting and killing a big cow moose and marking in the dreamtime one of its hooves so he could recognize it the next day. On his daylight hunt he recognised the path that he had taken in his dream, found the cow moose that he had marked in the dreamtime. Upon his return with his kill he invited the community to share in the meat and to marvel at the marks which were clearly apparent on its hoof.

Figure 9.3: Blueberry River Reserve: Hunting Map (Courtesy of author Hugh Brody)

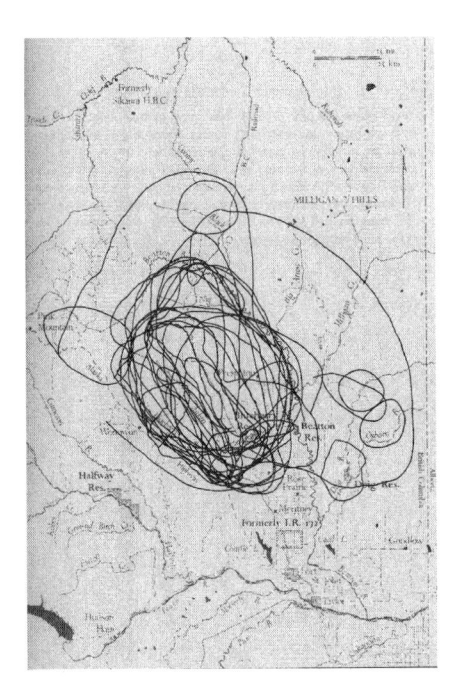

Dreams, visions and revelations arise from the Indigenous worldview that interrelationships are existent between all forms in the universe, animate and inanimate. Native philosopher Vine Deloria Jr, a member of the Standing Rock Sioux Nation, explained that the Indigenous spiritual and intellectual journey for knowledge is based on empirical observation of the physical world and through deep connection with and interference from the higher powers which arrive through sacred dreams, visions, prayer and ceremony and also through the experience of interspecies relations:

> It was historically common within Indigenous societies to have dreams in which other life forms, plants, animals, stones or other land elements would reveal essential knowledge of the properties that they contained. These forms, communicating through dreams, visions, or directly to the individual, would direct human beings in regards to how to behave towards that element or spirit, i.e. how to harvest it or use it for medicine or ceremony or for other more mundane personal needs. Many anecdotes, both oral and transcribed, have recounted interspecies relations and conversations between animals, birds, elements and human beings and as Deloria Jr. related, these relationships can be initiated by either the human or by the animal, element or spirit. (Deloria, 2006: 24)

In his writing about the Cheyenne Nation's understanding of communication, Karl S. Schlesier takes up the notion of interspecies communication. He writes,

> In Tsistsistas (Cheyenne) memories, animals talked with humans, took pity on them, protected and taught them, gave to them special power and knowledge, healed them from wounds and sicknesses, kept them alive with self sacrifice, and finally became human themselves to help them in great need. (Schlesier, 1987: 12)

This understanding of the interdependence linking humans and non-humans, which is echoed in many Indigenous cultures worldwide, is crucial to how Indigenous peoples experience the land. It also provides a very different slant on the meaning of the rights encoded in treaties between Canada and various First Nations, Inuit and Métis peoples: hunting and fishing, as well as the stewardship relations these involve go much further than an economy or resource dependencies. Spiritually and ontologically, human and non-humans are inextricably bound to the land. This may be an obvious statement but it foregrounds an entirely different relationship to the maps than those posited by European explorers, traders and industrialists who have seen maps as the means to great efficiencies of resource extraction.

Within the parameters of most Western modalities of thought this elemental interspecies communication of the Cheyenne and those occurring with other Indigenous nations, for example the Ojibway and Cree, is all but inconceivable. We can, however, turn to the language of quantum physics to assist us with grasping the possibility of a link between Western science and Indigenous knowledge. In *The After Death Experience: The Physics of the Non-Physical*, author Ian Wilson draws a comparison with quantum physics and briefly explains how 'subtle' knowledge or communication might be transmitted:

> According to quantum theory there are certain conditions under which, in the case of two very distant sub-atomic particles, if the behavior of one is altered the other can be expected to change instantaneously in exactly the same way, despite no apparent force or signal linking them. It is as if each particle 'knows' what the other is doing. (Wilson, quoted in Deloria Jr, 1989, p 112)

This concept of simultaneity may assist us in understanding how interspecies communication may be possible. If, as in Indigenous worldviews/science, it is understood that there is no separation between mind and body or between any of the constitutive elements of the universe, then in actuality there is no boundary or border to cross.

Mapping dialects: map sites of difference

Respecting the embodied basis of maps, that is understanding them as representations of 'being in place' or better 'being in space with others (human and other than humans)', we might argue for an understanding of mapping as a multidimensional, multifaceted system of relational coordinates that reflect the complexity of belonging. For Indigenous people and non-Indigenous people alike this complexity of belonging requires a renovated understanding of our finite and material experiences of space and time. As we strive to approach a particular map, or a better set of maps – for example, those charting a proposed Northern Gateway pipeline or those marking the potential devastation such a project might unleash – we might imagine positioning ourselves on a four dimensional map that is represented by a complex web of vertical and horizontal layers. We already belong to the space-time represented and move from layer to layer and ultimately include those positions that are not seen, since they are not on the physical plane but remain rather within the spiritual realm. In *Personal Geographies And Other maps of the Imagination*, art historian Katherine Harmon (2004: 11) asserts that 'Like memory, geography is associative … Part of what fascinates us when looking at a map is inhabiting the mind of its maker, considering that particular terrain of imagination overlaid with those unique contour lines of experience'.

Harmon goes on to suggest, 'The coded visual language of maps is one we all know, but in making maps of our world we each have our own dialect'. This idea raises important questions for the artists/mapmakers whose work takes us into the interstices of Indigenous and non-Indigenous ways of knowing. If coming to terms with a map is relational and/or culturally specific, then how do we work with this 'coded visual language'? How do we do this in a manner that resists reproducing a hegemonic universalism at the core of the colonial project or will to map. At what point does the visual make the leap to the verbal and become one's 'own dialect', as Harmon puts it? How and in what way does our mapped dialogue move beyond a culture or community, away from the local to the universal, and begin to claim to represent space (our own, other's) for those outside our immediate sociolinguistic enclave? It is in the shifting territory of dissonance, accent, inflection – the tension between location and dislocation – that our project begins. It is here that we hope to stay.

To better explain our understanding of the relational difference inherent in Indigenous mapping we might look to other media or mediating practices, such as photography and film-making. These visual technologies, often in concert with a colonial will to map and limit autonomy, have played a defining role in the hegemony of Western thinking about Indigenous peoples and the lands they are seen to inhabit. Analysing similarities in the practices of photographer Peter Pitseolak (1902–73) and filmmaker Zacharias Kunuk, D.W. Norman (2014) argues that these Inuit artists employ representational approaches that substantially alter the dialectic relationship of Inuit people to the land. Above any quantifiable metrics, they define the conditions of Inuit life and homeland, centring these reproductions not only around their own persistent presence, but around the direct connections to their land, their presence within and responses to land, marked out in time and oral narrative. These practices transform the dialogue from one of a people juxtaposed onto land, into one of a land defined by its people and their activities, productions and lived conditions and experiences throughout time. Norman argues for a decolonial media aesthetics that can respect the agency of Inuit artists across a century of photographic history. He writes, 'to know a land one must know its people, because their knowledge of it extends far beyond maps, ice charts and documentary images'. And it suggests that making sense of this relational dynamic involves direct experience or knowledge of people and their land: 'To know the people one must accept and understand their ways of experiencing the land, something not contained in any one method' (Norman, 2014: 70).

Shawnadithit was a young Beothuk woman who drew these maps in the winter of 1829 at a time in history when the Beothuk peoples were few in number, having succumbed to disease, genocidal killing and strategies of assimilation. This map speaks about the agency, observations and perspectives of the Beothuk. It suggests, as geographer Matthew Sparkes recounts, 'that the Beothuk were also observers and agents of geographic interpretation. Moreover, it reminds the contemporary critic that the Beothuk not only interpreted the land but the impact of colonialism on that land' (Sparkes, 1998, p 319).

In approaching maps through the lens of Indigenous cosmologies, we arrive at the distinction that Indigenous maps are representations of an

Figure 9.4: Sketch II, Shawnadithit, The Taking of Mary March on the North side of the Lake, VIIIA-556 (Courtesy of The Rooms Corporation of Newfoundland and Labrador, Canada, Provincial Museum Division)

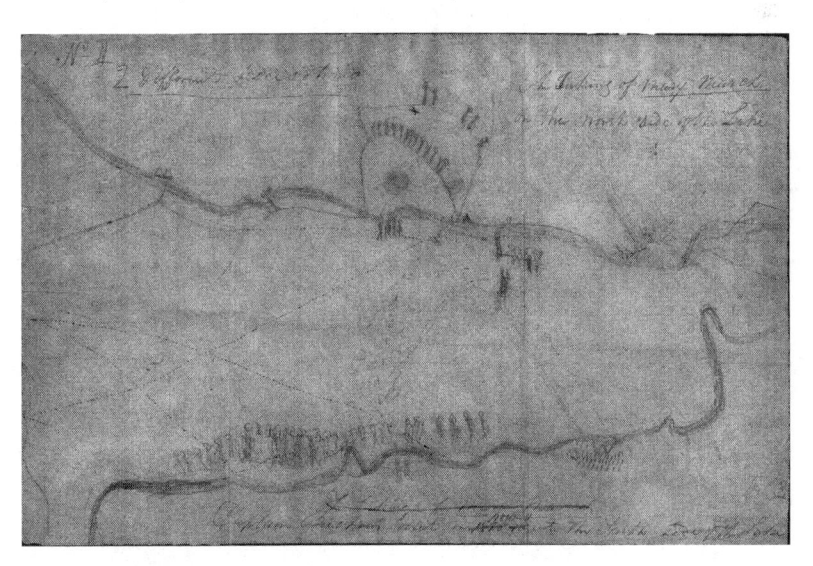

embodied living-through or dwelling-in experience, not an objective looking-at-experience, while understanding, of course, that this must include the knowledge that these maps also contain an unspoken projection or perspective of some sort. In analysing and understanding the conceptualisation and production of Aboriginal cartographies, one requires a grasp of the spatial concepts and senses of place of the mapmakers, as well as the language of signs and symbols (their semiotics) and the linguistic specificities of each map. In short, one must have a fundamental grasp of those cultural processes, ways of knowing and cosmological constructs within which meaning is produced and communicated by these Indigenous nations. One ultimately seeks to learn the language of the mapmaker. The Indigenous maps that we are interested in contextualising are mnemonic in nature: they are memory maps that embed within them Indigenous epistemologies and ontologies. The symbolic language found in these maps is often both a representation of a particular geography and an embodiment of a metaphysical relationship to place. Of great significance in Indigenous maps are Indigenous toponyms (place names) as they speak about a continuum of history, a way of signalling that the past is also a present. Having said this, the ramification of the changing of place names of Indigenous places through the colonial project has been particularly wrenching as this has proven to be one of the most strategic and successful means employed by colonialism to shift the nature of our places and impose the structure of theirs. This continues to remind us that, 'invasion is a structure, not an event' (Wolfe, 2006: 388). Through the changing of place names Indigenous stories have been erased, further obliterating Indigenous presence and entitlement as stewards of this land. Alyce Johnson's dissertation, 'Mnemonic Maps, Talking Landscapes: Spatially Narrated Kaajèt-Crow Clan, An Examination of K'àma Dzêa-Ptarmigan Heart as a Geospatial Narrative', makes clear that the elaboration of place names are cultural expressions and an excellent way to learn one's history, and that they help 'to situate one's self in a social consciousness of an ever present past' (Johnson, 2008: 242).

Three elements dominate tribal concepts of space: the primacy of place, the importance of land and community, and a strong connection between notions of time and space. For many Indigenous peoples and mapmakers, considering the context of the 'now,' the time in which we are embarking on our journey, involves a temporal realisation that time is fluid and overlapping. In relation to the Indigenous Yoruba concept of time, which is similar to the Native tribal philosophies in North America, Benjamin Ray (1976) emphasised the significance of the human journey in tribal consciousness and the relationships between Western linear time and the archaic timelessness of the Yoruba worldview as cyclical:

> Ordinary linear time would not exist in Yoruba consciousness, since conceptually, the human spirit is always coming into the world and returning in one un-ending cycle. On the other hand, since nothing ever repeats itself, and since from this ontological perspective there is always change of and transformation of body, of personality, of mission, of destiny, then existence in time would be more appropriately conceived in spatial terms as a spiral neither cyclical, nor linear. There is no time-out-of-time. (Ray, 1976: 41)

In our work, we find a link between Indigenous thinking about primacy of place or land-based ways of knowing, and critical theories of space as social production. In relation to Aboriginal space, we find Soja's concept spatial justice particularly helpful. Challenging normative assumptions about human need and patterns of consumption, Soja writes:

> Only when we abstract away from or ignore the spatiality of human life can we conceive of a situation in which individuals and collectivities are perfectly equal no matter how such equality is defined. Whether it be occupying a favoured position in front of a television set or shopping for food or finding a good school or choosing to live close to a job or achieving greater wealth and prosperity or finding a location to invest billions of dollars or, indeed, seeking great spatial justice, human activities not only are shaped by geographical inequalities but also play a role in producing and reproducing them. (Soja, 2010: 72)

For Soja, spatial justice hinges on understanding and redressing 'uneven geographies of power'. His work draws on the writings of Henri Lefebvre, Michel Foucault, Edward Said and David Harvey, among others, in order to demonstrate the ways in which the act of theorising social disparity is deeply embedded in pragmatic and programmatic actions in space. The actions take place, literally and figuratively, in specific sites that become crucial to not only the bridging of theory and practice but also linking urban and non-urban spaces across time. Waiting for a bus in Los Angeles, to take one of Soja's examples, cannot be completely disentangled from state boundaries and the flows of trans-urban flows of people and capital. Recognising the unjust plotting of transit routes as sites of racialised exclusions and neo-liberal politics radically alters how one might read the map of Los Angeles. Within Canada the work of Idle No More has served to remind us that the free transportation of goods and service on national railways, highways, bridges and borders is dependent on the will of the First Nations whose lands these traverse. In so doing, blockades and road closures allow fissures to appear on the surface of the map of Canada that challenge us to think about how we experience space and mobility.

In her discussion of a number of cultural theories that assist in clarifying the nature of Indigenous space, Katja Sarkowsky (2007) picks up on Soja's earlier discussion of Lefebvre's concept of three distinct types of space: 'firstspace' or 'quantifiable, fragmented material space', 'secondspace' as 'a mental construction', 'immaterial and unknowable in geography', and 'thirdspace' encompassing 'all spatial possibilities simultaneously' (Soja, in Sarkowsky, 2007: 32). Soja's notion of Thirdspace provides an important tool for thinking through the expansion of mapping techniques to include Indigenous maps and map making. Soja writes:

> Thirdspace is the space where all places are capable of being seen from every angle, each standing clear; but also a secret and conjectured object, filled with illusions and allusions, a space that is common to all of us yet never able to be completely seen and understood … Any attempt to capture this all-encompassing space in words and texts, for example, invokes an immediate sense of impossibility, a despair that the sequentiality of language and writing, of the narrative form and history-telling, can never do more than scratch the surface of Thirdspaces's extraordinary simultaneities. (Soja, 2010: 56–7)

In similar fashion, Homi Bhabha, in *The Location of Culture* (1994), articulates a different but related concept of 'Third Space' as a metaphorical location for the production of cultural meaning and difference. Bhabha advocates this space as a place of resistance and like Soja uses this 'Thirdspace' to formulate a spatial concept of cultural and political resistance and as a means of exposing the binary structures of power (Sarkowsky, 2007: 33). Read against the maps of a settler nation, such as Canada is, Indigenous maps provide a means of reframing how and what we tend to think of as the purpose of the map. If, as we have suggested, the embodied and relational presence of the mapmaker's racialised body remains in view, the map itself ceases to function within a representational logic of objective knowledge; the figure in the land that denies the abstract system of knowing or representing the colonial fantasy: terra nullius.

The 'Dreamwalk' map speaks about interstitial places which reflect Indigenous space and time as it traces the spatiality of bodies moving across the landscape. The circular nature of the lines depicts the thorough exploration of a place and suggests an extensive knowledge of the area mapped through circumambulating the area over and over. Although it does not read like a disciplinary cartographic drawing, it can still be considered 'a representation of space, still a picturing and still an embodiment of a geographical imagination' (Sparkes, 1998: 324).

Figure 9.5: Dreamwalk #1, by Mimi Gellman, 2010 (Courtesy of the artist)

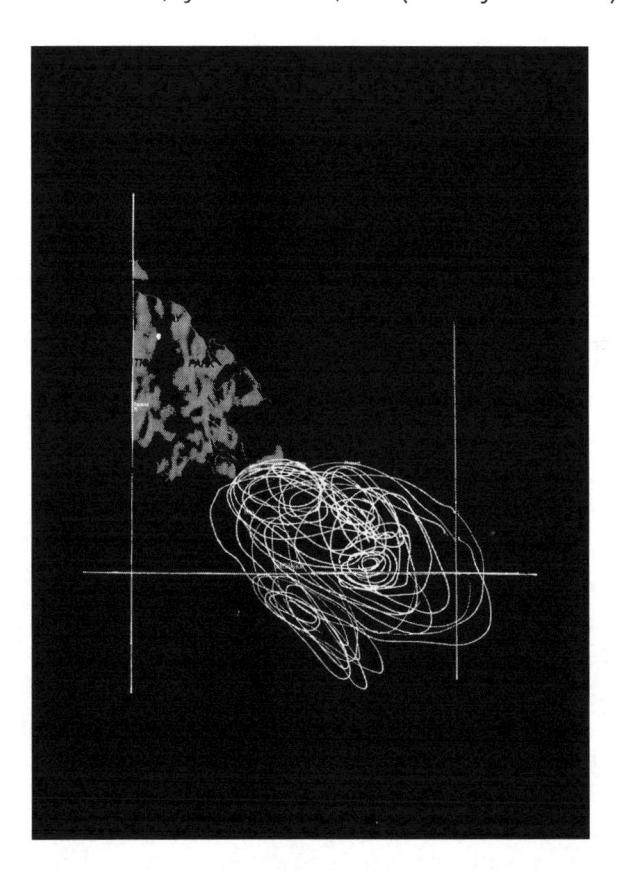

Relational mapping: walking away from a conclusion

> While we sleep, or try to sleep, the city travels with us – stowed in overhead bins, or shoved under the seat in front. Masterful striations, they hold laptops or pack mobile devices. Maps of the city no longer fold. They snap open and scroll. In the daylight, they bend us over faded displays. Together, you and I squint, pinch finger a direction, or we try to. (Lowry et al, 2013)

How maps are made and how they are read is of grave political significance: this is one of the brutal lessons of European encroachment on Indigenous lands and the continued impacts of the colonialist project. In this chapter, we have argued for a need to consider, if not reconcile, the ontological differences brought to bear on Indigenous and non-Indigenous/Western maps. With examples from various Indigenous sources we have attempted to draw attention to salient differences that we are using to guide our approach to the contested geographies that comprise the unseeded territories of British Columbia, where we live and work. The geographies that we took up through Trading Routes continue to inform our shared and divergent interests. The conflicting and conflicted comprehensions of the land borne across a variety of scales and cultural territories knit together conceptions of the local, Indigenous, non-Indigenous, regional, national, transnational and global in ways that both challenge and unite theorists and creative practitioners. To the extent that the Northern Gateway project has focused the energies of governments, developers, workers, and Band Councils, as well as non-governmental organisations, environmentalist, Aboriginal organisations and other citizen groups, it provides a key site for strategic resistance (a concentration of hegemonic forces?). While it might seem that the traditional territories of the Haisla, Haida, Tshimsham, or Dene – to name some of First Nations directly involved with the proposed Northern Gateway pipeline –are distant from usual geographies invoked by 'right to the city' movements, approaching the proposed pipeline in terms of a multi-sited and strategic engagement with an emergent urbanisation, as a vital zone of spatial (in)justice, is perhaps useful. The coupling of the Alberta oil fields and the transportation of Canadian fossil fuels (bitumen, crude oil, coal and liquid natural gas from BC) across North America and into the expanding/expansionary markets in Asia. China's voracious appetite for energy, and its attempts to move away from fossil fuels to renewable sources, is radically shifting Canada's national economic interests and will have an impact on federal government policies for decades to come. More than this, changing geopolitical contexts set the stage for a heightened awareness of Indigenous knowledge and leadership at the intersections of social planning, economic development and environmental organisation. Conciliations among Indigenous and non-Indigenous initiatives across municipal, provincial and national networks are redrawing maps of Canada, and we have attempted to argue how these are experienced at the level of quotidian, embodied relations.

This is an installation image from a series of nine bus shelter works that Maraya created in conjunction with a 2011 multimedia exhibition at Centre A, the Vancouver International Centre for Contemporary Asian Art. Mapping the global mobility of contemporary urban design and development that connects sites in Vancouver with Dubai, these images speak to the unhomely displacements of contemporary urban design and development. This poster was installed on Pender Street at the gates of Vancouver's Chinatown.

Figure 9.6: Maraya bus shelter poster

In the conclusion to *Seeking Spatial Justice* (2010), Soja proposes 'a strategic optimism' that links lessons learned in Los Angeles around the success of UCLA's Urban Planning programme to an ability to translate critical theory into social practice. Drawing on examples from the Los Angeles Bus Riders Union, Citizens for a Better Inglewood, which was able to pass local and state legislation to thwart Wal-Mart development, and Los Angeles Alliance for a New Economy (LAANE), among others, Soja recalls the positive inroads made by cultural theorists who were able to work together with and form coalitions with labour organisations and citizens' groups. For Soja these examples provide something of a blueprint for larger national and international initiatives that have been able to counter the powerful forces of neo-liberalisation. Linking Lefebvre's 'social-spatial dialectic' and 'right to the city' with an ever-growing need to consider (and act on) social justice, he writes 'Googling "right to the city" today … brings up nearly nine million entries.' The growing importance of these initiatives provides a way of thinking about the at times overwhelming forces of global capitalism.

To underline his conclusion, Soja quotes cites David Harvey's keynote address to the World Social Forum in Belém, Brazil, in February 2009. Harvey argues:

> We need in fact to begin to exercise our right to the city … to reverse this whole way in which the financial institutions are given priority over us … to ask the question what is more important, the value of the banks or the value of humanity … to take command of the capitalist surplus absorption problem. We have to socialize the capital surplus. We have to use it to meet social needs. (quoted in Soja, 2010: 198)

Extending and troubling Harvey's argument, Soja contends 'the right to the city must not be reduced to struggles against capitalism.' As he says:

> there are many other forces shaping these unjust geographies, such as racism, religious fundamentalism and gender discrimination, as well as spatial practices that are not necessarily designed only or always to reinforce class differences, such the drawing of electoral district or other boundaries, the siting of toxic facilities, the building of mass transit systems, the location of schools and hospitals, the formation of neighborhood associations, community gardening and food production, zoning laws, the residential clustering of particular occupations such as artists or engineers. (Soja, 2010: 199)

To this map Soja is drawing, which is grounded in Los Angeles and the collations formed through and around UCLA's Urban Planning, we might add our own concerns with justice for First Nations, Inuit, and Métis living in or alongside Canada.

Indigenous struggles remain unnamed in Soja's expansion of Harvey's Marxian project. Nevertheless, there are crucial overlaps with the geography/geographies he describes and those invoked in this chapter, particularly around environment devastation, food production, education, social services and voter identity. The question that remains for us is one of how we might productively build new coalitions, among artists, academics, community leaders, that is respectful of land-based knowledge systems. Of the languages we do not speak. Of the rivers we have yet to visit. And most importantly, how do we approach this dialogue in a manner that resists or reverses the ocular-centric drive of colonial expansion that suggests that if you see something officially represented, you can rightfully take it? Thus, comparing and sharing our different maps, what new stories can we tell? The geopolitics of Trading Routes, the jumping off point of this collaborative chapter, continues to frame our mutual interests and individual investigations of the intersections or folds of creative practice and critical engagement. Increasingly the incommensurability of maps, the fact that Indigenous and non-Indigenous thinking do not line up, that our maps do not necessarily scale, that their registers are out of sync is the point. Our differences, the ruptures in the surface of an idea of a territory or a migration route, of a province, First Nation or Canada, whatever map we choose to work from, requires a dialogic approach to incompatible sight lines. In sharing maps we share ontologies and, as this chapter has done for its authors, this sharing motivates us to keep going. Reconciliation is not an end point, a destination, but a process, a journey we walk together and apart, trading maps as we go.

TEN

Adapting to the future: vulnerable bodies, resilient practices

Deirdre Heddon and Sue Porter

Introduction

TONY:	Right, I think this is recording.
TERRY:	Here we are
GLENISE:	At the start of our walk in Badocks wood.
PAUL	So here we are at – what's this place called?
JOHN:	No 1 the Harbour Side.
SHARON:	OK, so today's walk is going to be around the Bristol docks.

(Heddon, 2015: 179)[1]

In this chapter, we are concerned with the contribution of arts-based approaches to support participation in service of a fairer society. As illustration, we offer an account of the project 'Walking Interconnections: Researching the Lived Experience of Disabled People for a Sustainable Society' and the interventions that the project and its outcomes have staged not only in environmental discourse and debate about inclusive public space, but also in representations of walking practices. We start by describing and contextualising Walking Interconnections, before going on to consider the arts-based approaches used within the project and the research findings they enabled.

Walking Interconnections brought together disabled people and sustainability practitioners to share walking encounters in public places. Through mapping, talking, walking and reflecting together they entered each other's life-worlds. Their experiences are caught in photographs, maps and *Going for a Walk,* a verbatim play crafted by Deirdre Heddon from the recorded conversations of the walkers. Throughout the chapter, we include co-researchers' voices using excerpts from *Going for a Walk*.

The Walking Interconnections project

'Walking Interconnections: Researching the Lived Experience of Disabled People for a Sustainable Society' was a two-year-long interdisciplinary research project funded by the UK's Arts and Humanities Research Council (AHRC), as part of their research theme 'Connected Communities'.[2] It responded to the demonstrable lack of connection between disability and environmental movements (Imrie and Thomas, 2008; Abbott and Porter, 2013).[3] More pointedly, it was motivated by the marginalisation of disabled people within and by environmentalist discourse. Such discourse most often presumes, figures and thus reiterates a normative, undifferentiated and able-bodied subject. Sarah Ray's insightful identification of a 'corporeal unconscious' within USA environmental thought (Ray, 2009: 261) has resonance in our location of writing, Britain. Walking Interconnections set out to explore disabled people's everyday practices of resilience.

As suggested by the project's title, a key method of research used in Walking Interconnections was walking. While the project's intention was not, at the outset, to challenge discourses of walking *per se* – though walking is often part of environmentalist agendas – Heddon's ongoing interest in walking as a mode of aesthetic practice led to an additional focus on the ways in which representations of walking in critical literature are similarly exclusive. While recognising that the visibility of disabled people as knowledgeable and resilient subjects is important politically and practically, we also acknowledge that resilience, as a mode of practice and aspiration, carries its own politics and offers vulnerability as productive resistance to neoliberal subjectivities.

As part of the AHRC Connected Communities programme, Walking Interconnections developed as a collaboration between academics and a community led organisation, The West of England Centre for Inclusive Living (WECIL). The project was led by four academic investigators: Dr Sue Porter (University of Bristol), Professor Deirdre Heddon (University of Glasgow), Dr Shawn Sobers (University of West of England) and Dr Suze Adams (University of West of England). The academic researchers were drawn from across the fields of social science, arts and humanities. The research team also involved two non-academic partners: environmentalist practitioner Alison Parfitt, and peer support co-ordinator for WECIL, Anna Wheeler. The project worked with 19 co-researchers (with the support of personal assistants). While Heddon and Porter are the authors of this article, much of the research on which it draws was created by all those involved in the project: Tony Benson, Liz Crow, Dale Durrant, Hayley Hellings, Tom Henfrey, Anais Leger,

Sue Liebow, Sharon Millard, Glenise Morgan, Karen Morgan, Neil, Paul Noone, Courtney Planter, Raheela Raza-Syed, Soledad Riesta, Terry Searle, Rosalind J. Turner and Julie Whittaker.

Context

LIZ: OK, so we've come past the nature reserve and got onto a track that we were both getting really quite enthusiastic about, it's one of those very sustainable tracks, tramped down earth and my trike has coped just about with the loose gravel surface on it. And beyond this gate we've come to what looks lovely, real potential for open countryside but we've come to one of those kissing gates which is impassable. I would probably get stuck in and left there because I think I would get wedged. And there's a lovely big gate next to it – but unfortunately that's padlocked – so that's the end of this route. So – now we are going to backtrack. (Heddon, 2015: 183)

Led by a team of four researchers drawn from across the arts and social sciences, the key aim of Walking Interconnections was to identify disabled people's wisdoms (Leipoldt, 2006) as these relate to debates about and planning towards environmentally and socially sustainable societies. By sustainable we mean the ability to sustain life on earth.[4] Key aspects of the transformation towards sustainability are the abilities to cope with and adapt to new challenges arising from changing environments (John and Kagan, 2014: 61). The project developed strategically from earlier scoping work undertaken by David Abbott and Sue Porter, extending the literature review and small focus group surveys documented in their essay, 'Environmental hazard and disabled people: from vulnerable to expert to interconnected' (2013). In that essay, the authors ask whether disabled people's experiences might enable them to become valuable contributors to planning initiatives directed towards sustainability, rather than marginalised by the dominant perception of disabled people as singularly vulnerable.

One catalyst for this scoping study was the perceived vulnerability of disabled people in the event of environmental hazard, acknowledging too that extreme weather events, as a result of climate change, are rising (Fischer and Knutti, 2015). A contextualising background was recognition that disabled people *were* vulnerable – that is, disproportionately affected in crises situations. However, Abbott and

Porter's (2013) contention is that such vulnerability is a product of both neglect (for example, structural attitudes position disabled people as the least worth saving) and design (for example, the needs and skills of disabled people are not fully acknowledged because planning responses are often ableist in their assumptions, privileging normative notions of bodily abilities). Problematising the perception of vulnerability, Abbott and Porter propose an alternative hypothesis, one which pays attention to disabled people's 'intricate, daily negotiations with risk, hazard and barriers'. As they argue, 'disabled people may have lived experiences which bestow expertise which could significantly contribute to discussions about and planning for environmental risk' (p 840). Tactically appropriating and redeploying environmentalist rhetoric, Abbott and Porter remind the reader that it is wasteful to marginalise those knowledge resources that might well offer innovative ways to view and understand our relationships with each other, including more-than-human others.

Focusing attention on the contributions that disabled people can make to sustainability discussions and planning, Abbott and Porter's essay seeks also to move beyond the more established debates around issues of access (Abbott and Porter, 2013). While there is no denying the continued existence of environmental injustice enacted through uneven geographies that serve to exclude, or at the very least challenge, certain bodies in certain (many) spaces (Imrie and Thomas, 2008: 478), Abbott and Porter (2013) are interested in what those bodies and minds do in those spaces, whether easily accessible or not; and, significantly, what that doing can teach us.

In the concluding paragraph of their essay, Abbott and Porter (2013) confirm their impression that disabled people's 'wisdom', gained through everyday experience, *may* well relate to: 'overcoming barriers; responding to risk; understanding the importance of the relational; and, appreciating the limits rather than the limitlessness of things' (p 851). They also admit to a desire to explore this hypothesis in the future and, more specifically, to develop methods that would enhance dialogue between disabled people and environmental activists. Walking Interconnections is positioned here as the sequel to that scoping study, moving beyond the review stage and from the theoretical and hypothetical to the everyday and practical. Members of the WECIL Peer support group were participants in a focus group in the scoping study and their input shaped both that essay and the Walking Interconnections project.

From marginal to valuable

TONY: There's this bridge, that's a footbridge, so these are all footpaths, these purple coloured things on the map, so we could maybe investigate that?
SUE: As long as we've got some options in case it doesn't work.
(Heddon, 2015: 179)

Our commitment to identifying and communicating the values of disabled people's everyday knowledges corresponds with the recent work of Rosemarie Garland-Thomson, particularly her essay, 'The Case for Conserving Disability' (2012). Two points made by Garland-Thomson are especially pertinent to Walking Interconnections: (1) 'disability is inherent in the human condition' and, (2) disability is 'a potentially generative resource rather than [an] unequivocally restrictive liability' (2012: 339). Recognising disability as inherent to all people – 'the transformation of flesh as it encounters world' and 'the body's response over time to its environment' (2012: 342) – Garland-Thomson proposes radically that 'what we call disability is perhaps the essential characteristic of being human'. Given this, disability is neither 'unusual [n]or avoidable' but instead is firmly a part of each of our lives. Garland-Thomson's discussion of disability as an evolving practice of a body located in time complements the work of her essay 'Misfits: a feminist materialist disability concept' (2011), where the body is located in space too. Garland-Thomson proposes disability as

> a shifting spatial and perpetually temporal relationship [which] confers agency and value on disabled subjects at risk of social devaluation by highlighting *adaptability, resourcefulness, and subjugated knowledge* as potential effects of misfitting (2011: 592, emphasis added).

In her extension of social constructionist theory towards dynamic materiality, Garland-Thomson shares much with the non-representational approach some cultural geographers take to exploring co-constitutive body-landscape relations, moving from disembodied thought to embodied thinking, action and relations. As Anderson and Harrison (2010: 7) summarise, 'Insisting on the non-representational basis of thought is to insist that the root of action is to be conceived less in terms of willpower or cognitive deliberation and more via embodied and environmental affordances, dispositions and habits'. From this frame of reference, nothing is fixed or given, since everything is in relation and in a perpetual state of becoming, 'dynamic phenomena produced through entangled and shifting forms of agency inherent in all materiality' (Garland-Thomson, 2011: 592). From here, one does not perceive a disabled person excluded from a fixed and settled world but approaches, instead, the process of world-making.

For Garland-Thomson, 'misfit' is a 'critical keyword' that denotes an encounter in which the relationship between two things is one of disjunction and incongruence (2011: 592). The benefit of this approach is that the 'problem' is inherent to neither of the two things, but rather their juxtaposition. With a shift in spatial and temporal context, there might well be a fit rather than a misfit. As she writes, 'Misfit emphasizes context over essence, relation over isolation, mediation over origination' (2011: 593). 'Misfitting' is offered as a way to theorise disability as a becoming that emerges from material arrangements which materialise disabled subjectivity at the same time as they materialise misfitting spaces (for example, the relation between a wheelchair user and a stair) (2011: 594). Misfitting opens up a space to (re)claim agency and to negotiate different relationships.

Disability's value – a value that prompts Garland-Thomson to argue for conserving disability – begins to emerge here also: 'fitting' tends to erase consciousness of the always-contingent in-between, the dynamism of our relations. This dynamism is brought home through the performance of misfitting because it affords an opportunity to become sensitised to material experience, igniting 'a vivid recognition of our fleshiness and the contingencies of human embodiment' (2011: 598). Misfitting reveals that the world is far from 'stable, predictable, and manageable' (2011: 598). Garland-Thomson closes 'Misfits' by listing six reasons why disability – misfits – should not be extirpated but should rather be valued as a 'form of human variation'. The sixth of these has the most bearing on Walking Interconnections and is worth quoting at length:

> The moral understandings, subjugated knowledge, or ethical fitting that can emerge from what might be called socially conscious, or even theoretically mediated, misfitting can yield innovative perspectives and skills in adapting to changing and challenging environments. Acquiring or being born with the traits we call disabilities fosters an adaptability and resourcefulness that often is underdeveloped in those whose bodies fit smoothly into the prevailing, sustaining environment. This epistemic status fosters a

resourcefulness that can extend to the nondisabled and not yet disabled as they relate to and live with people with disabilities (Garland-Thomson, 2011: 604).

Walking interconnections

ANAIS: Why did I volunteer? Because I was interested in the aspect of action research – something different, going outside, experiencing, reporting about what you felt outside and how you experience your environment.

LIZ: As a long-term wheelchair user and a trike user I'm looking always for new routes but there's a risk in trying out a new route that you don't know it's passable until you've tried it and if you don't know it's passable can you try it? So for me there's the potential of having a hike and trike buddy to try out a couple of new routes with, to try and extend the repertoire and see what the experience of doing the route is with somebody else.

TOM: When you are new to a place you learn a lot from walking around with people who know it. I felt it would be very interesting to learn about the place itself from the perspective of somebody who is experiencing it in quite a different way from me.
(Heddon, 2015: 178)

Walking Interconnections adopted a participatory research approach, with arts-based methods utilised as both research tools and outputs. Recognising the typical disconnection between two communities, disabled people and sustainability practitioners (see Abbott and Porter, 2013; Imrie and Thomas, 2008), we saw value in the exchange of experiences between them. This is not to suggest that there are not people who identify as both disabled and as environmental activists. However, research to date does suggest that there is little collaboration between these two communities. We recognise also that 'community' is a complex term, and one that risks homogenising differences and erecting boundaries. While many of our disabled co-researchers were drawn from a peer support group facilitated by WECIL, and in that sense might be regarded as a definable 'community', other co-researchers self-identified a performed identity, without necessarily being part of a constituted community. Our commitment to participative enquiry and our project's location within the AHRC's Connected Communities thematic prompted us to position our 'subjects' as co-researchers.[5] Over the course of a year we worked with 19 co-researchers from the Bristol area, who self-identified as either disabled or as environmental activist. We asked each co-researcher to invite another co-researcher to accompany them on a walk of their choice, exchanging experiences of the environment by walking together.

Each participant sketched a map of their proposed journey before and after the walk and they were all invited to select and use creative prompts from a 'Walking Guide' devised by academic co-researcher and artist, Dr Suze Adams. The Walking Guide functioned as a list of activities, instructions, foci of attention and suggestions for photo and film interpretation of the walk or, more prosaically, 'a collection of moves' to be performed.[6] The prompts in the Walking Guide, indebted to the popular *Mis-Guides* published by Devon-based artists' collective Wrights & Sites,[7] were intended to provide frames through which co-researchers could pay attention to the environment (for example, taking photographs of three orange things encountered while walking) and at the same time to gather data from each walk (for example, photographic documentation of surfaces encountered). In total, the project has an archive of some 900 photographs. Each walking pair or trio carried a camera and a digital voice recorder. After the walks co-researchers analysed together the walks they had undertaken, surfacing insights through sharing knowledge. Walkers reviewed and annotated the maps they had drawn before and after each walk and selected 'significant' moments depicted in the photographs taken, discussing their choices and what the images represented or meant to them with the full research team. The audio material of conversations – more than 25 hours recorded on the move – was transcribed by Heddon and used to create a 30-minute verbatim audio play, *Going for a Walk*. The play was shared in draft form with the co-researchers and once consent was given for the script to be made public, co-researchers were invited to participate in a workshop with Heddon before the play was audio recorded, with co-researchers invited to read their own part.[8] The play and an exhibition of selected images and walkers' maps were used to communicate the project to a range of stakeholders, including the Environment Agency, Bristol City Council Civil Protection, Public Health and Sustainability units, Neighbourhood Partnerships, Walking for Health, and the Schumacher Institute, and later at workshops,[9] festivals and conferences including The Glass-House Debate.[10]

Walking as a participatory research method

TOM: Taking it at a different pace and being more observant and sharing things. I noticed a lot of things that I hadn't spotted before down here, details of even obvious things.

ANAIS: If I was on my own I wouldn't have experienced the walk in this way at all. I feel it becomes really practical, there is a strong practical side to it, whereas when I walk with my partner, we just discuss abstract stuff, we don't really realise where we walk, how we interact with the ground, this kind of stuff.

DALE: I hadn't realised how many different types of walking surface there were. It seems as if there was only two but actually there's four or five. There's cobbles, there's tarmac, there's roads, and a sort of paved area as well.

TOM: I've become much more aware of the different people passing through this area. How it works. The diversity of things bringing people in. I've always seen it more as a route for passing through.
(Heddon, 2015: 187)

Our choice of walking as a key research method in Walking Interconnections developed in part out of Heddon's previous interest in the capacity of walking to foster collaboration and facilitation of non-threatening dialogic exchange (Heddon and Turner, 2010; Heddon, 2012). Walking as a research methodology also follows in the footsteps of Jon Anderson's 'walking and talking' interviews (Anderson, 2004), Carpiano's 'go along' interviews (Carpiano, 2009), Ingold and Lee's peripatetic ethnography (Ingold and Lee, 2008) and Heddon and Turner's 'interviews on the move' (Heddon and Turner, 2010, 2012). In contrast to researchers such as Anderson, Carpiano and Heddon and Turner, who have used walking as an envelope through which to conduct interviews between researcher and research subject, in Walking Interconnections our 'subjects' were positioned as co-researchers, and their conversation, image making and mapping created the data.

Edensor notes that walking offers a perspective from which life can be both grasped and understood, but also through which identity can be transmitted (Edensor, 2000: 81). Walking can be both performative and communicative, focusing attention on the kinaesthetic, mobile and sensory/felt dimensions of lived experience (Pink et al, 2010). In addition to walking being conducive to collaboration and dialogue, in the context of exploring people's everyday practices walking is an embodied performance that allows reflection on people's affective relationships to and with place (see for example Ingold and Vergunst, 2008; Patterson, 2009). Geographers Andrews, Hall, Evans and Colls (2012) recently issued an appeal to researchers to pay different attention to forms of embodiment and urban mobility. As they note, and as our own research design aimed to acknowledge, for many people – and for an increasing percentage of the population – walking is undertaken 'through the use of wheelchairs, sticks, scooters, and walking frames', or through slow walking (2012: 1928). Andrews et al, surmising that most work on walkability in the social sciences is focused on issues of access, argue that 'new research needs to be developed paying particular attention to different forms of embodiment, mobility, movement activities, and the places, experiences, agency and cultures involved' (2012: 1930).

Walking offers itself as a research method particularly useful to the generation of qualitative data which gestures towards the affective and emotional, as much as towards more tangible issues of access. Through Walking Interconnections, we were interested in our co-researchers' navigation of place alongside the affective dimensions and shifting dynamics of people–people and people–place relations. Walking Interconnections' co-researchers, prompted by the Walking Guide and the dialogic structure of the walk, were walking and *thinking bodily* about their interaction with the environment, nature, space, community and belonging. Walking locates bodies in space, but at the same time is mobile, offering at the outset a certain propensity towards an attitude of always-in-relation. In the act of walking, as one moves through space and is in relation to space, one is always engaged in an unsettled process of becoming, just as place too is always in the process of becoming in relation to the ones who move through it. Following Rosemarie Garland-Thomson, we are interested in the relationship of flesh to world, with walking offering a key way to explore those relationships. Walking, as our research reveals, has its own particular, contextual practices – that is, ways of *walking-worlding*.

Interventions into walking discourse

While Andrews et al's (2012) appeal to move away from an ingrained focus on access towards an exploration of embodied practices was issued to health geographers specifically, their request to attend to 'different forms of embodiment' could well be directed to researchers in the arts and humanities too. Walking as an embodied practice has been much explored recently from within different disciplinary perspectives, including anthropology, architecture, design, art and performance.[11] This critical interest in walking has been matched by a popular one, with articles in newspapers extolling the virtues of walking, exhibitions and art festivals dedicated to programming and reviewing the use of walking in art, and an ever increasing number of walking festivals launched across the UK.[12] Strikingly, in spite of the variety of locations in which 'walking' is engaged and discussed, the form it takes as a practice seems decidedly homogenous.

In previous research, Heddon and Turner (2012) have critiqued the exclusive and excluding nature of writing about walking, specifically aesthetic walking. As they note in 'Walking women: shifting the tales and scales of mobility', the constant but unacknowledged reiteration of a particular genealogy, which references mainly male writers and artists, produces something of a canon and orthodoxy of walking practice and theory. The persistent positioning of walking as 'individualist, heroic, epic and transgressive' serves to marginalize other types of practices and the critical insights that these prompt (Heddon and Turner, 2012: 224). Whether the location is urban or rural, the scene set is most often a 'wilderness' to be conquered and tamed. Heddon and Turner's aim was not to deny such features as the heroic or adventurous in aesthetic practices, but rather to revise the tropes through mobilising scales – spatial and temporal. What is deemed adventurous, or daring, or innovative is very much dependent on context; creating relations rather than escaping them, making work in familiar locales, or simply working outside might be usefully reframed as courageous and innovative acts. In any case, Heddon and Turner sought to press the point that a key political potential of walking might very well lie in its practice of relation- and social-making (2012: 236).

Though Heddon's previous research therefore calls for and demonstrates attention to gender differences, noting that the seemingly unmarked body figured in much walking criticism is decidedly male, what remains vastly understated and under explored is that this body is also able-bodied/non-disabled. Heddon's work in the field of walking aesthetics is part of the spatial turn in criticism evidenced across the humanities and social sciences since the 1990s, which explains in part the emergence of walking as a legitimate academic focus. However, the subject of walking is curiously normative. Writing from within the discipline of urban design, for example, Filipa Matos Wunderlich references pace and routine in his paper presented at the Walk21-VI conference (2005):

> Walking as both an experienced and observed activity in urban space involves regularity and routine. It is performed rhythmically step after step, after step, after step, after step.

Architectural theorist Jane Rendell writes in a similar vein:

> There is a kind of thinking that corresponds to walking, one that follows an itinerary, keeps up a certain pace and remains in constant motion, moving from one thing to another, engaging only in passing (Rendell, 2008: 185).

Ingold and Vergunst propose that walking is 'an accomplishment of the whole body in motion' and demand that we 'pay attention to experiences of tactile, feet-first, engagement with the world' (2008: 2). In summary, even where walking is the specific focus of analysis, much remains taken for granted and presumed to be in common, including rhythms, paces, speeds, movements, atmospheres; indeed, bodies and the very act of walking itself.

These presumptions about walking prompt fundamental questions: what is walking and who is walking? Such homogeneity also, though, fosters certain answers. As one of our co-researchers, Liz Crow – a wheelchair user – commented on the Walking Interconnections blog in June 2013, she bit her 'tongue at the word walking (because I'm not, am I?)' (Crow, 2013a). Notably, six months further into the Walking Interconnections project, Crow's use of the word walking, admittedly still somewhat hesitant, does indicate an importantly expanded signification:

> Speaking personally, so many years of medical history have been of doctors telling me I should walk – that is, functionally, place one foot in front of the other in order to move from one point to another. In almost 30 years of using a wheelchair, I've never yet seen a doctor who understood that that's not what walking ever represented to me. It was moving through space, connecting with natural and social environments, relationships, meditation, relaxation, pleasure, mental health, tactility, and more. Those are the really important features of walking and it remains all of those things when I 'walk' with wheels (Crow, 2013b).

Crow goes on to explain to the reader of this blog why she chose a recreational walk to undertake as part of the Walking Interconnections project. What Crow makes clear is that, ordinarily, any type of walking she does requires careful planning, what she refers to as 'the dry stuff'. Participating in Walking Interconnections, and walking with a non-disabled partner, allowed her a moment of reprieve from that auxiliary and 'joyless' activity, and to experience the pleasure of walking. As she writes, 'The point for me of Walking Interconnections was to explore liberation from that; it was about reconnecting with all those other things that walking always represented to me and that the medics never knew'. Going on a walk, in some contexts, is to generate greater dependency on people rather than less, precisely to mitigate risk and realise pleasure.

Walking Interconnections allows for a disruption of the taken for granted and the unstated. Discussing with our co-researchers their experiences, and listening to their audio recordings, it is clear that, at least for some of the time, for some people – indeed, for increasing numbers of people – there is no rhythm to walking that it is easy to fall into, because the sometimes precarious inter-relationship of body and environment prevents flow; walking is varied in its tempo, with obstacles looked out for, detected and navigated, or not; pace is disjointed and fragmented because necessarily punctuated with essential periods of stillness allowing the body to rest and recover; when one's attention is always scanning for the challenges ahead, preparing to negotiate them, and then skilfully doing so – or not – there is little time to allow the mind to drift off into diversions. As Crow notes in her earlier blog entry, 'what should be pleasure is predominantly anxiety. Pleasure is mainly a thing of hindsight rather than in the moment. ... [E]ven at its best there is always an undercurrent of fear' (Crow, 2013a).

For many people, and for increasing numbers of people, going for a walk does not bring feet into contact with ground. The connection is wheels to ground. Is the wheelchair user's experience of walking – with the haptic running from ground to wheels through arms and to the rest of the body – any less 'environmental' than the walker whose shoe soles touch pavement? The phenomenological analytic underpinning much of the writing about walking, motivated by an exploration of the relationships between bodies immersed in places, shares the corporeal unconscious noted by Ray (2009). This tends to conjure unproblematised relations between a singular walking body and a connection and intimacy with the world, which is surely one aspect of a predominant environmental ethic. For Ingold (2010), steps and breath are connected to air and ground. But for the walker in a wheelchair, the body itself is simultaneously mobile and static and one cannot presume, for example, that the body moving through space in a wheelchair is made warm; atmosphere and weather are experienced – known, felt – differently.

The constant reiterations of embodiment lying in particular foot-to-ground phenomenological experience perhaps explains Crow's stated frustration during a walk for the AHRC's Connected Communities Festival held in Cardiff Bay (in 2014). As we explored the environment, mapping out an accessible route for participants, Crow perceived that a steep bank next to the path prevented her from really getting close to nature, over there – as if nature, or the environment even, was out of bounds to her. We would argue that it was not the bank that excluded Crow from getting close to nature but ideas of nature; where it lies, and how (particular but unmarked) bodies connect to or access it.[13] Challenging nature's location and every body's connection to it – every body's immersion it – is surely part of a sustainability ethic, one that might well also challenge the perceptible disconnection between the disability and environmental movements.

Embodied wisdoms

SUE:	I think we are going to get knocked over in a minute. [Referring to the bikes].
TONY:	I think this is probably the first time I've walked along this path. Whereas before I've always been one of the people on a push bike.
JULIE:	That's obviously another walk.
ANAIS:	You couldn't go there?
JULIE:	No. I don't think it would be a good idea with the scooters.
ANAIS:	There is a step there.
SUE:	Oh, sorry [getting out of the way of a man on a bike].
PAUL:	Oh, cobbles.
RAHEELA:	I hate them.
JULIE:	With a scooter I have to be aware of everything, people around me, children, everything.
SUE:	Is it safe for me to come out and get closer? I don't want you to get mowed down.[…]
SUE:	[Referring to bikes] It's very dangerous here, isn't it?

TONY: You have to give way, but I think the problem of this is that when you are on a pushbike you begin to think of this as a motorway for bicycles.
SUE: It feels like a motorway for bicycles.
X [MAN ON BIKE]: Excuse me.
SUE: Oh, sorry! [getting out of the way]
(Heddon, 2015: 184)

Walking Interconnections sought to identify the skills and strengths that make up disabled co-researchers' wisdom. Leipoldt (2006) writes of disabled people's experience in making real choices; moving beyond the rhetoric of rights to value individual choice; acknowledging limits, judging what to accept and what is open to change; skilfully 'riding the wave', rather than seeking to control it; bearing up through committed relationships, with oneself, others and the environment; and, creativity in living, and personal transformation.

Our co-researchers' analysis of the walking together experience identified repeated practices of risk taking, deviation, adaptability, problem solving, persistence and creativity. This mixture of 'practical' skills such as risk assessment and problem solving, and developed 'traits' such as persistence (often referred to by co-researchers as stubbornness) and creativity, map well onto definitions of resilience. For example, the Rockefeller Institute's tabulation of resilience features, 'qualities needed to evolve and emerge stronger' in the 'face of acute shocks and chronic stresses', though attached to an abstract notion of 'a city', shares a correspondence with our findings.[14] Our disabled research participants demonstrated variously the capacity to be: 'Accepting of uncertainty and change'; 'Reflective'; 'Adaptive'; 'Robust'; 'Resourceful' and 'Diverse (flexible)'.[15] Based on our research, we would add to this list of resilient qualities 'Persistent', 'Committed', 'Attentive' and 'Interdependent'. Garland-Thomson (2012: 346) offers several examples of similar assets, including strategic planning and time management skills, navigational skills used by blind people and people with low-vision, and sign language which can communicate across long distances. Appreciation of these skills supports our original challenge to the notion of disabled people as *only* vulnerable, recognising a set of abilities held in different measure across our group of co-researchers.

While the project has allowed us to understand more about different forms of resilience in support of the transition to a sustainable society, it has also highlighted aspects of social injustice, some of which have otherwise been too easy to overlook, for example illustrating the absence of the disabled body within spaces typically coded as explicitly 'environmental' – including heritage sites and 'natural' landscapes'. Of the 900 photographs taken while walking in public areas, it is startling that only a tiny number of these show any other visibly disabled people. One risk when researching with disabled people is that the more textured aspects of ableism get flattened into a reactive focus on physical access – such as the use of stiles, small kissing gates, and ornamental cobbles in heritage areas – losing the subtleties of insidious exclusion. The body is the fleshy substance of citizenship (Wiseman, 2014). Simply addressing physical barriers with, usually limited, 'special provision' sends out clear social messages about what constitutes a normal body, and who is a full citizen.

Walking Interconnections demonstrated that 'ability' is a dynamic definition for all human subjects, shifting depending on relations with and to space and time (some people feel more energetic in the morning, more vulnerable in the cold, and so on). Meekosha and Shuttleworth (2009: 65) write that

> [h]ow societies divide 'normal' and 'abnormal' bodies is central to the production and sustenance of what it means to be human in society. It defines access to nations and communities. It determines choice and participation in civic life. It determines what constitutes 'rational' men and women and who should have the right to be part of society and who should not.

Logically, the citizen is embodied, and the (private) body performs its citizenship in the public sphere. Lister points out that citizenship has traditionally been associated with the 'public' sphere and the body with the 'private' sphere, resulting in the distancing of the body from citizenship. This demarcation has resulted in the exclusion of particular groups of people from being able to achieve full citizenship based on corporeal difference (Lister, 2003). This public/private division mirrors the more simplistic social model interpretations of disability/impairment, where the social environment is blamed entirely. The social model of disability has been criticised for denying the embodied realities of pain, fatigue and other effects of impairment for many disabled people. In Wiseman's study of disabled young people,

> The everyday negotiation of feelings of 'sameness' and 'difference' were found to be important in understanding how participants felt about themselves in relation to their everyday citizenship. Families and friends were instrumental

in promoting feelings of 'sameness' while feelings of 'difference' emerged in relation to inaccessible toilets, … clothes shops and through negative interactions with non-disabled others. Citizenship and inclusion were invalidated where participants were made to feel 'out of place' because of corporeal difference (Wiseman, 2014).

Walking Interconnections' co-researchers reported similar feelings of acceptance and 'sameness' with their walking partners, sustained by the walking and talking. The dialogue produced by this 'being in place together' enabled their exploration of 'difference' occasioned by their different embodied experience of the environment they were walking in. In this way the 'personal' experience of individuals with impairments was reunited with the 'public' persona of disabled citizens. As noted earlier, Walking Interconnections arose from an awareness of a lack of connection between disability and environmental movements and one thing our research revealed was the failure to find common cause. This lack of connection between communities appeared to have led to local planning for shared routes being primarily responsive to vociferous cycling campaigns, rather than being equitably informed by the needs of other groups. In this way, we found the uplift in cycling initiatives has impacted negatively on disabled people's experiences of supposedly shared walking/cycling routes. The design of the space, as one of our non-disabled co-researchers, himself a cyclist, pointed out, allowed some cyclists to treat the whole space as if commuting on a motorway, putting pedestrians and wheelchair users at risk.

As well as skills noted above, co-researchers also demonstrated strengths, by which we mean the more relational aspects of resilience, such as acceptance of the necessity and desirability of interdependency. For example, disabled walkers, recognising rather than denying their vulnerability, utilised the relationship with their walking companions to experiment and to be playful; as one walker said, 'as a disabled person you have to break the rules sometimes'. Another participant reflected on the benefit of having someone to walk with; should things get really rough, her companion walker could go for help. While interdependency signals shared vulnerability, it also paradoxically permits greater liberation and, in this context, experimentation and risk taking.

In reflecting on the notions of interdependence and relationality, we found that the dominant discourse of 'independence', particularly as this is attached to the field of disability policy and practices, but also more generally in current discourses in relation to what constitutes a 'good citizen' and a 'good life', belies the reality and necessity of interdependence – interdependence offering alternative and useful conceptions of 'sustainable living'. Repeatedly observed in our project were interdependencies' attendant practices of trust, negotiation, reciprocity, mutuality and co-operation.

Resilient knowledge

Roz: Off to our right is a bird hide which is up several steps. And then in front of us is a steep, short incline which leads to the sea wall path which is like a dyke path, it's not a formal path. We're just about to have a conversation about how adventurous Liz feels because we are talking a very narrow pathway. My feeling is what we need to do is go up to the top of here so you can take a look and go, 'oh my god, you're having a laugh' or 'actually, yes let's give it a go'.
(Heddon, 2015: 183)

Recasting vulnerability as an environmental ethic contests the story of the subject as self-sufficient and singular. Recognising vulnerability's relationship to interdependency perhaps goes someway to addressing recent critiques of the 'resilience agenda'. As the term resilience gains in currency – 'whatever it is, it appears to be everywhere' (Anderson, 2015: 60), scholars have noted that it is not politically neutral. For MacKinnon and Derickson, for example, 'resilience is inherently conservative insofar as it privileges the restoration of existing systemic relations rather than their transformation' (2012: 262). They propose that 'capitalism is itself highly resilient at a systemic level' – the stresses and crises caused by the system and felt within the system are responded to by the system through 'periodic reinvention and restructuring' (2012: 261). To promote resilience is to accommodate and normalise the 'uneven effects of neoliberal governance', placing responsibility for dealing with crises onto individuals – or, in an extension of the Conservative-Liberal Democrat coalition government's Big Society – onto local communities (MacKinnon and Derickson, 2012: 257, 263). One outcome of 'resilient communities' is reduction in state support. Cretney (2014: 631) offers a more nuanced approach, identifying a number of different trends in resilience discourse, the third of which aims to resist complicity with neoliberalism: 'a countercultural form of activism that mobilises a specific articulation of resilience and transformation'.

In the context of Walking Interconnections, we would propose that a countercultural form of activism resides, on the one hand, in the very *articulation* of resilience and transformation, a performative act of resistance by those normally positioned as vulnerable and a drain on resources; and, on the other, in balance with this recognition of resilient skills and practices, an appreciation of vulnerability's contribution *to* resilience. Our co-researchers' resilience is very much dependent on their vulnerability and their interdependence, that is, on relationality rather than individualised response. From this perspective, resilience recognises the value of vulnerability rather than seeking to overcome it. While interdependency is perhaps more apparent because more explicit in the relationships of (some) disabled people (some of the time), as Judith Butler insists, as 'socially constituted bodies' (2004: 20), 'we are fundamentally dependent on others' (2004: xii).

Vulnerability and interdependency are two sides of the same ontological coin, far removed from the idea of the 'masterful', omnipotent subject. Resilience built on the foundations of vulnerability and interdependence promotes not the individualised, independent, neoliberal subject rightly critiqued by MacKinnon and Derickson, but a relational subject, 'one' who is *in* community, both impressed upon and impressing upon (Butler, 2004: 27). Borrowing from Butler again, greater recognition of our 'inevitable interdependency' might very well provide the sustaining grounds (2004: 180) for a 'global political community' (2004: xii).

Such sustaining grounds are, we argue, essential to sustainability. Geographer Doreen Massey writes evocatively of an immaterial architecture, the architecture of social relations (2001: 462), noting that these social relations are practices, and as such are embodied and material. Interdependency is a practice too, equally embodied and material, an openness of one to the other. Acknowledging our vulnerability and an 'ethics of relationship' (Shildrick, 2000: 216) might just allow all of us to practice our interdependency better, a process of resilience necessary to sustaining a diversity of assembled lives, including human ones.

Conclusion

Roz: If we had to choose three words that would describe the walk, what would they be?

Julie: Full of life.

SHARON:	Accessible, brilliant, lovely scenery.
ANAIS:	Sunny, relaxing and exploration.
LIZ:	Revelatory
ROZ:	Enjoyable.
LIZ:	Warm
ROZ:	Thought provoking.
LIZ:	Opening out, or opening up.
ANAIS:	Hot, continuity, and post-industrial.
JULIE:	Hot, historical, and water.
SOL:	I would say, mindful, because I felt really present, really there enjoying with you in the moment, so I would say present or mindful, energising.

(Heddon, 2015: 187–8)

This chapter has sought to demonstrate the potential contribution of participatory arts-based methods to increase participation for a fairer society, influencing environmental discourse, debates on citizenship and inclusive public space, and conceptions of resilience. In doing so we have also explored the need to critically review the methods themselves, in this case walking, and how its theory and practice has been largely informed by the assumptions of an ableist culture. The Walking Interconnections project contributed to individual and group agency; framing and presenting the issues in ways (such as the exhibition, audio play and guided walks) that were successful in raising awareness and developing relationships, so impacting on planners and policymakers, as well as the wider community. Extending our dialogic, participatory approach, at our initial sharing of our research in November 2013, we invited attendees – ranging from city councillors to non-governmental organisation workers – to reflect on the insights that emerged as they encountered our multi-modal research outputs. These were written by attendees onto the reverse side of postcards of Bristol. Comments included: 'An awareness of how barriers (kissing gates etc.) have a premise of keeping things out, without thought of who is going through; the need to incorporate access at an early stage of planning'; 'The enormous potential for cyclists and people with disabilities to work together to address the areas of conflict and for mutual benefit'; 'it's not about physical barriers (or their removal) but about everything: birds, light, relationships, sustainability, etc.'. Walking Interconnections sought to use arts-based methods to enable our co-researchers to perform as experts and, as importantly, to recognise that expertise, to understand themselves *as* experts. The comments collected at the first dissemination event made tangible to our co-researchers the impact and thus value of their knowledge.

Coda

Though a collaborative project, Dr Sue Porter initiated Walking Interconnections. Sue passed away suddenly and unexpectedly in January 2017. A friend and colleague of many, her commitment, expertise, humour and resilience are much missed across diverse communities and landscapes. It was my immense pleasure and privilege to work with Sue on Walking Interconnections and on this co-authored essay. Sue's impact on my research and its direction of travel is immeasurable. I am deeply grateful.

Professor Dee Heddon

Notes

[1] *Going for a Walk* is a 30 minute audio play, intended to be listened to while walking. The content of the play is taken entirely from words spoken by Walking Interconnections co-researchers, and arranged into a play by Heddon. The play can be listened to/downloaded at http://walkinginterconnections.com/audio-play-going-for-a-walk/ It is also published in *Studies in Theatre and Performance* (Heddon, 2015).

[2] For further information on Connected Communities, see www.ahrc.ac.uk/research/fundedthemesandprogrammes/crosscouncilprogrammes/connectedcommunities/

[3] Discourses of environmental health *do* forge a relationship between environmentalism and disability: toxic environments are held responsible for debilitating illness with evidence of such illnesses an environmental call to arms. Alison Kafer (2013), while acknowledging 'the exploitation of bodies and environments', at the same time notes the ableist and normalising assumptions often circulating in this relationship: 'illness and disability appear almost exclusively as tragic mistakes caused by unnatural incursions into or disruptions of the natural body and the natural environment'.

[4] We have already failed, of course, since many species have not been sustained; environmental crisis is not a feature of the future but of the present.

[5] The AHRC's Connected Communities funding call was explicit that research projects were conducted with communities, with an intention also to mobilise interconnections between communities, www.ahrc.ac.uk/research/fundedthemesandprogrammes/crosscouncilprogrammes/connectedcommunities/visionandoverview/

[6] See Walking Interconnections, 'Sharing a Walk: an arts-based methods approach', http://walkinginterconnections.com/wp-content/uploads/2013/02/Sharing-a-Walk_toolkit_v2.pdf

[7] See http://www.mis-guide.com/mg.html

[8] Actors were also employed to stand in for co-researchers who did not want to read their part.

9. Subsequently the project has contributed to Emergency/Civil Protection planning, the Rockefeller 100 Resilient Cities launch and agenda setting and European Green Capital action groups.
10. www.theglasshouse.org.uk/project/to-a-more-ambitious-place-voices-of-the-glass-house-debate-series-201415/
11. In April 2015, the AHRC-funded project 'Footworks', a research group attached to the Walking Artists Network, held a workshop and symposium with the University of Falmouth to explore the future of art and walking, entitled 'Where to?' (see https://footworkwalk.wordpress.com/) More than 70 abstracts were submitted for consideration.
12. See articles extolling the benefits of walking in *The New Yorker* ('Walking helps us think', 3 September 2014, www.newyorker.com/tech/elements/walking-helps-us-think) and *The New York Times* ('The Benefits of a Lunch Hour Walk', 21 January 2015, http://well.blogs.nytimes.com/2015/01/21/stressed-at-work-try-a-lunchtime-walk). 'Walk On: 40 Years of Art Walking' launched in London in 2013 and has subsequently toured to Sunderland, Birmingham, Southport and Plymouth (see http://walk.uk.net/portfolio/walk-on). Deveron Arts in Aberdeenshire launched its Walking Institute in the same year (see www.deveron-arts.com/the-walking-institute)
13. In fact, what was 'over there' was a man-made saltmarsh.
14. These resilient features could be tied to both engineering and ecological models of resilience, that is, the capacity to bounce back or to change and adaptation.
15. Two other qualities noted by the Rockefeller Institute – 'Inclusive' and 'Integrated' – are less easily detached from the model of resilient city and attached to a person.

Conclusion: Reflections on contemporary debates in co-production studies

Aksel Ersoy

Introduction

While community oriented studies continue to be a part of the language of the Arts, Humanities and Social Sciences, co-production is now proliferating furiously in research. It has become a new buzz word for a new set of instruments or a new way of working to produce sometimes effective research and sometimes better service quality in the UK and beyond. Co-production of research is believed to offer something different as it provides opportunities for experimenting with ideas from different disciplines to emphasise the dimensions of meaning, discourse and textuality. In other words, it emphasises the ontological work of new categories to be able to explore where knowledge resides, how problems are framed and how research can be mobilised in enacting new realities and research. While a growing body of research of co-production has started to exist between the social sciences, the humanities and the arts practices, they have blurred the boundaries of disciplinary subjectivities. The concept of co-production offers new ways of experimentation, where politics, knowledge, actors and actants are continually in flux. However, there is still a lack of case studies that would open up the field and illustrate in practice what the tensions and challenges of co-production are. This book has offered nuanced critical reflection about those tensions and challenges as well as providing practical examples.

This chapter aims to locate the contribution to this book in relation to process oriented research and its relationship with the impact agenda. It starts with discussing the key contours of the terrain over recent decades. It does so under the theme of co-production of research and the impact agenda. The third section focuses on the process oriented research and draws out three key messages from the chapters comprising this book. First, research on co-production opens up new materialist imaginaries of both concepts through conceptualising local knowledge, analysing impact and its enabling conditions. Second, it advances new theoretical agendas for co-produced research by developing original interfaces between social sciences, arts and humanities. Third, it opens up the multiple temporalities of communities, exploring experimental relationship with links between present, past and future in search of alternative temporalities of representation. Finally, the chapter notes the importance of remaining reflexive and open minded in response to future trends and setting research agendas.

An analysis of process-oriented research and its agency

The concept of co-production has been around for many years in the public domain but recently it has experienced a revival. After partnership working became dominant in the early 2000s, a number of policy documents shifted their focus on the delivery of public services. In England, a new partnership emerged between New Economics Foundation (NEF – a British thinktank that promotes social, economic and environmental justice) and NESTA (an independent charity that works to increase the innovation capacity in the UK). These organisations came together to develop the evidence base on co-production to promote a more positive environment for co-production in public services and policymaking. According to this partnership, co-production means 'delivering public services in an equal and reciprocal relationship between professionals, people using services, their families and their neighbours. Where activities are co-produced in this way, both services and neighbourhoods become far more effective agents of change' (Boyle and Harris, 2009: 11). The concept was referred to shift the balance of power relations, responsibility and resources from 'professionals' to individuals by inviting people into the delivery of their own services. Following 'the Manifesto for Coproduction', which set out to define and explain the concept by offering a range of possibilities if embraced by public services (Stephens et al, 2008), co-production became central to the process of growing the core economy by fostering equal partnership, transforming the dynamics between the public and public service workers and acknowledging different types of knowledge and skills (Boyle and Harris, 2009).

In Wales, the concept has had two different reactions. On the one hand, it has been adopted as a method that involves communities and professionals to be more effective and achieve sustainable outcomes. According to Dineen (2013), co-production is based on a philosophy that values individuals, builds on their own support systems and considers their place in the wider community. This approach requires a move away from service-led or top-down approaches to one of genuine citizen empowerment, involving service users and their communities in the co-commissioning, co-design, co-delivery and co-evaluation of services. There has been a growing consensus in Wales that co-production is a way forward, especially in services for health and wellbeing. In 2013, Carwyn Jones, the First Minister of Wales, stated that he and ministerial colleagues recognise the imperative and opportunity to see more co-production and other forms of public participation in the design and delivery of public services.[1] The concept became embedded in a number of policies and programmes, among which the Social Services and Well-being (Wales) Bill 2013 has become central to the transformation of social services by setting out the core legal framework for social services, care and support. Gwenda Thomas, Deputy Minister of Wales for Social Services, emphasised early intervention on social services that require greater cooperation, partnership working and the co-production of services between local authorities, the third sector, the independent sector and other partners.[2] In his speech, Mark Drakeford, Minister of Wales for Health and Social Services, stated that co-production is a vital tool for developing a better NHS in Wales.[3]

On the other hand, there have also been some critiques towards the language of co-production in Wales. In the annual conference of Wales Council for Voluntary Action in November 2014, Leighton Andrews, Minister of Wales for Public Services, explained his reservations about the concept. In a more radical way, he banned the word co-production in the Department of Public Services. Even though he has referred to the 'Commission on Public Service Governance and Delivery' Report which necessitates strategies shifting towards co-production to be able to reform the public sector,[4] Andrews has preferred to talk about community control and participatory democracy. Nevertheless, co-production still remains influential in public policy. Recently, the Wales Public Services 2025 programme has started to look at the economic, demographic, social and environmental pressures that Wales will face in the next 10 to 15 years. This is an independent programme, hosted by Cardiff University, undertaking a range of projects in partnership with organisations such as NESTA, Carnegie UK Trust and the Big Lottery Fund. The report aims to provide a more detailed picture of the current contradictions in the fiscal environment in the short term and rising demand over the long term (Jeffs, 2013). Within the report, co-production has been referred to as a more radical approach to efficiency and is used to meet existing demand more efficiently and with less effort.

In Scotland, the institutional dimension of co-production has been taken up widely and it remains an important element of public policymaking at the moment. On a simple level, co-production is defined as involving people in the delivery of public services. This helps people change their relationship with services from dependency to genuinely taking control. It helps improve public ownership and helps services improve by increasing their relevance.[5] In a recent interview organised by the Scottish Coproduction Network in January 2015,[6] Sir Peter Housden, Permanent Secretary to the Scottish Government, emphasised the importance of co-production to reforming public services in Scotland, empowering communities and reducing inequalities. According to him, co-production is 'a complete different way of thinking'. He argues that the Scottish Government's programme is looking to embed the notion of co-production in the whole way it thinks about the delivery of public services via ongoing dialogue and engagement with those people who will be receiving those services. He acknowledges the potential for empathy, innovation and engagement coming from people, which has become 'the core part of the Scottish approach to public services'. Alongside the Scottish Government, networks and partnerships such as the Scottish Coproduction Network and the Joint Improvement Team remain key players in promoting the importance of the concept. Co-production has become embedded in a wide range of Scottish Government policies and legislation.

Even though it is hard to say exactly when the term co-production started to be used in research, it is possible to see some tipping points in terms of how the language was adopted in higher education. Probably the most striking example above all is that co-production of research has been used very widely and comfortably in the context of the 'Impact Agenda' in the UK. Since the outcomes of the Research Assessment Exercise (RAE) in 2008 gave way to the Research Excellence Framework (REF), there has been an increasing focus on impact assessment. While universities have started to comply with the impact assessment mechanisms being put in place by Higher Education Funding Council for England (HEFCE) and the research councils such as the Economic and Social Research Council (ESRC) and the Arts and Humanities Research Council (AHRC), public engagement strategies have become more essential for universities. Community oriented impact has been taken up in the REF and universities are expected to produce excellent research as well as remaining 'accountable' publicly (Pain et al, 2011). Co-production has started to be used as a buzz word by research institutions to be able to respond to the demands of the impact agenda (Durose et al, 2012).

Although co-production of research fitted very comfortably with the language of public engagement, some academics remain sceptical. The institutional expectation of the REF impact agenda has been the most obvious example behind this scepticism as it has threatened the ethical commitment of co-production of research by economising or predefining a certain kind of relationship between the academy, society and nature. Moreover, many case studies drawn as a part of 'Pathways to Impact' have been problematic due to the standard metric systems and the reporting process being used after research is conducted (Pain et al, 2015). Nevertheless, it would be a mistake to frame the impact agenda solely in negative terms. Even if some academics in social sciences and humanities are left to do community participation to be able to demonstrate the non-economic impact of their research, the impact agenda has also brought in a more positive spin for those who are actually willing to engage with communities. Therefore, the impact agenda has in a way legitimised that desire among a previously hostile senior management team. In that respect, the UK AHRC-funded Connected Communities (CC) programme, for example, is explicitly designed to promote collaboration between academics and 'communities'. By 2014, more than 900 partnership projects were funded with community partners and 150 community heritage projects were supported through partnership with the Heritage Lottery Fund (HLF).[7] There are other funding models emerging. Taking the example of the HLF and the AHRC, there have been some parallel funding processes going on where the HLF funds the community organisations and the AHRC funds the academic research so that people are building alliances, not always in straightforward ways but in ways that are emerging. For example, a small number of coordinating centres have been funded to commemorate the centenary of the First World War since 2013. While the coordinating centres are expected to act as beacons for community outreach, engagement and collaboration, they will lay the foundations for the creation of sustainable relationships and practices between academic and public historic research. Another study looked at the gender dimension of co-produced research under the CC programme (Enright et al, 2016). It has been argued that the co-production agenda has encouraged academic women in the UK to use their established community relationships, inter-personal skills and emotional labour to create alternative ways of performing research.

At a wider scale, when the Royal Geographical Society (RGS) (with the Institute of British Geographers, IBG) announced its annual conference theme as 'Geographies of Coproduction', more than 1800 participants showed interest in the topic to discuss the difficulties, challenges and multiple dimensions of interdisciplinary research. Even though the conference was held in London (UK), almost 40% of the participants came from outside the UK.[8] What was more striking was the number of other contributors who came along and presented their research: 9.7% of the UK participants came from institutions outside academia. They included museums, artists, community centres, charities, voluntary organisations and research institutions. In fact, their contribution was more than that from Scottish and Welsh universities combined. This shows that the theme coproducing appealed to non-academic audiences as well as the academic community. Within these discussions, co-production of research has also been associated with other community practices such as action research or participatory action research, the origins of which go back to the early 1970s. In his book *Pedagogy of the Oppressed*, for example, Paulo Freire (1970) provided guidelines for readdressing power inequalities through learning approaches in a learning environment. His idea was to provide counter-hegemonic approaches to knowledge creation so that 'oppressed' communities could challenge more powerful interests and perspectives. Building on traditions of feminist, post-colonial, critical race and participatory action research praxis, researchers are now seizing opportunities to push community oriented research beyond the technocratic rationality that currently takes place. Within these debates, participatory approaches have become an important part of the geography discipline as the process of knowledge production is broken open. As Nik Theodore has also picked up,[9] there is now a demand for a different kind of relationship based on shared inquiry and insights that cannot be achieved without collaboration. The discipline of geography cannot defend its boundaries anymore. Wynne-Jones et al (2015) argued that new theoretical insights and new practices are being worked out in participatory working even if they sometimes create tensions in the discipline.

In this context, co-production has been used as a new technique for accountability and forging closer relations between different groups. It not only blurs the boundaries between the 'researcher' and the 'researched' but also it enables a greater tendency towards engaging 'beyond text' tools, using arts, media, storytelling, performance and photography to widen its audience and impact (Beebeejaun et al, 2014). Nevertheless, as Jasanoff (2006) argues, the co-productionist perspective can be predictive in the same way that good history is predictive: it may not be a reliable guide to exactly how things would play out in the future; yet, without its benefits, there is a danger of applying the same epistemological blinders. In the research context, it enables spaces for collaboration, reflection, knowledge creation and dialogical learning; and fills a gap where interdisciplinary studies have been soul-seeking in recent decades.

Advancing the debates

As has been illustrated within the chapters of this book, the research on co-production has not appeared in linear directions. It has incorporated different perspectives from various actors during the project timeline. While this process has facilitated mutual learning and ongoing relationships, it has also challenged the traditional understanding of knowledge creation, which is based on individualistic, hierarchical and most of the time bureaucratic systems. The chapters in the book indicate a more horizontal and interactive knowledge creation and governance system where multiplicity and interdisciplinarity matter. This understanding also echoes with literature within the field on the subject of engagement, acknowledging the role of transparency, reflection and clarity to ensure effectiveness of the process (Rowe and Frewer, 2000). Most importantly, the case studies presented in this book diverge with the linear progress models embedded as a part of the impact agenda that imposes top-down criteria and priorities. They highlight relational and reciprocal conceptions of research outcomes revaluing the importance of participatory action research approaches that hinder value-based rationality and research partnership.

In terms of the project evaluation, the impact of co-production goes beyond the narrowly identified criteria of social (and natural) sciences and emphasises more inclusive and process oriented engagement. This emphasis on process can generate positive engagement and facilitate interactions among the project participants. Also since research remains experimental during the process, collaborative projects under the framework of co-produced research express and reflect on how they might reimagine alternatives. They connect with both the desire and the mobilisation of alternative futures. As a result, the impact of co-produced research captures a learning culture and a learning organisation that can provide enabling conditions to experiment and innovate without concerns about making mistakes. This way of thinking pushes the way Research Council UK, HEFCE and universities have framed the concept of 'research impact'.

However, without strong leadership, the engagement activities are unlikely to achieve impacts among the wider organisation. One of the common challenges within collaborative research is the nature of change in funding and human resources. The project leads need to be aware of alternative arrangements to manage a sustainable programme. Hence, the research becomes more dynamic and evolutionary, and it builds on existing conditions. Describing how the research might look on the ground, understanding the challenges and the messiness, and capturing people's experiences of being involved require a sound framework, strong leadership and trust among the partners. Nevertheless, this does not mean strong leadership is the only vital component of engagement. The impact of any collaboration should be viewed not as an outcome of research but as a praxis during which certain hierarchies do not exist in practice. This stimulates a long-term engagement where impacts occur both during the process and afterwards. Therefore, the nature of impact cannot be quantified by the current impact agenda as it is open, dynamic and subject to change in time.

The contributions within the book have illustrated that collaborative research can advance the research in co-production in at least three ways. First, they open up new materialist imaginaries of both concepts through conceptualising local knowledge, analysing impact and its enabling conditions. The chapters offer original readings of diverse understandings of co-produced research, highlighting the ways in which knowledge can be conceptualised through collaborative governance; impact can be deconstructed into its conditions; and resilience can become an internal part of the impact agenda. For instance, in Chapter One, Marina Chang and Gemma Moore demonstrate that knowledge can be created through a more horizontal and interactive governance system that challenges the masculinist views of knowledge creation as a part of the impact agenda. In Chapter Two, Alex Haynes highlights the potential impact that can be generated throughout the research process and discusses role of negotiations, compromises and collaborations as a part of collaborative research. In Chapter Three, Judy Willcocks talks about the role of museums and the potential for creating real impact in the long term. In Chapter Four, Sue Cohen, Allan Herbert, Nathan Evans and Tove Samzelius discuss the settings and process of the research project they have been involved in. They talk about the changing dynamics of collaborative partnership and the role of institutional arrangements to sustain long-term impact of research programme. In Chapter Five, Catherine Wilkinson uses audio artefacts as a part of her research and argues that impact is defined in relation to how we approach participation in a participatory research project.In the second half of the book, the chapters advance new theoretical agendas for co-produced research by developing original interfaces between social sciences, arts and humanities. These chapters draw out the political potential of conceiving arts praxis, rehearsals and theatre as essentially contingent and unsettled, showing how new interfaces and approaches, conceived as performative, excessive and unstable, can provide an enduring platform for interdisciplinary studies. Overall, they push the impact agenda away from an output oriented activity towards an emergent system in which learning processes, ethics and other unconventional engagements are recognised as final products. In Chapter Six, Penny Evans and Angela Piccini reflect on the role of arts practices and the aesthetic dimension of arts-based inquiry as opposed to science itself. They highlight how impact can be produced in collaboration rather than being formulated as part of the project output. In Chapter Seven, Edizel and Evans use cultural ecosystem mapping as a tool and argue that such collaborative tools challenge top-down, expert-led change that is associated with 'impact'. In Chapter Eight, Kayte McSweeney and Jay Stewart discuss the role of power and empowerment associated with gender variance. They highlight the need for a value-based approach and practices as a part of the impact agenda. In Chapter Nine, Glen Lowry and Mimi Gellman use Indigenous maps and illustrate how 'Indigenous thinking' can push the binary view of the 'researcher' and the 'researched' described by conventional ways. In the final chapter, Deirdre Heddon and Sue Porter demonstrate the potential contribution of participatory arts-based methods by using walking as a methodology. They advocate the revaluing of participatory action research methods as they recognise the value of more intangible aspects such as vulnerability and hence provide meaningful shifts in terms of what participants consider as the 'impact'.

Discussion and conclusion

Discussions on co-production reveal that we still have not reached a consensus on the difference between co-production of research and co-production of public services. In fact, there is a constant iteration between these two different but connected arenas. While co-production of services remains as the successor of the long tradition of partnership and contractualism, and it has been used to explore how public services are delivered in new ways in new times, co-production of research raises concerns about inclusion and uses different ways with which to leverage experiences of people or institutions in diverse constituencies. It raises the question of how we do what we do. It offers an opportunity to explore process oriented research without pre-supposing the outcomes of those engagements. Nevertheless, it would be a mistake to think that there is no difference of substance among the groups or networks of people who are studying co-production of research. In fact, the concept has multiple genealogies and urges us to explore different sorts of co-productions varying from earlier forms of participatory research strategies such as participatory action research. The shift towards 'co-productions' not only allows contextual factors to mould the discipline of arts, social sciences and humanities but also, and equally, enables new encounters to loop back and reflect our understanding of the interdisciplinary research. Co-production of research enables us to enter those spaces that would allow us to negotiate what counts as important. It provides different entry points by being a sequential and development process. But more importantly, as Nik Theodore argues, it provides a set of ethical commitments which remains at the heart of co-produced research.

From an institutional perspective, it is quite apparent that the language of co-production has been used substantially, even though there have been some critiques in the domain of public services. In England, NESTA and NEF remain the key players. They came together in 2009 to develop the evidence base on co-production to promote a more positive environment for co-production in public services and policymaking. In Scotland, there has been an increasing interest in the concept and the Scottish Government is keen on exploring how co-production can be embedded in public services in times of austerity. In Wales, co-production has been a way forward especially in services on health and wellbeing. In terms of co-production of research, there are also similar expectations. In the UK, the mechanisms for measuring and embedding 'community oriented impact' have begun to take hold through the REF and bodies designed to support universities in their public engagement strategies such as the National Co-ordinating Centre for Public Engagement (NCCPE), The Wellcome Trust, Catalyst Public Engagement Beacons, and embedded university public engagement departments are becoming more widespread. Meanwhile, new streams have opened up within the AHRC programme, designed to promote collaborative endeavours and co-production between academics, artists, public service providers and a range of community groups. Co-production has become institutionalised in those kinds of ways, when we see city councils, national governments, international organisations and even within multinational corporations such as KPMG, PwC and Arup. The concept is proliferating furiously and moving in the consulting circles.

The difficulty is that, since co-production is now everywhere, we are not clear about the difference between co-production of services and co-production of research. While the risks of institutionalisation continue, it remains important to question whether co-production can be used as a new lens for academics and if it makes us think differently. Moreover, it is important to recognise that the concept cannot be seen as a cheap way out both in public services and research. It comes with commitments such as time and trust, so it would not give a straightforward answer in terms of policy. Even though there have been attempts to do it otherwise, a number of case studies have highlighted that the decision making is down to the organisation that holds the budget. So the challenge is to move away from the hierarchical structures in policy and research, even though it is difficult in practice. Co-production brings in hard questions that we need to grapple with in terms of shifting our thinking. It is a transformation of experience into policy or a transformation of research into action and change. However, instead of intellectualising the concept, it should be celebrated without asking how change happens. This would stop academics finding community organisations to identify what to work on in response to a funding opportunity and encourage engagement and collaboration as a core part of knowledge practices at universities. Otherwise, there might be a danger of doing it wrong.

The final point is that, although the institutionalisation of the concept would be problematic and lead to the underestimation of the ethos through the way co-production has been taken up in the process, it would be naïve to jettison the role of institutions completely. There might be opportunities that institutionalisation can offer. Universities can offer different ways of knowing and bring together a whole range of voices in discussions. They can offer mechanisms for knowledge creation and then turn that into a question of metrics. Therefore, 'either/or's might not be the right ways of doing co-production both in public domains and research. We need to be moving away from the easy binaries that often critical social scientists have worked with about radical/not radical or power/resistance and the like. To be able to do this, we need to be reflexive and constantly question the structures that we have. If something becomes normalised, then we have to find new ways of being able to question our practices. For the moment co-production offers us maybe a way forward but it is not set in stone.

Notes

[1] https://allinthistogetherwales.files.wordpress.com/2013/07/first-minister-reply-to-aitt-4th-june-2013.pdf

[2] His speech was on 'Giving people a stronger voice and more control over services will result in better care' on 28 January 2013, http://www.assembly.wales/Laid%20Documents/PRI-LD9181-EM-R%20-%20Social%20Services%20and%20Well-being%20(Wales)%20Bill%20-%20REVISED%20EXPLANATORY%20MEMORANDUM-28012014-253328/pri-ld9181-em-r-e-English.pdf

[3] His delivered his statement on 'Publication of the Chief Medical Officer for Wales' Annual Report for 2012–13' on 9 October 2013, http://gov.wales/about/cabinet/cabinetstatements/2013/cmo1213/?lang=en
[4] See Welsh Government (2014).
[5] See NHS Tayside (2010: 13).
[6] 'Co-production in Scotland: In conversation with Sir Peter Housden, Permanent Secretary to the Scottish Governement', www.coproductionscotland.org.uk/resources/in-conversation-with-the-permanent-secretary
[7] http://closedprogrammes.hlf.org.uk/HowToApply/whatwefund/FirstWorldWar/Pages/AHRC.aspx
[8] The data was requested from RGS-IBG and analysed by the author.
[9] Prof Nik Theodore presented his paper on 'Subject Spaces: On the Ethics of Coproducing Urban Research' on 9 June 2015 at the University of Bristol, UK. The audio recording is available at http://bristol.ac.uk/ias/vidaud/events

References

Abbott, D. and Porter, S. (2013) Environmental hazard and disabled people: from vulnerable to expert to interconnected, *Disability and Society* 28(6): 839–52.

Ahmed, S. (2006) *Queer Phenomenology – Orientations, Objects, Others*, Durham, NC: Duke University Press.

Allegue, L., Jones, S., Kershaw, B. and Piccini, A. (eds) (2009) *Practice-as-Research in Performance and Screen*, London: Palgrave.

Amsden, J. and Van Wynsberghe, R. (2005) Community mapping as a research tool with youth, *Action Research* 3, 357–81.

Anderson, B. (2015) What Kind of Thing is Resilience?, *Politics* 35(1): 60–6.

Anderson, B. and Harrison, P. (2010) The promise of non-representational theories, in P. Harrison, *Taking-place: non-representational theories and geography*, London: Ashgate.

Anderson, J. (2004) Talking whilst walking: a geographical archaeology of knowledge, *Area*, 36(3): 254–61.

Andrews, G., Hall, E., Evans, B., Colls, R. (2012) Moving beyond walkability: On the potential of health geography, *Social Science & Medicine* 75(11): 1925–32.

Arendt, H. (1998) *The Human Condition*, Chicago: Chicago University Press.

Arnold-Foster, K. and Speight, C. (2010) Museums and Higher Education: A Context for Collaboration, in B. Cook, R. Reynolds and C. Speight (eds), *Museums and Design Education: Looking to Learn, Learning to See*, Farnham: Ashgate, pp 1–10.

Askins, K. and Pain, R. (2011) Contact zones: participation, materiality, and the messiness of interaction, *Environment and Planning D: Society and Space* 29(5): 803–21.

Australian Research Council (2015) Research impact principles and framework, http://www.arc.gov.au/research-impact-principles-and-framework

Banks, M. (2001) *Visual Methods in Social Research*, London: Sage Publications.

Barry, A., Born, G. and Weszkalnys, G. (2008) Logics of Interdisciplinarity, *Economy and Society* 37 (1): 20–49

Bauer, M.W., Allum, N. and Miller, S. (2007) What can we learn from 25 years of PUS survey research? Liberating and expanding the agenda, *Public Understanding of Science* 16 (1): 79–95.

Beebeejaun, Y., Durose, C., Rees, J., Richardson, J. and Richardson, L. (2014) 'Beyond text': Exploring ethos and method in co-producing research with communities, *Community Development Journal*, 49(1): 37–53.

Beierle, T.C. (2002) The quality of stakeholder-based decisions, *Risk Analysis* 22: 739–49.

Belfiore, E. and Bennett, O. (2008) Autonomy of the Arts and Rejection of Instrumentality, in E. Belfiore and O. Bennett (eds), *The Social Impacts of the Arts*, London: Palgrave Macmillan, pp 176–90.

Benjamin, W. (1968 [1936]) Hannah Arendt (ed) *The work of art in the age of mechanical reproduction*, Illuminations, London: Fontana, pp 214–18.

Bhabha, H. (1993) Beyond the Pale: Art in the Age of Multicultural Translation, in E. Sussman (ed), *Biennial Exhibition*, Whitney Museum of American Art, Abrams, New York.

Bhabha, H. (1994) *The Location of Culture*, London: Routledge.

Bickers, R., Cole, T., Carstairs, J., Nourse, N., McLellan, J., Insole, P., Piccini, A., Miller, K., Skinner, R., Jones, M., Gulliver, M., Williams, J. and Eisenstadt, N. (ed) (2015) Thomas, M., Anderson, C., Warren, J., Bristol, The People of, and Eisenstadt, N. *Know your Bristol on the move*, Bristol: Centre for Public Engagement, University of Bristol.

Bion, W. (1961) *Experiences in Groups*, London: Tavistock.

Bishop, C. (2012) *Artificial Hells: Participatory Art and the Politics of Spectatorship*, London: Verso.

Boon, T., van der Vaart, M. and Price, K. (2014) Oramics to electronica: investigating lay understandings of the history of technology through a participatory project, *Science Museum Group Journal* 2, Autumn.

Boyle, D. and Harris, M. (2009) *The challenge of coproduction. How equal partnerships between professionals and the public are crucial to improving public services*, London: Nesta.

Brody, H. (2004) *Maps and dreams: Indians and the British Columbia frontier*, British Columbia: Douglas and McIntyre Ltd.

Brookes, I., Archibald, S., McInnes, K., Cross, B., Daniel, B. and Johnson, F. (2012) Finding the words to work together: developing a research design to explore risk and adult protection in co-produced research, *British Journal of Learning Disabilities* 40, 143–51.

Bryman, A. (2008) *Social Research Methods*, 3rd edition, Oxford: Oxford University Press.

Bunning, K., Kavanagh, J., McSweeney, K. and Sandell, R. (2015) Embedding plurality: exploring participatory practice in the development of a new permanent gallery, *Science Museum Group Journal* 4, Autumn.

Butler, J. (2004) *Precarious Life: The Powers of Mourning and Violence*, London: Verso.

Byrne, A., Canavan, J. and Millar, M. (2009) Participatory research and the voice-centred relational method of data analysis: Is it worth it?, *International Journal of Social Research Methodology*, vol 12(1): 67–77.

Cahill, C. (2007) Doing research with young people: Participatory research and the rituals of collective work, *Children's Geographies*, 5(3): 297–312.

Cahill, C., Sultana, F. and Pain, R. (2007) Participatory ethics: Politics, practices and institutions, *An International E-Journal for Critical Geographers*, 6(3): 304–18.

Cajete, G. (2000) *Native Science: Natural Laws of Interdependence*, Santa Fe, NM: Clear Light Publishers.

Cameron, D. (2016) Speech on 'Education of disadvantaged children, support for families and mental health services', Prime Minister's Office, 11 January.

Carpiano, R.M. (2009) Come take a walk with me: The "Go-Along" interview as a novel method of studying the implications of place for health and well-being, *Health & Place* 15(1): 263–72.

Carpentier, N. (2011) *Media and Participation: A Site of Ideological-democratic Struggle*, Bristol: Intellect.

Castells, M. (1991) *The Informational City: Economic Restructuring and Urban Development*, London: John Wiley & Sons.

Cauchi-Santoro, R. (2016) Mapping community identity: Safeguarding the memories of a city's downtown core, *City, Culture and Society* 7, 43–54

Chalfen, R. (1987) *Snapshot Versions of Life*, Ohio: Popular Press, Bowling Green State University.

Chan, K.M., Satterfield, T. and Goldstein, J. (2012) Rethinking ecosystem services to better address and navigate cultural values, *Ecological Economics* 74, 8–18

Chang, M. (2013) Growing a commons food regime: theory and practice, PhD thesis, University College London.

Chang, M. and Meusburger, L. (eds) (2011) *The Food Junctions Cookbook: Living Recipes for Social Innovation*, London: University College London.

Chávez, V. and Soep, E. (2005) Youth radio and the pedagogy of collegiality, *Harvard Educational Review*, 75(4): 409–34.

Cheddie, J. (2012) Embedding shared heritage: Human rights discourse and the London Mayor's Commission on African and Asian Heritage, in R. Sandell and E. Nightingale (eds), *Museums, Equality and Social Justice*, Abingdon: Routledge, pp 270–80.

Church, A., Fish, R., Tratalos, J., Haines-Young, R., Mourato, S., Stapleton, L., Willis, C., Coates, P., Gibbons, S., Leyshon, C., Potschin, M., Ravenscroft, N., Sanchis-Guarner, R., Winter, M. and Kenter, J. (2014) UK National Ecosystem Assessment Follow-on, Work Package Report 5: Cultural ecosystem services and indicators, UNEP-WCMC, LWEC, UK.

Clark, T. (2008) 'We're over-researched here!' Exploring accounts of research fatigue within qualitative research engagements, *Sociology*, 42(5): 953–70.

Clifford, J. and Marcus, G. (1986) *Writing Culture: The Politics and Poetics of Ethnography*, Berkeley: University of California Press.

Clifford, J. and Marcus, G. (1988) *The Predicament of Culture: Twentieth Century Ethnography, Literature and Art*, Cambridge, MA: Harvard University Press.

Clifford, J. and Marcus, G. (1997) *Routes: Travel and Translation in the Later Twentieth Century*, Cambridge, MA: Harvard University Press.

Cinderby, S. (1999) Geographic Information Systems for participation: The future of environmental GIS?, *International Journal of Environment and Pollution*, 11(3): 304–15.

Cinderby, S. (2010) How to reach the "hard-to-reach": the development of Participatory Geographic Information Systems (P-GIS) for inclusive urban design in UK cities, *Area* 42: 239–51. doi:10.1111/j.1475-4762.2009.00912.x

Coates, P., Brady, E., Church, A., Cowell, B., Daniels, S., DeSilvey, C., Fish, R., Holyoak, V., Horrell, D., Mackey, S., Pite, R., Stibbe, A. and Waters, R. (2014) Arts & Humanities Perspectives on Cultural Ecosystem Services (CES), Arts & Humanities Working Group (AHWG): Final Report, April.

Comunian, R. and Gilmore, A. (2015) *Beyond the Creative Campus: Reflections on the evolving relationships between higher education and the creative economy*, London: Kings College London, www.creative-campus.org.uk/final-report---beyond-the-creative-campus.html

Cooke, B. (2001) The social psychological limits to participation?, in B. Cooke and U. Kothari (eds) *Participation: The new tyranny?*, London: Zed Books.

Cooke, B. and Kothari, U. (eds) (2001) *Participation: The new tyranny?* London: Zed Books.

Connected Communities Symposium (2015) *Utopias, Futures and Temporalities: Critical Considerations for Social Change*, Bristol, May, https://connected-communities.org/index.php/events/event/utopias-futures-and-temporalities-critical-considerations-for-social-change-symposium/

Corbett, J., Rambaldi, G., Kyem, P., Weiner, D., Olson, R., Muchemi, J., McCall, M. and Chambers, R. (2006) Overview: mapping for change – the emergence of a new practice, Participatory Methods, *Participatory Learning and Action* 54: 13–19.

Cox, S.M., Kazubowski-Houston, M. and Nisker, J. (2009) Genetics on stage: Public engagement in health policy development on preimplantation genetic diagnosis, *Social Science & Medicine* 68: 1472–80.

Crawhill, N. (2008) *The role of participatory cultural mapping in promoting intercultural dialogue – "We are not hyenas"*, Paris: UNESCO.

Cretney, R. (2014) Resilience for Whom? Emerging Critical Geographies of Socio-ecological Resilience, *Geography Compass* 8/9: 627–40.

Crow, L. (2013a) Planning and 'Walking', 13 September, http://walkinginterconnections.com/blog

Crow, L. (2013b) On Functional and Recreational Walking, 3 December, http://walkinginterconnections.com/blog/

Darbyshire, P., MacDougall, C. and Schiller, W. (2005) Multiple methods in qualitative research with children: More insight or just more?, *Qualitative Research*, 5(4): 417–36.

Davis, M. and Holcombe, S. (2010) Whose ethics? Codifying and enacting ethics in research settings, *Australian Aboriginal Studies*, 2: 1–9.

DEFRA (2011) *UK National Ecosystems Assessment* (NEA), London: DEFRA.

DEFRA (2014) *UK National Ecosystems Assessment Follow-on* (NEAFO), London: DEFRA.

Dalal-Clayton, B. and Bass, S. (2002) *Sustainable development strategies: A resource book*, London: Earthscan.

deLemos, J.L. (2006) Community-based participatory research: changing scientific practice from research on communities to research with and for communities, *Local Environment*, 11(3): 329–38.

Deloria, V. (2006) *The World We Used to Live In*, Golden, CO: Fulcrum Publishing..

Dentith, A.M., Measor, L. and O'Malley, M.P. (2009) Stirring dangerous waters: Dilemmas for critical participatory research with young people, *Sociology*, 43(1): 158–68.

Department for Work and Pensions (2015) Households Below Average Income, An analysis of the income distribution 1994/95–2013/14, Table 4.5db.

Dineen, R. (2013) Putting co-production at the heart of public services in Wales, *Guardian*, 2 May, www.theguardian.com/social-care-network/2013/may/02/co-production-public-services-wales

Dixon, B. and Facer, K. (2016) *Creating Living Knowledge*, London: AHRC.

Donington, K., Hanley, R. and Moody, J. (eds) (2016) *Britain's memory of slavery: Local nuances of a 'national sin'*, Liverpool: Liverpool University Press.

Dorling, D. (2014) *Inequality and the 1%*, London: Verso.

Dunbar-Hester, C. (2008) Geeks, meta-geeks, and gender trouble: Activism, identity, and low-power FM radio, *Social Studies of Science*, 38(2): 201–32.

Durose, C., Beebeejaun, Y., Rees, J., Richardson, J. and Richardson, L. (2012) *Connected communities: Towards co-production in research with communities*.

Durose, C and Richardson, L. (2015) (ed) *Designing public policy for co-production: Theory, practice and change*, Bristol: Policy Press.

Duxbury, N., Garrett-Petts, W.F. and MacLennan, D. (2015) Cultural mapping as cultural inquiry: Introduction to an emerging field of practice, in N. Duxbury, W.F. Garrett-Petts, and D. MacLennan (eds), *Cultural Mapping as Cultural Inquiry*, New York: Routledge, pp 1–44.

Edensor, T. (2000) Walking in the British Countryside: Reflexivity, Embodied Practices and Ways to Escape, *Body & Society* 6(3/4): 81–106.

Enright, B., Facer, K. and Larner, W. (2016) Reframing Co-production: Gender, relational academic labour and the university, in E. Jupp, J. Pykett and F. Smith (eds) *Emotional states: Sites and spaces of affective governance*, London: Routledge.

Evans, G. (2015) Designing legacy and the legacy of design: London 2012 and the Regeneration Games, *Architectural Research Quarterly* 18: 353–66. doi:10.1017/S1359135515000081

Evans, G. (2013) Cultural Planning and Sustainable Development, in G. Baker and D. Stevenson (eds), *The Ashgate Research Companion to Planning and Culture*, London, New York: Routledge, pp 223–8.

Evans, G. (2005) Measure for Measure: Evaluating the Evidence of Culture's Contribution to Regeneration, *Urban Studies* 42: 959–83. doi:10.1080/00420980500107102

Evans, G. and Foord, J. (2008) Cultural mapping and sustainable communities: planning for the arts revisited, *Cultural Trends* 17: 65. doi:10.1080/09548960802090634

Facer, K. and Enright, B. (2016) *Creating Living Knowledge*, Bristol: University of Bristol, pp 5, 95, 106–19.

Facer, K. and Pahl, K. (2017) (ed) *Valuing interdisciplinary collaborative research: Beyond impact*, Bristol: Policy Press.

Feldman, A. (1998) Implementing and assessing the power of conversation in the teaching of action research, *Teacher Education Quarterly*, 25(2): 27–42.

Fish, R. and Church, A. (2013) *A conceptual framework for Cultural Ecosystem Services Working Paper*, Exeter: Centre for Rural Policy Research: University of Excter.

Fischer, E. M. and Knutti, R. (2015) Anthropogenic contribution to global occurrence of heavy-precipitation and high-temperature extremes, *Nature Climate Change* 5: 560–4.

Fleetwood, N. (2005) Authenticating practices: Producing 'The Real' in youth videos, in S. Maira and E. Soep (eds) *Youthscapes: The popular, the national, the global*, Philadelphia: University of Pennsylvania Press, pp 55-72.

Florida, R. (2002) *The Rise of the Creative Class. And How It's Transforming Work, Leisure and Everyday Life*, New York: Basic Books.

Florida, R. (2005) *Cities and the Creative Class*, London: Routledge.

Foucault, M. (1976) *The History of Sexuality: An Introduction* (Vol 1), New York: Vintage Books.

Foucault, M. (1995) *Discipline and Punish: The Birth of the Prison*, translated by Alan Sheridan, New York: Vintage.

Foucault, M. (2003) *Society Must Be Defended: Lectures at the College de France, 1975–1976*, translated by David Macey, New York: Picador.

Fox, R. (2013) Resisting participation: critiquing participatory research methodologies with young people, *Journal of Youth Studies*, 16(8): 986–99.

Frederickson, N. and Petrides, K.V. (2008) Ethnic, gender and socio-economic group differences in academic performance and secondary school selection: A longitudinal analysis, *Learning and Individual Differences* 18: 144–51.

Freeman, J. (1970) The Tyranny of Structurelessness, www.jofreeman.com/joreen/tyranny.htm

Freire, P. (1970, 2001, 2005) *Pedagogy of the Oppressed*, London: Continuum.

FreshMinds (2008) Establishing a baseline for public engagement: Guiding your strategy.

Funtowitz, S. and Ravetz, J. (1993) Science for the post-normal age, *Futures* 25: 739–55.

Gadamer, H. (1992) *Truth and method*, second revised edition, NY: Crossroad.

Gallagher, M. (2008) 'Power is not an evil': Rethinking power in participatory methods, *Children's Geographies*, 6(2): 137–50.

Gardner, H. (2006) *Multiple intelligences: New horizons in theory and practice*, New York: Basic Books.

Garland-Thomson, R. (2011) Misfits: a feminist materialist disability concept, *Hypatia* 26 (3): 591–609.

Garland-Thomson, R. (2012) The case for conserving disability, *Bioethical Inquiry* 9: 339–55.

Geertz, C. (1973) *The Interpretation of Culture*, New York: Basic Books.

Geertz, C. (1983) *Local Knowledge*, New York: Basic Books.

Gell Man, M. (2009) Interstitial travel, A personal phenomenology of walking and mapping, Master of Visual Studies Thesis, Toronto: University of Toronto.

Gell Man, M. (2016) The exploding archive, Research Praxis PhD, in progress, Queen's University.

Goffman, E. (1959) *The presentation of self in everyday life*, London: Penguin Books.

Goodchild, M.F. (1992) Geographical information science, *International Journal of Geographical Information Systems* 6, 31–45

Government of Canada (2008) Statement of apology to former students of Indian Residential Schools, 11 June, www.aadnc-aandc.gc.ca/eng/1100100015644/1100100015649

Govier, L. (2010) *Leaders in co-creation? Why and how museums could develop their co-creative practice with the public, building on ideas from the performing arts and other non-museum organisations*, University of Leicester, www2.le.ac.uk/departments/museumstudies/rcmg/publications

Gramsci, A. (1978) *Selections from the Prison Notebooks*, edited by Q. Hoare and G. Nowell Smith, London: Lawrence & Wishart.

Gramsci, A. (2005) *Selections from the Prison Notebooks*, London: Lawrence & Wishart Ltd.

Grand, A., Davies, G., Holliman, R. and Adams, A. (2015) Mapping public engagement with research in a UK university, *PLoS ONE* 10 (4): 1–19.

Grover, S. (2004) Why won't they listen to us? On giving power and voice to children participating in social research, *Childhood*, 11(1): 81–93.

Habermas, J. (1987) *The theory of communicative action: a critique of functionalist research*, translated by T. McCarthy, Vol. 2 Lifeworld and System, London: Polity Press.

Halberstam, J. (2011) *The Queer Art of Failure*. Durham, NC: Duke University Press.

Hall, M.H. and Reed, P.B. (1998) Shifting the burden: how much can government download to the non-profit sector, *Canadian Public Administration* 41(1): 1–20.

Hallett, L. (2012) Measuring Community Radio Audiences. ECREA Radio Evolution: Technology, Contents, Audiences Conference Proceedings, pp 377–86.

Hannan, L. and McNulty, P. (2013) *Bridging the Gap: Scoping Exercise Report*, London: Share Academy, www.londonmuseumsgroup.org/wp-content/uploads/2013/06/Share-Academy-Scoping-Exercise-Report-Final.pdf

Haraway, D. (1988) Situated knowledges: the science question in feminism and the privilege of partial perspective, *Feminist Studies* 14 (3): 575–99.

Harmon, K. (2004) *You Are Here: Personal Geographies and Other Maps of the Imagination*, Hong Kong: Tributary Books.

Harris, C. (2008) *The Reluctant Land: Society, Space and Environment in Canada before Confederation*, Vancouver: University of British Columbia Press.

Harrison, T. (2000) Urban policy: addressing wicked problems, in H. Davies and S.M. Nutley (eds) *What Works: Evidence Based Policy and Practice in Public Services*, Bristol: Policy Press.

Hawkes, J. (2001) *The Fourth Pillar of Sustainability: Culture's Essential Role in Public Planning*, Melbourne: Common Ground.

Hausman, B.L. (1995) *Changing Sex: Transsexualism, Technology and the Idea of Gender*, Durham, NC, and London: Duke University Press.

Heddon, D. (2012) Turning 40: 40 turns. Walking & friendship, *Performance Research*, 17(2): 67–75.

Heddon, D. (2015) Going for a walk: a verbatim play, *Studies in Theatre and Performance* 35(3): 177–88.

Heddon, D. and Turner, C. (2010) Walking women: interviews with artists on the move, *Performance Research* 15(4): 14–22.

Heddon, D. and Turner, C. (2012) Walking women: shifting the tales and scales of mobility, *Contemporary Theatre Review* 22(2): 224–36.

Herbert-Cheshire, L. (2000) Contemporary strategies in rural community development in Australia: a governmentality perspective, *Journal of Rural Studies* 16(2): 203–215.

Hirsch, J. (1981) *Family Photographs: Content, Meaning, and Effect*, Oxford: Oxford University Press.

Ho, P.S.Y. (2013) Introduction to the Special Section – Remapping the erotic: Interrogations from Asia, *Sexualities*, 16(1/2): 3-11.

Holcombe, S. (2008) Constraints on researchers acting as change agents, in J. Hunt, D.E. Smith, S. Garling, and W. Sanders (eds) *Contested governance: Culture, power and institutions in indigenous Australia*, CAEPR Research Monograph No 29, ANU E Press, Canberra, pp 55-71.

Holloway, S. and Valentine, G. (2000) *Children's geographies: Playing, living and learning*, London: Routledge.

Hooks, B. (1992) *Black Looks: Race and Representation*, London: Turnaround.

Hussain, R. and Moore, G. (2012) *The UCL-led Beacon for Public Engagement Final Evaluation Report*, London: Public Engagement Unit, UCL.

Iervolino, I. (2014) 'Learning to change for the better', Who Am I? Hacking into the Science Museum, Science Museum report (unpublished).

Imrie, R. and Thomas, H. (2008) The interrelationships between environment and disability, *Local Environment* 13(6): 477–83.

Ingold, T. (2010) Footprints through the weather-world: walking, breathing, knowing, *Journal of the Royal Anthropological Institute* 16(1): 121–39.

Ingold, T and Lee, J. (2008) *Ways of Walking: Ethnography and practice on foot*, London: Ashgate.

Innes, M., McDermont, M., and Larner, W. and Ersoy, A. (2016) *The instrumentation of governance: how regulation is being reconfigured in advanced liberal societies*, Working Paper.

Irish, S. (2010) *Suzanne Lacy: Spaces Between*, Minneapolis, MN: University of Minnesota Press.

Jackson, A. (2015) *Share Academy Evaluation: Final Evaluation Report*, London: Share Academy, www.londonmuseumsgroup.org/wp-content/uploads/2015/07/Share-Academy-Final-Evaluation-Report-2015.pdf

Jasanoff, S. (2006) *States of knowledge: The co-production of science and the social order*, London and New York: Routledge.

Jeanneney, J. (2007) *Google and the Myth of Universal Knowledge: A View from Europe*, London: University of Chicago Press.

Jeffs, M. (2013) *Future pressures on Welsh public services: Financial, demand and other cost pressures to 2025 and a review of potential responses*, Report by Welsh Public Services, www.walespublicservices2025.org.uk/files/2016/03/Mark-Jeffs-WPS2025-Summary-Report1.pdf

John, B. and Kagan, S. (2014) Extreme Climate Events as Opportunities for Radical Open Citizenship, *Open Citizenship* 5(1): 60–75.

Johnson, A. (2008) *Mnemonic maps, talking landscapes: Spatially narrated Kaajèt-Crow Clan: an examination of K'àma Dzêa-Ptarmigan Heart as a geospatial narrative*, unpublished dissertation, University of British Columbia.

Johnson, A. (2011) *Mnemonic maps, talking landscapes: Spatially narrated Kaajèt Crow Clan, an examination of K'àma Dzêa-Ptarmigan Heart as a geospatial narrative*, dissertation, Trent University.

Joseph, M. (2002) *Against the Romance of Community*, Minneapolis, MN: University of Minnesota Press.

Kafer, A. (2013) *Feminist, Queer, Crip*, Bloomington: Indiana University Press.

Katz, J. (1997) Ethnography's warrants, *Sociological Methods & Research*, 25(4): 391–423.

Knowle West Media Centre (2014) *Approach to community development and measuring impact.*

Lannin, L., Bent, C., Jackson, A., McNulty, P., Willcocks, J. and Chatterjee, H. (2014) Deepening the remit of education: exploring the benefit of collaborative partnerships between museums and higher education, *Journal of Education in Museums* 35: 53–63.

Lacy, S., Jacob, M.J., Phillips, P.C., Gablik, S., Májozo, E.C., Gómez-Peña, G., Lippard, L.R., Baca, J.F., Kelley, J., Kaprow, A. et al (1995) *Mapping the Terrain: New Genre Public Art*, Seattle: Bay Press.

Larner, W. and Butler, M. (2005) Governmentalities of local partnerships: the rise of a 'Partnering State' in New Zealand, *Studies in Political Economy* 75 (Spring): 85–108.

Latour, B. (1993) *We have never been modern*, translated by Catherine Porter, Cambridge MA: Harvard University Press.

Leavy, P. (2015) *Method Meets Art: Arts-Based Research Practice*, London, The Guildford Press.

Ledwith, M. (2011) *Community Development: A Critical Approach*, Bristol: Policy Press.

Lefebvre, H. (1974) *The Production of Space*, translated by D. Nicholson-Smith, Oxford: Blackwell.

Lehr, J.L., McCallie, E., Davies, S., Caron, B., Gammon, B. and Duensing, S. (2007) The value of "dialogue events" as sites of learning: An exploration of research and evaluation frameworks, *International Journal of Science Education* 29(12): 1467–87.

Leipoldt, E.A. (2006) Disability experience: a contribution from the margins towards a sustainable future, *Journal of Futures Studies* 10(3): 15–32.

Leshner, A. (2003) Public engagement with science, *Science* 299 (5609): 977.

Levitas, R. (2013) *Utopia as Method*, London: Palgrave Macmillan.

Lewis, P. (1976) *Bristol Channel and Community Television*, London: Independent Broadcasting Authority.

Li, W. (2005) Community decision-making: participation in development, *Annals of Tourism Research* 33(1): 132–43.

Lister, R. (2003) *Citizenship: Feminist Perspectives*, London: Palgrave Macmillan.

Literat, I. (2013) Participatory mapping with urban youth: The visual elicitation of socio-spatial research data, *Learning, Media and Technology*, 38(2): 198–216.

Longley, A. and Duxbury, N. (2016) Introduction: Mapping cultural intangibles, *City, Culture and Society* 7: 1–7

Lowry, G., Levin, M.S. and Tsang, H (Maraya) (2013) Talk/performance text excerpt. Speculative Cities Symposium, University of British Columbia, Vancouver. May 07.

Lowry, G., Levin, M.S. and Tsang, H (Maraya) (2015) Maraya as visual research: mapping urban displacement and narrating artistic inquiry, in N. Duxbury, W.F. Garrett-Petts, and D. MacLennan (eds) *Cultural mapping as cultural inquiry*, New York: Routledge: pp 319–37.

Lovink, G. (2011) *The Society of the Query and the Googlisation of our Lives: A tribute to Joseph Weizenbaum*, 15th Karlsruhe Dialogues, Karlsruhe Institute of Technology, www.zak.kit.edu/downloads/Lovink_8_fertig.pdf

Luke, R., Clement, A., Terada, R., Bortolussi, D., Booth, C., Brooks, D. and Christ, D. (2004) The promise and perils of a participatory approach to developing an open source community learning network, In Proceedings of the eighth conference on Participatory design: Artful integration: interweaving media, materials and practices. ACM. 1. pp 11-19.

Lynch, B. (2015) *Our Museum: A five-year perspective from a critical friend*, Summary Report, Paul Hamlyn Foundation.

Mackinnon, D. and Derickson, K.D. (2012) From resilience to resourcefulness: A critique of resilience policy and activism, *Progress in Human Geography* 37(2): 253–70.

Makagon, D. and Neumann, M. (2009) *Recording culture: audio documentary and the ethnographic experience*, Thousand Oaks, CA: Sage Publications.

Mandel, J.L. (2003) Negotiating expectations in the field: gatekeepers, research fatigue and cultural biases, *Singapore Journal of Tropical Geography*, 24(2): 198–210.

References

Maraya (Tsang, Levin and Lowry) Gallery Installation and Public Art Project. Centre A, the Vancouver International Centre for Contemporary Asian Art. November 5 – December 17, 2011. http://centrea.org/2011/11/maraya/

Marinetto, M (2003) Who wants to be an active citizen? The politics and practice of community involvement, *Sociology* 37(1): 103–20

Massey, D. (2001) Living in Wythenshawe, in I. Borden, J. Kerr, J. Rendell, and A. Pivaro (eds), *The Unknown City: Contesting Architecture and Social Space*, Cambridge, MA: MIT Press, pp 458–75.

McDermott, F. (2002) *Inside group work: A guide to reflective practice*, Crows Nest NSW: Allen and Unwin.

McDermont, M., Cowan, D. and Prendergrast, J. (2009) Structuring governance: A case study of the new organizational provision of public service delivery, *Critical Social Policy* 29 (4): 677–702.

McDermont, M. and the Productive Margins Research Forum (2012) *Productive Margins Research Initiative Case for Support*, www.productivemargins.ac.uk/files/2016/01/august-2012.pdf

MEA (Millennium Ecosystem Assessment) (2005) *Ecosystems and human well-being: Synthesis*, Washington, DC.: Island Press.

Mebratu, D. (1998) Sustainability and sustainable development: historical and conceptual review, *Environmental Impact Assessment Review* 18: 493–520.

Meekosha, H. and Shuttleworth, R. (2009) What's so "Critical" about Critical Disability Studies?, *Australian Journal of Human Rights* 15(1): 47–75.

Merleau-Ponty, M. (1962) *1908–1961: Phenomenology of Perception*, New York: Humanities Press.

Meyer, M. (2010) The rise of the knowledge broker, *Science Communication* 329(1): 118–22.

Merriam, S.B. and Simpson, E.L. (2000) *A guide to research for educators and trainers of adults*, Malabar: Krieger.

Moeran, B. (2007) From participant observation to observant participation, in S. Ybema, D. Yanow, H. Wels and F. Kamsteeg (eds) *Organizational ethnography: Studying the complexities of everyday life*, London: SAGE Publications, pp 139–56.

Mohan, G. (1999) Not so distant, not so strange: The personal and the political in participatory research, *Ethics, Place and Environment*, 2(1): 41–54.

Monti, D.J. (1992) On the risks and rewards of 'going native', *Qualitative Sociology*, 15(3): 325–32.

Moran, J.M. (2002) *There's No Place Like Home Video*, Minneapolis, MN: University of Minnesota Press.

Murray, C. (2006) Peer led focus groups and young people, *Children and Society*, 20(4): 273–86.

National Co-ordinating Centre for Public Engagement (NCCPE) (2010) *The Engaged University: A Manifesto for Public Engagement*, www.publicengagement.ac.uk/sites/default/files/Manifesto%20for%20Public%20Engagement%20Final%20January%202010.pdf

Newman, J. (ed) (2005) *Remaking governance: Peoples, politics and the public sphere*, Bristol: Policy Press.

Newman, J. (2010) Towards a pedagogical state? Summoning the 'empowered' citizen, *Citizenship Studies* 14(6): 711–23.

NHS Tayside (2010) *Health Equity Strategy 2010: Communities in Control*, www.nhstaysidecdn.scot.nhs.uk/NHSTaysideWeb/idcplg?IdcService=GET_SECURE_FILE&Rendition=web&RevisionSelectionMethod=LatestReleased&noSaveAs=1&dDocName=prod_217621

Norman, D.W. (2014) Control Mapping: Peter Pitseolak and Zacharias Kunuk on Reclaiming Inuit Photographic Images and Imaging, *Decolonization: Indigeneity, Education & Society* 3(1): 48–72.

Noorani, T. (2013) *Law School*, Bristol: University of Bristol.

Nowotny, H., Scott, P. and Gibbons, M. (2001) *Re-thinking science: Knowledge and the public in an age of uncertainty*, Cambridge: Wiley-Blackwell.

Nyden, P. (2006) The challenges and opportunities of engaged scholarship, in L. Silka (ed), *Scholarship in action: Applied research and community change*, Washington, DC: US Department of Housing and Urban Development, pp 11–26.

O'Neill, P. and Wilson, M. (2010) *Curating and the Educational Turn*, London: Open Editions.

O'Riordan, T. (2001) *Globalism, Localism and Identity: Fresh perspectives on the transition to sustainability*, London: Earthscan Publications.

Ontario-MCP (2010) *Cultural Resource Mapping: A Guide for Municipalities*, Municipal Cultural Planning Incorporated (MCPI), http://www.ontariomcp.ca/toolkits/CulturalResourceMapping_digital.pdf

Ostrom, E. (1996) Crossing the great divide: Coproduction, synergy, and development, *World Development* 24: 1073–87.

Pain, R. (2003) Youth, age, and the representation of fear, *Capital & Class*, 27(2): 151–71.

Pain, R. (2004) Social geography: Participatory research, *Progress in Human Geography*, 28(5): 652–63.

Pain, R. and Francis, P. (2003) Reflections on participatory research, *Area*, 35(1): 46–54.

Pain, R. and Kindon, S. (2007) 'Participatory geographies', *Environment and Planning A*, 39(12): 2807–12.

Pain, R., Kesby, M. and Askins, K. (2011) Geographies of impact: Power, participation and potential, *Area* 43: 183–8.

Pain, R., Whitman, G., Milledge, D. and Lune Rivers Trust (2012) *Participatory Action Research Toolkit: An Introduction to Using PAR as an Approach to Learning*, Durham, UK: Department of Geography, Durham University, www.dur.ac.uk/resources/beacon/PARtoolkit.pdf

Pain, R., K. Askins, S. Banks, T. Cook, G. Crawford, L. Crookes, S. Darby, et al. (2015) *Mapping alternative impact: Alternative approaches to impact from co-produced research*, Durham: Centre for Social Justice and Community Action, Durham University.

Patel, Z., Greyling, S., Parnell, S. and Pirie, G. (2015) Co-producing urban knowledge: experimenting with an alternative to 'best practice' for Cape Town, South Africa, *International Development Planning Review*, 37(2): 187–203.

Paterson, M. (2009) Haptic geographies: Ethnography, haptic knowledges and sensuous dispositions, *Progress in Human Geography*, 33(6); 766–88.

Peat, F.D. (1996) *Blackfoot physics: A journey into the Native American universe*, London: Fourth Estate.

Perkins, C. (2007) Community mapping, *The Cartographic Journal* 44(2): 127–37.

Perry, B. and Atherson, M. (2017) Beyond critique: The value of co-production in realising just cities?, *Local Environment – The International Journal of Justice and Sustainability*, pp 1–16.

Piccini, A.A. and Insole, P. (2013) Your place or mine? Crowdsourced planning, moving image archives and community archaeology, *Archäologische Informationen*, 36: 31–43.

Pink, S., Hubbard, P., O'Neill, M. and Radley, A. (2010) Walking across disciplines: from ethnography to arts practice, *Visual Studies* 25(1): 1–7.

Plieninger, T., Dijks, S., Oteros-Rozas, E. and Bieling, C. (2013) Assessing, mapping, and quantifying cultural ecosystem services at community level, *Land Use Policy* 33, 118–29. doi:10.1016/j.landusepol.2012.12.013

Polk, M. (2015) (ed) *Co-producing knowledge for sustainable cities: Joining forces for change*, London: Routledge.

Pratt, G. and Johnston, C. (2013) Staging testimony in Nanay, *Geographical Review* 103(2): 288–303.

Rambaldi, G., Kyem, P.A.K., McCall, M. and Weiner, D. (2006) Participatory Spatial Information Management and Communication in Developing Countries, *The Electronic Journal of Information Systems in Developing Countries* 25.

Rancière, J. (2006) *The Politics of Aesthetics*, London: Continuum.

Ravn, S. and Duff, C. (2015) Putting the party down on paper: A novel method for mapping youth drug use in private settings, *Health & Place*, 31: 124–32.

Ray, B.C. (1976) *African religions: Symbol, ritual, and community*, Englewood Cliffs, NJ: Prentice-Hall.

Ray, S.J. (2009) Risking bodies in the wild: the "corporeal unconscious" of American adventure culture, *Journal of Sport and Social Issues* 33(3): 257–84.

Read, S. (2012) *A Map of Alkborough Flats and the Humber Estuary to explore the processes impacting upon the decision to establish a Managed Realignment Site*, AHRC Landscape & Environment Programme, Impact Fellowship.

Rendell, J. (2008) *Art and Architecture: A Place Between*, London: Routledge.

Rhoten, S. and Calhoun, C. (eds) (2011) *Knowledge Matters: The Public Mission of the Research University*, New York: Columbia University Press.

Richardson, L. (2000) Writing: A method of inquiry, in K. Denzin and Y. Lincoln (eds) *Handbook of Qualitative Methods*, Thousand Oaks: Sage Publications, pp 923–48.

Rogers, J., Irini, P. and Andrew, P. (eds) (2014) *Open Collaborative Making: A Digital Perspective*, London: Uniform Publications.

Rowe, G. and Frewer, L. (2000) Public Participation Methods: A Framework for Evaluation, *Science, Technology and Human Values* 25(3): 3–29.

Rowe, G. and Frewer, L.J. (2005) A typology of public engagement mechanisms, *Science, Technology & Human Values* 30(2): 251–90.

Ryan, R.L. (2011) The social landscape of planning: Integrating social and perceptual research with spatial planning information, *Landscape and Urban Planning* 100: 361–3.

Said, E. (1978) *Orientalism*, London: Vintage Books.

Sandell, R. (2002) *Museums, Society, Inequality*, Abingdon: Routledge.

Sandell, R. and Nightingale, E. (2012) *Museums, Equality and Social Justice*, London and New York: Routledge.

Sanderson, P. and Thomas, P. (2014) Troubling identities: race, place and positionality among young people in two towns in northern England, *Journal of Youth Studies*, 17(9): 1168–86.

Sarkowsky, K. (2007) *AlterNative Spaces: Constructions of Space in Native American and First Nations' Literatures*, Heidelberg: Winter.

Schlesier, K.H. (1987) *The Wolves of Heaven: Cheyenne Shamanism, Ceremonies and Prehistoric Origins*, Norman: University of Oklahoma Press.

Sedgwick, E.K. (1994) *Tendencies*, New York and London: Routledge.

Siepmann, C.A. and Reisberg, S. (1948) 'To secure these rights': Coverage of a radio documentary, *The Public Opinion Quarterly*, 12(4): 649–58.

Shildrick, M. (2000) Contagious Encounters and the Ethics of Risk, *Journal of Medical Humanities* 21(4): 215–27.

Sillitoe, P. (2007) Anthropologists only Need Apply: Challenges of Applied Anthropology, *The Journal of the Royal Anthropological Institute* 13(1): 147–65.

Silko, L.M. (1996) *Yellow Woman and a Beauty of the Spirit*, New York: Touchstone.

Simon, N. (2010) *The Participatory Museum*, San Francisco: Museum 20.

Skeggs, B. (1997) *Formations of Class and Gender: Becoming Respectable*, Theory, Culture and Society series, London: Sage.

Skeggs, B. et al (2002) 'Oh goodness, I am watching reality TV': Techniques for telling the reflexive self, in T. May (ed) *Qualitative research in action*, London: Sage.

Skelton, T. (2008) Research with children and young people: exploring tensions between ethics, competence and participation, *Children's Geographies*, 6(1): 21–36.

Smeets, R. and Yoshida, R. (2005) *Cultural mapping and the safeguarding of the intangible cultural heritage*, Paris: NESCO.

Soja, E.W. (1996) *Thirdspace: Journeys to Los Angeles and other real-and-imagined places*, Cambridge, MA: Blackwell.

Soja, E.W. (2010) *Seeking spatial justice*, Minneapolis: University of Minnesota Press.

Soja, E. (2013) *Seeking social justice*, Minneapolis: University of Minnesota Press

Solnit, R. (2005) *A Field Guide to Getting Lost*, New York: Viking.

Sparkes, M. (1998) Mapped bodies and disembodied maps, in H.J. Nast and S. Pile (eds) *Places through the body*, London and New York: Routledge.

Spivak, G.C. (2010) Can the subaltern speak?, Reprinted and revised in R. Morris (ed) *Can the subaltern speak? Reflections on the history of an idea*, New York: Columbia University Press.

Stephens L., Ryan-Collins J. and Boyle D. (2008) *Co-production: a Manifesto for Growing the Core Economy*, London: New Economic Foundation (NEF).

Stewart, S. (2007) *Cultural mapping toolkit*, Vancouver: Creative City Network of Canada and 2010 Legacies Now.

Stilgoe, J. (2003) *Citizen Science*, London: DEMOS Publication.

Stilgoe, J., Lock, S.J. and Wilsdon, J. (2014) Why should we promote public engagement with science?, *Public Understanding of Science* 23(4): 1–15.

Smith, L.T. (1999) *Decolonizing methodologies: Research and indigenous peoples*, London: Zed Books.

Swantz, M. (1996) A Personal position paper on participatory research: Personal quest for living knowledge, *Qualitative Inquiry*, 2(1): 120–36.

Theodore, N. (2015) Subject spaces: on the ethics of co-producing urban research, University Seminar, University of Bristol, Bristol.

Trench, B. (2008) Towards an analytical framework of science communication models, in D. Cheng, M. Claessens, T. Gascoigne, J. Metcalfe, B. Schiele and S. Shi (eds), *Communicating Science in Social Contexts: New Models, New Practices*, New York: Springer, pp 119–38.

Truth and Reconciliation Commission of Canada (2015) *Honouring the truth: Reconciling for the future*, Executive summary of final report, Winnipeg: Truth and Reconciliation Commission of Canada.

Tuckman, B.W. (1965) Developmental sequence in small groups, *Psychological Bulletin* 63(6): 384–99.

UNESCO (2009) Culture and sustainable development, *Examples of Institutional Innovation and Proposal of a New Cultural Policy Profile*, Culture 21.

Valentine, G. (1999) Being seen and heard? The ethical complexities of working with children and young people at home and at school, *Ethics, Place and Environment*, 2(2): 141–55.

Van Blerk, L. and Ansell, N. (2007) Participatory feedback and dissemination with and for children: reflections from research with young migrants in southern Africa, *Children's Geographies*, 5(3): 313–24.

Van Kerkhoff, L.E. and Lebel, L. (2015) Coproductive capacities: Rethinking science-governance relations in a diverse world, *Ecology and Society*, 20(1): 14.

Vromen, A. and Collin, P. (2010) Everyday youth participation? contrasting views from Australian policymakers and young people. *Young*, 18(1): 97–112.

Warner, M. (ed) (1994) *Fear of a Queer Planet: Queer Politics and Social Theory*, Minneapolis, MN: University of Minnesota Press.

References

Warner, M. (ed) (2005) *Publics and counterpublics*, New York: Zone Books.

Weber, M. (1978) *Economy and Society*, Berkeley, CA: University of California Press.

Weller, S. (2006) Tuning-in to teenagers! Using radio phone-in discussions in research with young people, *International Journal of Social Research Methodology*, 9(4): 303–15.

Welsh Government (2014) *Commission on Public Service Governance and Delivery: Full Report*, www.lgcplus.com/Journals/2014/01/21/d/r/x/Commission-on-Public-Service-Governance-and-Delivery-Wales.pdf

Wilkinson, C. (2017) Going 'backstage': observant participation in research with young people, *Children's Geographies*, 1–7.

Wilson, I. (1989) (1st US edn) *The after death experience: The physics of the non-physical*, New York: Morrow.

Wiseman, P. (2014) Everyday embodied citizenship and disabled young people, August, UofG Sociology, www.glasgowsociology.com/everyday-embodied-citizenship-and-disabled-young-people

Wolfe, P. (2006) Settler colonialism and the elimination of the native, *Journal of Genocide Research* 8(4): 387–409.

Wright, D.E. and Mahiri, J. (2012) Literacy learning within community action projects for social change, *Journal of Adolescent and Adult Literacy*, 56(2): 123–31.

Wunderlich, F.M. (2005) Walking and rhythmicity: sensing urban space, Walk21-VI Conference, Zurich, http://discovery.ucl.ac.uk/1314823/1/Wunderlich_1314823_Walking%20and%20rhythmicity_Matos_edited%26proofread1.pdf

Wyman, M. (2004) *The Defiant Imagination: Why Culture Matters*, Vancouver: Douglas & McIntyre.

Wynne, B., Stilgoe, J. and Wilsdon, J. (2005) *The Public Value of Science*, DEMOS Publication.

Wynne-Jones, S., North, P. and Routledge, P. (2015) Practising participatory geographies: potentials, problems and politics, *Area*, doi: 10.1111/area.12186

Zimmerman, P. (1995) *Reel Families: A Social History of Amateur Film*, Bloomington: Indiana University Press.

Index

References to figures are in *italics*

A
Abbott, D. 181–2
Adams, Suze 180, 186
Agbetu, Toyin 56
Ahmed, S. 144–5
Anderson, B. 183, 196
Anderson, J. 187
Andrews, G. 188
Andrews, Leighton 203
Arabic-speaking women's group 34–8, 41–4
　impacts identified by the women 39–40
Arnolfini Gallery, Bristol 107, 109
Arts and Humanities Research Council (AHRC) 110, 180, 186, 192, 205, 210
Arts Council England 48, 49, 55, 103, 139
Australia *see* collaborative research

B
Banks, M. 29–30
Bass, S. 120
Beacon for Public Engagement (UCL) *see* university public engagement
Beierle, T.C. 123
Benjamin, W. 102
Bishop, C. 99, 102, 103
Boyle, D. 202
Bristol Channel (TV channel) 112
Bristol Method 3
Bristol One Parent Project (BOPP) 62–3
Bristol University *see* community groups and universities; regulatory aesthetics; walking practice, and disability
Brody, H. 165
Butler, J. 197
Byrne, A. 89

C
Cahill, C. 86, 87
Cajete, G. 163, 164–5
Calthorpe Project 18–20
Cameron, D. 77
Camley Street Nature Park 17
Canada *see* mapping (of contested geographies)
Cardiff University 114–116, 203
see also community groups and universities
Carpiano, R.M. 187
Castells, M. 134
Central Saint Martins, London 50–3
Chan, K.M. 122
Chávez, V. 87
Cheddie, J. 56
Cinderby, S. 124
Close and Remote 77, 79
co-production
　advancing the debates 207–9

concept of 1–3, 202–4
funding models 205
and impact agenda 204–10
and institutionalisation 210–11
of research 204–11
of research and of public services 209–11
Coates, P. 122–3
Cohen, Sue 61, 65, 66, 68, 73, 74, 76–7, 78–9, 83
collaborative research 29–45
　and Arabic-speaking women's group 34–8, 39–40, 41–3, 44
　creating a shared space 41–2
　definition 30
　dynamic nature of 44
　enabling conditions for impact 41–4
　impacts of 38–45
　intuitive methodology 43–4
　key findings of 30–1
　methodology 30–1, 43–4
　and Persian women's group 31–4, 39–40, 42–3
　shared agenda 42–3
　value of 44–5
community groups and universities 61–84
　academic lead 72–3
　aims of programme 61–2
　arts practice as research method 73–4, 76–8
　background of community groups 62–4
　equality and time 69–72, 80–1
　and ethics 82–4
　hybrid community researcher 81–2
　impact and challenges of 80–4
　impact of regulatory systems 78–80
　interdisciplinary tensions 74–8, 82–4
　recruitment process 78–80
　research process 72–8
　sites of experimentation 64–9
community-oriented research 4–5
community radio *see* participatory research
Comunian, R. 49, 58
Cox, S.M. 99, 102
Cretney, R. 196–7
Crow, L. 190–1, 192
Culhane, Anne-Marie 116
Cultural Capital Exchange 49
Cultural Ecosystem Services Framework 125, *126*
cultural mapping 119–35
　benefits of 132–5
　concept of 122–3, *123*, 125
　creative methods of 123–4
　and Cultural Ecosystem Services Framework 125, *126*
　and culture 121–3

233

and engaging with water communities 124–33
in festivals 129–33, *130–1*, *133*, 134
in focus groups 126–9, *127–8*
and sustainability 120–3
types of interactions 130–2

D

Dalal-Clayton, B. 120
DeLemo, J.L. 87
Deloria Jr, V. 166
Derickson, K.D. 196
Dineen, R. 202
disabled people *see* walking practice, and disability
Doherty, Claire 103
Donington, K. 53
Drakeford, Mark 203
Dunbar-Hester, C. 87–8
Duxbury, N. 123, 125, 129, 135

E

Edensor, T. 187
Elliott, Eva 76
Enright, B. 117
ethics 82–3
evaluation
  and regulatory aesthetics 104–5
  and university public engagement 14–15, 19–20, 22–3, 26–7
Evans, G. 129
Evans, Nathan 61, 65, 66, 76, 81–2, 84
Evans, Penny 103

F

Facer, K. 117
Fleetwood, N. 93
Florida, R. 102
Food Junctions Cookbook 20–1
Food Junctions Festival *16*, 17–18
Foodpaths Movement *16*, 18–20
Forum model 64–5, 114–15
Foucault, M. 146
Francis, P. 86, 96
Fraser, Mike 108, 109
Frederickson, N. 55
Freeman, J. 117
Freire, P. 206
FreshMinds 13–14
Frewer, L. 12

G

Garland-Thomson, R. 183–5, 193
Garneau, David 157, *157*
Gellman, M. 158
Gendered Intelligence *see* museums and gender identity
Geographic Information Systems (GIS) 122, 123, 124
Geographies of Coproduction 205–6
geography (discipline of) 1–2, 205–6
Gilmore, A. 49, 58
Google Cultural Institute 50–3
Govier, L. 147

H

Hackney Museum and Archives 53–6
Hackney Wick Festival 130, *130*
Hallett, L. 91
Haq, Nav 109
Haraway, D. 145
Harmon, K. 168
Harris, C. 156–7, 158
Harris, M. 202
Harrison, P. 183
Harvey, David 176
Heddon, D. 179, 180–1, 183, 185, 186–7, 189, 193, 196, 198
Herbert, Allan 61, 65, 66, 69, 70, 75, 76, 79–80
Higher Education Funding Council for England (HEFCE) 12–13, 47, 207
Ho, P.S.Y. 86
Hooks, B. 56
Hopkinson, David 113
Housden, Sir Peter 204
Hussein, Moestak 75–6
hybrid community researchers 81–2
Hydrocitizenship project 125

I

indigenous people *see* mapping (of contested geographies)
Ingold, T. 187, 190, 191
interdisciplinarity 74–8, 82–4
intuitive methodology 43–4

J

Jackson, A. 58
Jasanoff, S. 2, 206
Jeanneney, J. 51
John, B. 181
Johnson, A. 170
Jones, Carwyn 203

K

Kagan, S. 181
Katz, J. 86
KCC Live *see* participatory research
Kindon, S. 86
Know your Bristol on the Move 106, 110–14, 117
Knowle West Media Centre (KWMC) *see* regulatory aesthetics
Knowle West TV 112–13, 117
knowledge
  and arts practices 100
  horizontal and interactive system 22
  and power 146, 149
  University of Local Knowledge (ULK) 106, 107–10, 117

L

Lacy, Suzanne 107–8, 109
Lannin, L. 48
Larner, W. 1
Latour, B. 99
Lee, J. 187
Lee Valley, London *see* cultural mapping
Leipold, E.A. 193

Index

Leshner, A. 11
Lewis, P. 112
Life Chances agenda 77–8
Local Roots/Global Routes: the Legacies of Slavery in Hackney 53–6
Longley, A. 123, 125, 129, 135
Love the Lea Festival 130, 131, *131*, 134
Lowry, G. 174
Luke, R. 97

M

MacKinnon, D. 196
Mahiri, J. 91
Makagon, D. 93
Malbeuf, Amy 161, *161*
mapping (of contested geographies) 155–77
  collaborative approach 159–60
  and colonialism 155–8
  dialects of 167–73, *169*, *173*
  and indigenous worldviews 160–7, *161*, *165*
  and notion of space 172–3, *173*
  relational mapping 174–7
Massey, D. 197
McDermont, M. 64, 69, 114
Meekosha, H. 194
Merleau-Ponty, M. 162
Meyer, M. 49
Millennium Ecosystem Assessment (MEA) 121–2
Moeran, B. 87, 88
Mohan, G. 86
Monti, D.J. 87
Murray, C. 90
museums and gender identity 137–53
  background of Gendered Intelligence 138
  establishing the partnership 139–41
  ethnographic research approach 147–8
  legacy of 150–2
  and object displays 144–6
  and partnership working 146–50, 152–3
  the project 141–4
  see also universities and museums

N

National Co-ordinating Centre for Public Engagement (NCCPE) 11, 13, 58–9
NESTA 202, 210
Neumann, M. 93
New Economics Foundation (NEF) 202, 210
Nightingale, E. 148
Norman, D.W. 168–9
Nyden, P. 44

O

observant participation 87–8
Olden, Matt 115
O'Riordan, T. 43
Ostrom, E. 3

P

Pain, R. 86, 96
Participatory Action Research (PAR) 4–5
Participatory Geographic Information Systems (PGIS) 119, 124

participatory mapping *see* cultural mapping
participatory research 4, 85–97
  concept of youth-led 86–7
  critique of methodology 94–7
  dissemination 93–4, 97
  and focus groups 88–94
  methodology 85
  observant participation 87–8
Peat, D. 160
Peckham Cultural Institute 50–3
pedagogy of collegiality 87
Persian women's group 31–4, 42–3
  impacts identified by the women 39–40
Petrides, K.V. 55
Piccini, Angela 73–4, 76
  see also regulatory aesthetics
policy co-production 2, 3
Porter, S. 181–2
Productive Margins 106, 114–16, 117
  see also community groups and universities
public engagement in higher education *see* university public engagement

R

Rambaldi, G. 124
Rancière, J. 102–3, 106, 115
Ray, B. 170–1
Ray, S. 180, 191
regulatory aesthetics 99–118
  background of community groups 99–100
  context of 102–3
  and data 105
  evaluation 104–5
  and expectation 109–10
  and flow of money 117
  Key Performance Indicators 105
  Know your Bristol on the Move 106, 110–14, 117
  KWMC's contexts 103–5
  and personal relationships 117–18
  planning forms 105
  Productive Margins 106, 114–16, 117
  projects 106–16
  research questions 101
  and structures 117
  University of Local Knowledge (ULK) 106, 107–10, 117
regulatory systems, impact of 78–80
Reisberg, S. 93
Rendell, J. 190
Research Excellence Framework 1, 204–5
Reveal Festival 17–18
Richardson, L. 97
Rowe, G. 12
Royal Geographical Society 1–2, 205–6

S

Said, E. 144
Saltus-Hendrickson, Roiyah 77
Samzelius, Tove 61, 65, 66, 70, 71, 73, 74, 76, 80–1
Sandell, R. 148
Sarkowsky, K. 172
Schlesier, K.S. 166

Science Museum, London *see* museums and gender identity
Scotland 204, 210
Sedgwick, E.K. 146
Share Academy *see* universities and museums
Shildrick, M. 197
Shuttleworth, R. 194
Siepmann, C.A. 93
Silko, L.M. 161–2
Simon, N. 52, 147
Single Parent Action Network (SPAN) *see* community groups and universities
Situations 103–4
Skeggs, B. 145
Smith, L.T. 96, 97
Soep, E. 87
Soja, E. 155, 156, 171–2, 175–7
Solnit, R. 162
South London Gallery 50–3
South Riverside Community Development Centre (SRCDC) *see* community groups and universities
Sparkes, M. 169, 173
Spivak, G. 145
Stewart, S. 121, 123
sustainability
 cultural mapping 120–3
 university public engagement 25–6
 walking practice, and disability 180–2, 197

T

Theodore, N. 82–3, 206, 210
Thomas, Gwenda 203
Thomas-Hughes, Helen 65–6
Three Mills, National Mills Weekend 132, *133*, 135
Trading Routes project *see* mapping (of contested geographies)
Trench, B. 12
Trevor, Tom 107, 109
Turner, C. 187, 189

U

universities and museums 47–59
 background to 47–8
 case studies 50–6
 challenges and benefits of collaboration 57–8
 impact of collaboration 52–3
 Local Roots/Global Routes: the Legacies of Slavery in Hackney 53–6
 next steps 58–9
 Peckham Cultural Institute 50–3
 pilot projects 48
 power relationships 49
 Share Academy background 48–50
 see also museums and gender identity
University College London (UCL)
 legacies of British Slave-ownership project 53–6
 see also university public engagement
University of Bristol *see* community groups and universities; regulatory aesthetics; walking practice, and disability

University of Glasgow *see* walking practice, and disability
University of Local Knowledge (ULK) 106, 107–10, 117
University of the West of England
 and University of Local Knowledge (ULK) 106, 107–10, 117
 see also walking practice, and disability
university public engagement 9–28
 achievements of Beacon for Public Engagement 14
 benefits of 11–12
 concept of 10–13
 enabling conditions for 23–7
 evaluation 14–15, 19–20, 22–3, 26–7
 Food Junctions Cookbook 20–1
 Food Junctions Festival *16*, 17–18
 Foodpaths Movement *16*, 18–20
 framework for 12
 importance of 9
 launch of Beacon for Public Engagement 12–14
 lessons learned 22–3
 in practice *16*, 16–21
 types of 12
urban water communities *see* participatory mapping

V

Vergunst 190

W

Wales 202–3, 210
walking practice, and disability 179–99
 background to project 180–1
 and citizenship 194–5
 context 181–2
 and dissemination 186, 198–9
 impact of 198–9
 participatory research approach 185–8
 and resilient knowledge 196–7
 and sustainability 180–2, 197
 using skills of disabled people 192–6
 valuing of disability 183–5
 walking discourse 188–92
Warner, M. 144
water communities *see* participatory mapping
Watson, Debbie 73
West of England Centre for Inclusive Living (WECIL) *see* walking practice, and disability
Wilson, I. 167
Wiseman, P. 194–5
Wolfe, P. 170
women's groups *see* collaborative research
Wright, D.E. 91
Wunderlich, F.M. 189–90
Wyman, M. 99, 102
Wynne-Jones, S. 206

Y

youth-led participatory research *see* participatory research